Set Free
A Lifelong Christian's Overdue Discovery

TABLE OF CONTENTS
Preface (6)
Why This Book Was Written (8)
Introduction (p13)

PART I – WE ARE OUR OWN HANDICAP

CHAPTERS 1-11
SETTLING

Chapter 1: Settling for Too Little – The Role of Faith (p33)

Chapter 2: It Doesn't Have to Be This Way (p38)

Chapter 3: An Increased Appetite (p40)

Chapter 4: Stopping at Faith Is Lazy (p42)

Chapter 5: Settling for Too Little–The Role of Self-Saving Financials (p45)

Chapter 6: Isn't Being Grateful Enough? (p49)

Chapter 7: Exalting the Glory of Christ, Our Purpose (p53)

Chapter 8: We Are Far Too Easily Pleased – Our Bar Is Too Low (p56)

Chapter 9: A Cost-Benefit Analysis (p61)

Chapter 10: Which Do You Despise? (p66)

Chapter 11: Improving Our Vision (p74)

CHAPTERS 12-17
HOLDING ON

Chapter 12: Saved but Never Dying (p80)

Chapter 13: Self-Assertion (p86)

Chapter 14: Waiting Expectantly (p90)

Chapter 15: Erasing Us (p93)

Chapter 16: Releasing – God Waits on Us? (p96)

Chapter 17: If/Then (p99)

PART II – TRANSITIONING TO TRUTH

CHAPTERS 18-35
THE COMPONENTS OF TRANSITIONING TO TRUTH

Chapter 18: A Personal Turn (p103)

Chapter 19: The Holy Spirit Experience (p106)

Chapter 20: A Traceable Pathway (p109)

Chapter 21: Who Am I? (p113)

Chapter 22: Clarifier: Man's Writings / God's Word (p117)

Chapter 23: Under the Influence: In Whose Spirit Are We Living? (p120)

Chapter 24: Adam's Upper Hand (p123)

Chapter 25: A Savior Saves; A Lord Owns (p126)

Chapter 26: Spurring on Our Death (p131)

Chapter 27: An Ownership Problem (p136)

Chapter 28: Transcendence & Time (p142)

Chapter 29: Informed Faith Facilitates Giving Up (p144)

Chapter 30: Real Newness (p148)

Chapter 31: An Informed Theology – Narrowing the Focus (p151)

Chapter 32: Increasing Deliverance (p156)

Chapter 33: Depending on A Dead Man? (p160)

Chapter 34: Don't Make Him Strip You (p164)

Chapter 35: Heading Plateward: Rending Our Heart (p167)

PART III – WHAT IS TRUE OF YOU

CHAPTERS 36-41
FIRST – THE WORK OF THE BLOOD

Chapter 36: The Blood of Christ (p175)

Chapter 37: The Role of the Blood (p181)

Chapter 38: God Is Satisfied (p185)

Chapter 39: The Believer's Access to God (p187)

Chapter 40: Overcoming the Accuser (p192)

Chapter 41: The Wrath of God (p195)

CHAPTERS 42-46
SECOND – THE WORK OF THE CROSS

Chapter 42: The Cross of Christ (p206)

Chapter 43: The Role of the Cross (p209)

Chapter 44: As in Adam, So in Christ (p217)

Chapter 45: The Divine Way of Deliverance (p219)

Chapter 46: His Death and Resurrection – Representative & Inclusive (p222)

CHAPTERS 47-54
THIRD – RECKONING INTO CONFIDENT BELIEF

Chapter 47: The Paths of Progress: Knowing and Reckoning (p227)

Chapter 48: The Path of Progress: Knowing (p230)

Chapter 49: The Path of Progress: Reckoning (p241)

Chapter 50: Temptation and Failure – The Challenge to Faith (p245)

Chapter 51: Abiding in Him (p250)

Chapter 52: Nothing of the Old Can Inherit the New (p257)

Chapter 53: Remembering Burial Means an End (p260)

Chapter 54: Being Joined in Christ Means Resurrection (p263)

CHAPTERS 55-59
ROUNDING THIRD AND HEADING FOR HOME

Chapter 55: Presenting Ourselves to God (p265)

Chapter 56: Presenting Yourselves (p269)

Chapter 57: Recognizing God's Ownership – The End of the Beginning (p271)

Chapter 58: Servant or Slave? (p273)

Chapter 59: Sliding Home – Face First (p276)

CHAPTER 60
WALKING IN OBEDIENCE (p280)

APPENDIXES A-C (pp287-314)

A personal note from the author

    If you were to locate my personal copy of *Set Free*, you would find two critical, companion books bundled alongside it. Without the Bible and Watchman Nee's book, *The Normal Christian Life*, the book you are now holding would never have been written.

    I pray you have a Bible. If you do not own a Bible, and because there is no greater investment into the nourishment of the human soul, please consider contacting Bibles for America to get one FREE (https://biblesforamerica.org/place-order). If you want to get the most out of your copy of *Set Free*, know you will also need to secure your own copy of *The Normal Christian Life*. Get one for a few dollars at https://tinyurl.com/y8egoe8j or https://tinyurl.com/y83gb6n4.

    May God meet you in the pages that follow. He is ready.

— *Greg*

NOTE: All scripture references throughout this book are in the NIV unless otherwise noted.

Preface

Therefore, if anyone is in Christ, he is a new creation. The old has passed away; behold, the new has come. - 2 Cor. 5:17 (ESV)

God knew, pending my obedience, the writing of this book would be inevitable. I did not. For more than two years I tried *not* to write it. But finally, what had begun to flow up from my heart was forced out by the inward pressure. It has been born out of a kind of inward necessity. I thought a bit of sporadic journaling would be a satisfactory relief valve. I was wrong—it only made the burden heavier. I thought God and I had agreed that the path on which we had traveled was too deeply personal, holy and life-giving to adequately communicate in words ... and not to be mentioned beyond family. But it soon became evident my theme of brokenness and inadequacy was something God wanted to use to challenge today's self-resourcing, self-confident and mostly unbroken American Christian.

Now that you don't like me because of what I just wrote, I have to be honest. I want people to like me. Knowing what I was burdened to write would not be popular, I had to become willing to risk prescribing this strong and unrequested medicine regardless. For God was clearly burdening my heart with an initially bitter message; until we who have placed our faith in Jesus become broken and convinced of our *inabilities* in this life, we will never be set free to begin living a spirit-filled, selfless and deeply satisfying life.

If you are outside my encouraging and obliging family members, and have not already put this book down, you will likely find parts one and two to be disjointed and in need of a good editor. I have stitched its message together as best I can, but don't believe I have done so very well. Please forgive this inadequacy. In as much as this may be the case, however, it may lend itself better to what I pray will be a willingness to dwell upon many of the short chapters as if individual challenges. In fact, I encourage you to either agree or disagree with each successive chapter before continuing on.

Furthermore, I want you to know I claim for the book neither originality nor any degree of inspiration beyond what may be enjoyed by any who belong to Christ. Please do not read the words revelation or illumination to be more than a new awareness God was giving me through his awakened Holy Spirit in my life – not some 'new' word from God, for his Word has given us all we need for insight into all things (2 Timothy 3:16-17, Hebrews 4:12-13). As for originality, as Emerson once said, "Every man is a quotation from his ancestors." Without a doubt, the reader will detect on these pages traces of other's hearts. You will find many footnotes giving credit to others who have gone before me in our common zeal. All I can hope is that this book may be a right emphasis coming at a right time.

Admittedly, trying to trace the journey of God's merciful pursuit of my mind and heart on paper has been difficult. But, for reasons only God knows presently, I am confident he has asked that I do so. The road that has led me to the truths found in this book has been one more characterized by God's persistent pursuit than my prompt perception. I am humbled regularly by what I have yet to learn from the trustworthy hand of God.

As difficult as it has been to tell the story of the truths the Holy Spirit has taught me, it has been worth the effort if for only one reason: God is now exposing me to increasing numbers of lifelong Christians who are suffering from the same disorder God tenderly uncovered in my own life. I pray you are holding (or listening to) this book because God is preparing you for more than a *settled-for* Christian life.

The Holy Spirit's abiding and personal fellowship is something the Father intended for us after drawing Jesus to His side. But sadly, as my own story will illustrate, many lifelong Christians are achieving a moderate level of *acceptable spiritual success* without having fully surrendered the whole of their lives into Christ. This undetected self-sufficiency stifles the Holy Spirit's free movement within us. As a consequence, we eventually find ourselves disillusioned by our ongoing struggles to live a truly victorious Christian life.

The Counselor, as Jesus called him, must be an indispensable part of our new life in Christ if we are to live above the exceedingly low bar of spiritual expectancy that characterizes much of the western Church.

My life in Christ is an ongoing story—one needful of continual, daily surrender. But if, like me, you have known Jesus most of your life, have perhaps grown up in an American, Christian home filled with love, encouragement and affirmation, but have grown weary of your self-empowered journey as a Christian, you may benefit from some of what follows. I earnestly pray there will be great hope here for many who are truly hungering for more.

- *Greg*

Why This Book Was Written

It was a typically hot and humid summer day here in Indy as I sat in his comfortably air-conditioned office. I'd been running errands in the heat of the day and was grateful for this cool place where I could exhale for a few minutes. And although we were talking business, I was still grateful to sit there and rest–benefitting from his expertise.

The man in whose office I sat was yet another whose lifelong Christianity had been working. Beautiful wife – check. Three fairly well-behaved children – check. Time and money for recreation on the golf course – check. A nice suburban home with crown molding – check. A devoted dog to rest at his feet during the most productive hours of the work day, 9pm-midnight – check. The third generation in a lineage of strong, God-fearing Christian grandparents and parents – check.

And now, for many years, he had devoted himself to his career and was reaping the rewards of a loyal staff willing to leap tall buildings in a single bound for their collective clientele. Ah, yes! Life was good.

Right?

In an effort to edify him for his professional expertise and ability to make the complex simple to a layman such as myself, I casually asked him if he enjoyed what he did for a living.

Perhaps because our families had known one another for both of our lifetimes and the informality of our gathering felt safe, or perhaps because it was the end of another demanding work week and his guard was down … whatever the reason, to my surprise, a torrent of painful dissatisfaction and spiritual discontentedness began to flow freely.

I was, once again, hearing the all-too-familiar, soulish anguish of a lifelong Christian who was growing sick and tired of himself and his inability to live for something more deeply fulfilling than the pride of his own expectations.

> "I thought by now," continuing his self-diagnostic, "I'd feel a lot more fulfilled."

At this, I felt my own temperature begin to rise. For the past several years, I have heard this refrain from multiple lifelong Christians who have been victims of an incalculably low bar of spiritual expectation for their lives. Some have been pastors. Some businessmen. All who would consider themselves lifelong Christians. Is this really all the God who saved them from hell intended for them in this life? A 2-car garage and a late model SUV? A controllable, safe life? The respect of onlookers who just knew this guy (or gal) had it all together in his Christian walk? A self-empowered hike through eighty or so years? A growing study of the Bible until we can quote a hundred verses and enunciate the most challenging Hebrew names?

He continued.

> And what's wrong with me anyway? I can discipline myself to work late every night and put up with all kinds of people and personalities in my office and profession, but in every other place I keep acting like the same, immature idiot I've always been! And I'm *so* stinkin' selfish. Everything I do somehow comes around to benefitting me. I hate that!

He went on.

> And this phone! I'm great at using it, but *it* uses *me* really–I can almost get nauseous just thinking about it. There are lots of things like that. I'd like to just go on a retreat and leave my phone at home for three days. But I won't do it. I think I'd hyperventilate and slip into a coma or something. Man, I hate that I'm controlled by so many things...I can't even control myself!

> I call myself a Christian, but I have no power to do what I *want* to do. I feel like a slave. Deep down, I'm the same old crappy dude I've been for twenty-five years. And I hate my pride.

> Don't get me wrong...it's not like I'm an evil person right now, and I'm not struggling with anything dark or addictive or overtly sinful– at least not that I'm aware of. I'm just...well, maybe I'm not sure I'm

ever going to change. That kind of scares me—makes me feel defeated as a Christian. I want—no, I *need real* change. I need the supernatural God of this universe to grab me by the collar. I need to see Him! I *know* God wants more for me. But I'm powerless to get there.

And, changing the scene, I won't forget the moment I *first* saw my own frustrating condition gushing from the lips of *another* Christian man who was expressing what he thought to be his own, personal dilemma. In four words, and with a clarity I had been unable to put my finger on myself, this man's honest self-proclamation told me I wasn't alone. What I'd been experiencing for several years was now pouring from another self-exasperated soul who, like me, had known Jesus for many years.

The four words? "...so done with myself."

It was as if the Lord were giving me eyes to see right through this man; I could immediately empathize with and identify this man's spiritual condition...for it had been my own. When you come to the place where you look yourself in the mirror and say, "You know what, dude? I'm completely done with you!", you're closing in on the best strategy I know to recover your life–surrender, the letting go.

I now know the Lord was exposing me to this man's soulish anguish as the first in a long list of Christians to whom I would be exposed, all shouldering a common disease.

About this first of many such experiences, I wrote the following in my journal on Wednesday, September 30, 2012.

> Just about three weeks ago, in the midst of a closed-door conversation I was having with a member of my organization's management, I heard what has perhaps been the best description of such a readiness in a man's life to move from being a man saved by God to a man given over.
>
> At one point in our conversation, and following a most prolonged exhale, hands lifting to the top of his head to clasp together, this man looked me straight in the eye from behind his desk and said, "I am completely *done* with me. Greg, I have never in my life been so *done* with myself."
>
> It was for such a time as this, the Spirit of God had me in that place–for this man was ready. Ready for not just that which had already saved him from eternal death (for he is a member of the Body of Christ), but for that which could begin the journey toward the release of the Spirit of God in his members. He had most concisely

proclaimed he was prepared for the surrender of his bigger problem—the problem that is the very manufacture of the sins of our life; and that, our **selves**...our very sin **nature**...our **flesh**. O praise you, living God, for your willingness to break us. All that you love, you break.

But the real issue at stake in these rare and precious times of God's inbreaking is this; how do we respond? Most of us take a second, accepting deep breath and recommit ourselves to the grind (though it sounds more spiritual and optimistic to call it our earth-side call).

Oh, self-sick Christian, **it doesn't have to be this way**! The good news is that your transactional Christianity *can* become transformational Christianity. But to come to grips with what has become the pandemic lie of the devil that has us lifelong Christians living like the world around us, frustrated by our self-stunted growth while admittedly living in the strength of the old man who was *supposed* to have died when we came to Christ (what's up with that anyway), we will need to take a patient walk together into the source of our difficulty. To get to the bottom of what ails us, we cannot learn one more self-help technique. We cannot really understand God's compelling purpose for our lives until we understand the root of our sickness...as Christians!

And that is why I have written this book—to help lifelong Christians who have realized they are still missing something as they battle this life with all their strength.

I, too, had been missing something in my Christianity. And though I will continue to learn while on this now-fulfilling journey with Jesus for the rest of my life, I praise God that he has made me keenly aware of the root of my problem—why I'd been unable to sustain a *realness* in my walk with him. I don't think it is coincidence that my heart is burdened for the millions of Christians who are living good, but self-sick lives. When you find an antidote to a sickness, spiritual or otherwise, you deeply desire to offer it to others.

Initially, much of what is written on these pages was a therapeutic act of obedience out of the gratitude of my heart for where the Spirit of the living God had taken me. But lately, the Lord has allowed me to be exposed to increasing numbers of similarly frustrated Christians who are where I had been for many years, two examples of which I recounted above. I can see the signs now. And my soul longs to share what God has revealed about my ailment as a lifelong Christian. And yet it is humbling to know it is not mine, but the Holy Spirit's responsibility to do what he desires with the contents of these pages.

Now, one final but important thought.

If you are a type-A person and you just want the antidote, it may be frustrating for you to linger through the first thirty-five, short chapters. After all, you picked up this book because, in some regard, you are wondering if you can honestly be *Set Free* to live victoriously with your Savior. But, please understand we must first buy into what ails us as lifelong, American Christians. And this is what we will endeavor to do through the introduction, and then into the short chapters that make up the bulk of the first two parts of the book.

As you begin this book, you may intend to grab a few good tidbits and keep the train a rollin'. I am afraid much of the inadequacy of our spiritual experience can be traced back to what A.W. Tozer calls, "our habit of skipping through the corridors of the Kingdom like children through the market place, chattering about everything, but pausing to learn the true value of nothing."

As a personal admission, he confessed to something once that was good for me to admit as well.

> In my creature impatience I am often caused to wish that there were some way to bring modern Christians into a deeper spiritual life painlessly by short easy lessons; but such wishes are vain. No short cut exists. God has not bowed to our nervous haste nor embraced the methods of our machine age. It is well that we accept the hard truth now: the man who would know God must give time to Him. He must count no time wasted which is spent in the cultivation of His acquaintance.[1]

So to help us fight this tendency, and assuming you are open to having the Holy Spirit inquire deeply of your soul life, I have added "PAUSE to PONDER" points to conclude many chapters. Consider them pit stops. Remember, you have to STOP for a pit stop. Because this is true, it is not intended that you read more than a single chapter at a setting.

Join me in contemplating the pages that follow. You're not alone, my friend. I think you'll be glad to know there is a way out of the religion of Christianity, and into a deeply intimate fellowship with the God who is *still* chasing you down.

---

[1] A.W. Tozer, The Devine Conquest, Page 22

Introduction

How *does* a forty-six-year-old man, having lived with Jesus as his Savior for thirty-five of those years, discover something so new, so revolutionary about his identity in Christ that he feels as if he's been born again, AGAIN?

"It's not like God was on the periphery of my life," but rather, as Richard Foster relates in his book, Freedom of Simplicity, "it would be more accurate to say that I was on the periphery of His Life."[2] I can relate to that postulation.

I wasn't on the periphery of His life because I didn't care *or* because I hadn't accepted Jesus as my sufficiency *or* because I was living in willful sin *or* because I was distracted by a corporate job demanding all my time and energy...at least not any more.

I was on the periphery of His life because I knew too little of brokenness and too much of my well-disciplined efforts and self-confidence. I was on the periphery of His life because the life I was living was, to a great degree, still mine and not His. I was on the periphery of His life because I had been content with my efforts to please Him. I didn't know any better, actually. In Steven Curtis Chapman's words, I was content with playing in a puddle when I could have been swimming in the ocean.

There is much surrender yet to be discovered, but we, the triune God and I, are on a road I hadn't even known I was missing. Let me try to explain with an illustration from the life of fellow traveler, Kyle Idleman. He tells this story.

> Recently my wife and I and our four kids flew into the Atlanta airport from the island of Hispaniola where we had spent a month

---

[2] Richard Foster, Freedom of Simplicity; Chapter 5, Page 97

> on a mission trip. After landing, we grabbed our bags and began a long hike through the airport.
>
> When we travel, my wife and I share the responsibilities. One of us packs lots of stuff and one of us carries it everywhere. That's how we've worked it out.
>
> So I'm carrying about a half dozen bags through the airport. They are just hanging all around me. It's just a moving pile of bags with my head sticking out of the top. We turn to go down a hallway that is about 100 yards long. My wife and kids all get on a moving sidewalk, but I'm carrying a wide load and it's impossible for me to navigate the turn and I miss the on ramp.
>
> I wish you could have seen what it looked like from my perspective. They set the few bags they have on the moving sidewalk and just stand there watching me. I'm sweating like...well, like a man carrying a half dozen suitcases through the airport. I'm trying to keep up with the pace.
>
> We end up arriving at the end of the sidewalk at about the same time. But there's a difference. I'm frustrated, exhausted, and annoyed, and they are ready to keep moving. That's what our lives look like when we try the self-empowered hike, instead of the Spirit-filled walkway.[3]

That was me. I was trying to follow the Lord without having discovered what Jesus intended for us when he went away and told the disciples that it was actually *better that he leave them so that he could equip them* with his Spirit. He could then not merely be *with* them, but *in* them.

God knew that, eventually, we wouldn't be able to successfully follow him on our own, armed only with emotional inspiration, positive thinking or self-discipline. He knew that life would get long and our self-empowered living would become insufficient for us. In short, the normal Christian life Jesus intended for us wasn't going to work without our awakening to the power of his Spirit.

Now many of us shake our heads and agree with the likes of what I've just written; we think of other poor souls whose lives need the kind of help only the supernatural can provide. It's always easier to see in others what we cannot see in ourselves.

---

[3] Kyle Idleman, Not A Fan; Chapter 6, Pages 88-89

In addition, we grade our Christian lives on the curve. And so from the looks of things, we're doing pretty well! By comparison, we are subconsciously buoyed by the idea that the Lord must be fairly pleased with us. This makes us feel good about ourselves.

But in doing so, we miss that we have developed quite a successful self-life. And it is this self-life that has become too characteristic of the 21st century, self-sufficient, suburban, born-again Christian. It shows up in *all kinds* of places.

While we are aware that ours isn't a *perfect* walk with Jesus, we believe we can whip ourselves into shape…someday. And herein lies the problem; we don't see that our *self*-confidence breaks the heart of God.

We *are* a confident people.

In our substantially healthy self-confidence, we incessantly quench the Spirit of God from the scene of our individual and collective lives. And through it all, in perplexed solemnity, we wonder why God doesn't appear to be powerfully and notably moving in America.

This correlation between our confidence and God's silence is not a coincidence.

Let's narrow the frame a bit. If read in truly introspective honesty, is there any part of this next section to which you can relate? We'll maintain the plural pronoun for now – since doing so is less pointed. Besides, somewhere in my past I learned that "attack mode" may not always be the best way to win friends and influence people.

We are a confident people…

We are confident in our ability to accomplish things.

We are confident in our ability to get along in an assertive world.

We are confident in our work ethic.

We are confident in our roles as provider, homemaker or other worthwhile vocation.

We are confident in the dwellings which we have confidently purchased, that they will provide us with shelter and security.

We are confident in our transportation.

We are confident in our ability to fix, or have repaired, our cars, homes, lawnmowers, computers, washers and dryers, trimmers, leaking roofs, televisions, refrigerators, dishwashers, ovens, and microwaves (to name a few) so we can continue to be confident in our comfort.

We are confident in our ability to accomplish the necessary tasks each day, making it yet another of maximum productivity.

We are confident in our ability to learn—and to apply it to our lives.

We are confident in our ability to be culturally sensitive, relationally aware and service-oriented (when absolutely necessary), all of which provide us with confident, reciprocal relationships.

We are confident in our medical solutions for those rare, unforeseen inconveniences like infertility, that bad fall or that asthma problem.

We are confident in our ability to entertain ourselves with any number of worthwhile endeavors or pleasures.

We are confident in our ability to put balanced meals onto our dinner table—and, if not, in our ability to suck it up and work a second or third job...whatever it takes to keep up—or catch up.

In short, we post-modern Christians are a pretty resourceful bunch, pulling ourselves up from the old bootstraps when absolutely necessary—no guts, no glory, right? The land of the iron will, yes? And if we are lacking some important expertise, we can become better people through any one of a few hundred self-help systems.

Ok, question time.

In all our self-confidence, have we who claim to be followers of Jesus Christ left sufficient room for his desire to reveal to us the truth of our fundamental *insufficiency* in this life? Or are we primarily satisfied with grateful hearts, thanking Him for all of our 'self-hyphens?'

David Platt has observed the following, and included it in his book, *Radical*:

> We live in a land of self-improvement. Certainly there are steps we can take to make ourselves better. So we modify what the gospel says about us. We are not evil, we think, and certainly not spiritually dead. Haven't you heard of the power of positive thinking? I can become a better me and experience my best life now. That's why God is there—to make that happen. My life is not going right, but God loves me and has a plan to fix my life. I simply need to follow certain steps, think certain things, and check off certain boxes, and then I am good.
>
> Both our diagnosis of the situation and our conclusion regarding the solution fit nicely in a culture that exalts self-sufficiency, self-esteem, and self-confidence.[4]

Here are some of A.W. Tozer's satirical thoughts along these same lines:

> God simply wants to make us a good man or woman. Feelings of low self-esteem can be quickly eradicated by believing that, in Jesus, we can be the best we can possibly be. No matter what our problem is, Christ can make it go away. Christianity, according to this school of thought, is a sort of deluxe edition of life, and helps improve the all-important self-esteem issues that we might have. It helps us to feel better about ourselves.[5]

Now don't be too quick to brush these observations off in your own life. Pause here. If push comes to shove, in whom do you have greater confidence *for the daily throughput* of your life—God or yourself? For what purposes has your Christianity begun to serve you? Why *did* you become a Christian? Think practically.

Is your *contemplative* response to Platt's and Tozer's evaluations of the average Christian life one based in what you *believe* to be the right answer or one based *in actual practice*? And if asked, why would you say Jesus came to earth and then gave us his Spirit?

> The one school of thought holds that the Lord Jesus Christ came into this world in order to help us; that is to take us out of the conflicts and the twisted situations we get into during our lives. The thinking is that we are alright except for a few twists and turns here and there—which surely the Lord can straighten out. Man is basically good, except for a few little mistakes now and then. This thinking also holds that the purpose of Christianity is to make us better people.[6]

Again I ask, what role does Jesus actually play in your daily life? If you are truly interested in getting to the bottom of this, soldier on right here and now by reading the first couple pages in chapter 13 of A.W. Tozer's book, The Crucified Life, under the heading Two Contradictory Schools of Thought. Perhaps his simple and clear treatment of this topic will shed additional insight into your soul's honest inquiry. Why do you think the Lord Jesus came? How should your answer actually inform your life?

---

[4] David Platt, Radical; Chapter 2, Pg 31
[5] A.W. Tozer, The Crucified Life; Part 4, Chapter 13
[6] Tozer, The Crucified Life; Part 4, Chapter 13

Because the intent of this book is not to have you conquer it, but to work through it as a prayerful inquiry into God's development of your soul, it will be perfectly acceptable to move further into this writing *only after* you have come to some kind of an honest evaluation of this aspect of your life. Trust me, the next paragraph will wait a few days.

As the American Dream goes, we can do anything we set our minds to accomplish. As I write this, I am sitting in a Cracker Barrel in Morton, Illinois. While waiting for my table, I noticed a thoughtfully framed, warm picture of a porch which overlooks the ocean, a rocker beckoning a companion and an  American Flag draped over a nearby post. The tasteful, calligraphy scripted caption says, "*May I never wake up from the American Dream.*" How timely.

Now while this caption may not have been created by someone claiming Christianity, I wonder if it would have made a difference. In what do we stake our hope? What do we chase for satisfaction? Are we American Christians a deceived people? Are *we* living out our own personal versions of the American Dream or are we living *radically different* than the moral, kind-hearted people around us who, while being decent folks, yet belong to the world's system of self-preservation, wholesome, well-earned recreation, and rest? Is there enough contrast today between 'good folk' and reborn children of God?

When Jesus asked us to follow him, he asked us to pick up a personal cross of self-abandonment. Does the cross you are bearing look more like the American Dream or one pursuing a daily *death to self* for Christ's sake? Are you *in* the way more than out of the way as the Holy Spirit leads your life? Do you know? If you are not sure, your soul, while saved, is likely unbroken.

At this point, you could remind me of the old phrase, "Don't be so heavenly minded that you are of no earthly good." The only problem with that phrase is that it is unbiblical. The Bible says, "Set your mind on things above, *not* on the things that are on earth" (Col 3:2). Perhaps we're of too much earthly good to be of heavenly use?

I used to listen to Dennis Waitley's "The Psychology of Winning" repeatedly while on the road as a young, corporate salesman. Today, I am *still* trying to vanquish that self-buildup from my subconscious. While not all bad to be sure, my repetitive intake of that content was purposed to put a final nail in the coffin of any remaining wisps of self-doubt and personal or professional uncertainty I had not yet vanquished from my psyche as a twenty-something.

It's what we do as self-determiners. It's all part of suppressing our true human frailty–a frailty I now *embrace* because it gives me opportunity to taste the truth of our human condition apart from Christ. "Self-trust," says A.W. Tozer, "is the last great obstacle to living the crucified life."[7]

In sharp contrast to learning about how I can do all things to which I set my mind through repetitive self-encouragement, the Word of God tells me there is nothing good in me whatsoever apart from Jesus. And the Word of Truth tells me that I can do all things *through Christ* who gives me strength.

The truth is that I am fallen, lost and hopeless, and can in no way attain to usefulness as a Kingdom Citizen apart from Christ.

But again, our world tells us there is no limit to what we can accomplish when we combine ingenuity, imagination, and innovation with skill and hard work. We can earn any degree, start any business, climb any ladder, attain any prize, and achieve any goal. And *we* think we can best serve God in much the same way.

Yes, our greatest asset *is* our *own* ability! When we believe and trust in ourselves, of course thanking God along the way for such poise, no goal is too lofty to attain, and no hurdle too high to clear. For God has most surely given us *ability*!

But sadly, and *not* so tongue-in-cheek, we too often believe that our successful life results as a byproduct of *our* well-disciplined labor. And in doing so, we sin.

Rather, from the pages of John Stott's book, The Cross of Christ, here is a more accurate portrayal of who we are in ourselves, apart from Christ. In Paul's words and directly from Romans, this is our circumstance as the human race...as undeserving sinners.

> Sinners–it's the first word Paul uses to describe us, **failures** who have missed the target and invariably fall short of the glory of God (Romans 3:23). Next, we were **ungodly** (Romans 5:6), for we had not given God the glory due to His name, and there was no fear of

---

[7] Tozer, The Crucified Life; Chapter 9

God before our eyes (Romans 3:18). Paul's third descriptive epithet is **enemies** (Romans 5:10). That is, we were God's enemies as the NIV explains, for we had rebelled against His authority, rebuffed his love, and been defiant of his Law (Romans 8:7). The fourth and last word is **powerless** (Romans 5:6). It was when we were still powerless that Christ died for us. For we had no power to save ourselves. We were helpless.

These four words make an ugly cluster of adjectives.[8]

Lorenzo Scupoli (1530-1610) was one of those strange Catholics who during his lifetime was considered, more or less, a heretic because of his evangelical leaning. In his book, *The Spiritual Combat*, he wrote this:

> Let this be well impressed upon your mind; for our corrupt nature too easily inclines us to a false estimate of ourselves; so that, being really nothing, we account ourselves to be something, and presume, without the slightest foundation, upon our own strength.[9]

The Bible tells us we are to have *no* confidence in the flesh, counting it as loss (Phil. 3:3 & 7) while viewing the accomplishments and abilities of our flesh as garbage (3:8) for Christ's sake. Quite a contrasting picture, isn't it? To further nail this crucial reality home, I'd like to quote A.W. Tozer once more from his excellent work, The Crucified Life. Clarifications in brackets mine.

> This is a fault [presuming upon our own strength] not easily discerned by us, but very displeasing in the sight of God. For he desires and loves to see in us a frank and true recognition of this most certain truth; that all the virtue and grace within us is derived from Him alone who is the fountain of all good; and that nothing good can proceed from *us*, no not even a thought, which can find acceptance in His sight.

J.D. Greear says that, "The Gospel begins with our brokenness and inability, not our power and potential."[10] Billy Graham once said that, "Rarely is it someone's sin that keeps them from heaven—usually it is their good deeds."[11]

---

[8] John Stott, The Cross of Christ, Chapter 1
[9] Quoted from A.W. Tozer's, The Crucified Life; Chapter 9
[10] J.D. Greear, Jesus, Continued...; Chapter 17
[11] Quoted from J.D. Greear, Jesus, Continued...; Chapter 17

In the same way, says Greear, "It is our false sense of ability, not our inabilities, that keeps us from living in the power of the Spirit. Thinking we can get along fine apart from Him keeps us from the power available in Him (John 15:5). When you finally come to that place where you realize you have no true power, then you are ready to receive His. The great irony in the Christian life, you see, is that the way up is the way down. The lower we sink in ourselves, the higher we rise in Him."[12]

And so what happens when our self-confidence begins to waiver? What happens when we can no longer manipulate something to the "right" end? What happens when the loving, "can't stands it no more" God of our souls decides to remove some of our self-hyphens, our abilities, in order to turn our hearts toward something we cannot *do* in our own strength? What happens when we are stopped cold in our tracks for a season of God's choosing and are chosen to be laid waste by an all-consuming and jealous God?

What happens is what *can* become a rare and very precious thing. We can begin to discover our desperate need for our Savior–a reliance upon the One we have long *called* "Lord."

When our lives are humming along, or even when we hit speed bumps intended to turn our eyes upward and outside of ourselves, what we continue to lack in all of our personal poise is a desperation for the power of God. The modern, first-world Christian is terribly self-sufficient, and *God's* power is nothing more than an add-on to *our* strategies. We may not *say* this, but our actions betray us. We say, "I'm going to do…such and such, Lord. Please now, would you bless it?"

David Platt proposes something interesting in relation to our ability, apart from the power of the Holy Spirit, to build large and well-oiled churches. However, I am convinced his contemplation ails our personal lives as well. Most of us Christians can carry on the vast majority of our personal activities smoothly, efficiently–even successfully, never realizing that the Holy Spirit of God is virtually absent from the picture. We can so easily deceive ourselves into mistaking the *world's* evaluation of our effectiveness for the existence of a spiritually healthy, Spirit-infused life–when it is *not* there.

Along the same lines, A.W. Tozer makes this personal observation:

---

[12] J.D. Greear, Jesus, Continued…; Chapter 17

If the Holy Spirit were withdrawn from the church today, 95% of what we do would go on, and no one would know the difference. If the Holy Spirit had been withdrawn from the New Testament Church, 95% of what they did would stop, and everybody would know the difference. [13]

Once we begin to grasp that we possess nothing good in ourselves, that we desperately need the power of God's Spirit shed abroad in our hearts, and we receive this truth of our insufficiency from an in-breaking revelation of God, then we are finally setting foot onto the playing field, the domain, of the Holy Spirit. And if you're willing to comply, be ready to lose control. Be ready for some very unfamiliar terrain–territory known only to those who are–well, no longer so self-hyphenated.

When God chooses to lay waste to our self-sufficiency, promoting us into the more demanding and important role of bond-servant of Christ, we are on the right, though very unfamiliar and counter-cultural, track to becoming ones prepared for the awakening of the Holy Spirit in our lives. It is finally in this newness of position we become, in practice, more reliant on God than ourselves. And we should welcome this. It is in this promotion we make the move *from being atheists in practice to people truly reliant on God.*

But sadly, we too frequently miss our Lord's brooding pursuit over us.

Do you recall a time when you may have been physically laid up, incapable of functioning in your typically self-reliant, efficient, multi-tasking, healthy manner? Do you recall a time when the path you were being allowed to travel seemed to have more potholes than pavement?

If so, what did you do with that time or circumstance? What are you doing with it now? Are you pushing through it with great frustration, thinking only of all the things you should and could be *doing* were you not to have met with this unwelcomed stillness or struggle? Did it ever cross your mind that as a believer in Christ, you may just have been on the holy ground of the Spirit's pursuit?

I understand such times of unintended stillness or challenge can lead us to frustration or outright anger with God. He can take your emotion...for a time; as long as it is only for a time, after which such a continuing response may be an indication of a more serious problem–

---

[13] A.W. Tozer

hard heartedness or a callous lack of sensitivity to the Spirit's voice in your life.

> At times when something blows up in our face, we think it is all over instead of taking it as proof that we are not mature Christians. We need to take the blowup as proof that we are nearer our forever home today than we were yesterday. We need to understand that our heavenly Father is letting these things happen to us to wean us away from trusting ourselves and to move us to lean exclusively on the Lord Jesus Christ.
>
> [And in the worst case], when a Christian faces a difficult or extreme trial or temptation, he is tempted to throw in the towel and say, "God is no use. I'm just no good. You obviously don't want me–so I'm finished." All the while, he forgets that God wants to teach us through these trials and temptations, that self-trust is dangerous and unreliable.[14]

Again I must ask, are you too earthly minded that you are of little heavenly good?

Do you have *any* idea what you're missing when you behave so selfishly during a time of being involuntarily sidelined? These are times appointed by God for us which fall into a categorical heading J.D. Greear calls "white spaces."[15]

White spaces are typically the hardest parts of life to endure. They include the white space of silence, the white space of singleness, the white space of sickness or injury, the white space of unmet promises and unmet expectations, the white space of seemingly unimportant inactivity. Assuming you are not quenching the Spirit in your life with deliberate sin and you are living uprightly (Ps. 84:11 KJB), seeking God's face and remaining in the Word, these are times God is using to increase our faith and grow us into the men and women He desires for His self-glorifying purposes.

Are you in a white space right now? If you think these forays into your life are nothing more than irritable speed bumps of haphazard circumstance, keeping you from fulfilling your purpose in God's great economy, you are missing out on the Spirit's pursuit of your life. In

---

[14] Tozer, The Crucified Life; Chapter 8. Bracketed emphasis mine.

[15] J.D. Greear, Jesus, Continued; Chapter 14. Please do yourself a favor and READ THIS BOOK. When you get to chapter 14, and through the remainder of the book, be ready to listen to the Spirit of God. For what is God preparing you?

fact, you could not have made a more poor evaluation of your missed opportunity. *Losing periodic control of our lives is God's gift to us.*

For the Christian, *losing* control, since it isn't usually something we do by choice, should be recognized as God's pursuit of our lives. It is during these times we are in the cross-hairs of the One whom Francis Thompson called "The Hound of Heaven." In such times, the loving-kindness of God is being poured over us in hopes that we'll respond surrenderingly. If we respond with sensitivity toward the Spirit's inquisition of our hearts, the Holy Spirit can begin his work. If not, we risk wasting our life.

It was in such times of unanticipated stillness that he began giving me a greater understanding of who I am in Christ, leading to all sorts of discoveries.

This will be an ongoing theme of this book. And my heart's increased sensitivity to the Spirit was likely a byproduct of two things: First, my being ushered into weeks, and on two occasions several months, of physical stillness. And second, an unequaled investment of time in His Word.

Ok, time for some transparency.

As I read through what I *thought* was the final manuscript for this book, I got to this point right here and knew the Lord was prompting me to be more forthcoming in a personal matter than I'd intended. Originally, I was not prepared to share what follows so publicly.

I'm going to tell you something very few people know about me— at least before the writing of this book. Afterwards, you'll know why I'm so well acquainted with how it is that God often chooses to do his most deeply operative work during our times of unwelcomed stillness or pain. I'm not one for self-pity and certainly not one who wants others to hand me a crutch of excuse. Ok, I'm dancing around it; I wasn't going to tell you about this personal story because of my pride. There...I said it. It's *still* in there.

In the fall of 2002, I was supposed to die—or so said the doctors. It was the Lord's choice to *really* sideline me for the first time in my life. Through the experience, God had purposed to reveal to me something of a new level of personal insufficiency—something I carry with me to this day.

For reasons my doctors would only, in the end, refer to as "unknown origins," blood had pooled at the base of the basilica artery in my brain. The brain specialists were convinced I'd had an aneurism somewhere in the network of the brain and it was only a matter of hours until they'd expected to see me expired.

My cranial hemorrhaging initiated a flurry of activity behind the scenes once we arrived at the hospital. All I knew was that there seemed to be a lot of hushed conversations about me. Didn't they know I was in the room?

Because it seemed no one was letting me in on their secrets, I figured it wasn't that bad, and my main concern was getting out of the hospital so I could make good on my obligation to help lead worship the next day in church. It was, according to Lesli, a life-changing night at the hospital for the *both* of us.

Just recently, Lesli walked me through some of what she experienced on that long night.

> "While in the ER, Greg kept talking and being very friendly with the nurses...and singing. He *kept* singing, working through a particular song he'd been asked to prepare for the weekend.
>
> He may appear at times to be outgoing, but this was over the top.
>
> At the recommendation of the doctor, the staff ordered a CT scan. While waiting for the results, I wanted to call Richard (our worship leader at the time) to let him know Greg was *not* going to be able to sing that weekend.
>
> It was a Friday night and with services on both Saturday night and Sunday morning, I had to make the church aware of what was going on, and that plans for that weekend were going to have to change.
>
> Greg kept insisting he was fine—and he just *kept* singing. At the point where I informed the nursing staff that he was supposed to sing at church the next day, one of them assured me he wasn't going *anywhere*.
>
> When they brought me the CT scan and calmly tried to explain it to me, I was completely overwhelmed. They were basically telling me that my husband was in deep trouble. But I couldn't grasp it all. At that point I called one of Greg's brothers, Philip, since he had a medical background, and asked him to come to the hospital to help me understand what the nurses were telling me.
>
> As an extended family, we had rallied the troops that day and were in the process of moving our family of five from one apartment to another at the time when the back of Greg's neck and head had begun to burn like fire. Philip had found him soaking the back of his

head and neck under running cold water from the faucet in the upstairs tub. It didn't take Philip long to become concerned.

Consulting with me, Philip told me that we were going to have to talk Greg into going to the hospital—which, to no one's surprise, Greg resisted...until his dad and brothers *told* him he *was* going to comply. His family assured us they could get the rest of the boxes moved into the apartment without us while we got things checked out. And by this time, I think Greg detected enough concern from his brother's evaluation that he finally got into the passenger seat.

The nurses, and later the neurologists, went into more detail with Philip and I as they told us about the quantity and location of the blood at the base of Greg's brain.

They were planning to isolate the location of the hemorrhaging by doing a cerebral angiograph in order to detect the location and extent of the bleeding. This was apparently part of their preparation for the last resort in such cases—which, in Greg's case, had already been determined to *be* the case—brain surgery.

About this time, they began granting me some special privileges.

They granted me permission to join them and Greg in the room for the angiograph, believing that things could turn fatal at any moment. They wanted me to be with him. There was little protocol now. That scared me.

Eventually, we moved up to the ICU and while Greg was very aware, talking and carrying on conversations with occasional visitors, he had little knowledge of what he was really saying or the severity of the circumstance.

During the night, his parents came up to see him. He told them he wanted some food from Steak 'n Shake. Since ICU patients are not normally permitted to eat much of anything, the nurses called the doctors to inquire—and, once again, were given the variance. I was becoming increasingly aware that Greg's case was getting special treatment.

I felt as though everyone around us knew we were going to watch Greg die that night. I was scared to death. All I could do was sit by his bed, hold his hand and plead with God for his life.

Our three kids, daughter Jordan, 13, and sons Caleb and Isaac, 9 and 6, were with my mom and dad and wanted to come see their daddy. But the hospital wouldn't permit them to enter the ICU.

As the early morning hours wore on, my mom was becoming less agreeable. Actually, it was more like my mom was planning to bring the kids to see Greg, and I got the impression very little was going to stop her from bringing them to his bedside.

Around 5:30am, the nurses asked for the age of our kids, and then asked if someone could bring them to the hospital so they could see their daddy–to say goodbye, because the chances of his making it through surgery were, in their words, slim. I remember their naked honesty being so seemingly inappropriate.

Meanwhile, my conversations with Greg didn't help my mindset. He just continued to say that if it was his time to go, he was ready and that I'd be fine. Though I'm sure he was trying to console and love me, he wasn't doing a good job.

When the surgeons finally fully analyzed Greg's angiograph, they told us they were unable to locate the source of the bleed. They were incredulous. That much blood doesn't just come out of nowhere. There was, in fact, no longer any seepage anywhere for them to find. For the life of them, they could not locate where all of the blood had come from. The pool of blood was still there, clear as day and the size of a man's fist, but they had *no idea* how it got there.

Because of this, they determined there was no reason to conduct such a risky surgery.

Assuming they hadn't missed something, they figured whatever it was had closed itself back up. This meant they were going to monitor Greg for a day or two and, if nothing changed, were going to release him."

Release me? This was a miracle. I *now* know why God stopped me dead in my tracks that night, putting a complete stop to everything in my life but being alive. It wasn't so that I could know what pain was, dealing with the next several weeks flat on my back while the blood slowly dissipated itself down my spine, but so that I could experience the first of what was to become several complete stoppages of my "busy and productive" life.

It was as if God were saying, "Greg, now listen to me." He made sure I had no choice.

As I said, the ensuing recovery put me, literally, flat on my back for several weeks. The painful recovery put me into a position where I was, for the first time in my life, still—I mean *really still*...for a long time.

I was three months in recovery, but it was a holy time...a time I will never forget. God had my attention. And I leaned hard into Him in my complete helplessness. Anything less than a complete incapacity for this first stoppage time would have been insufficient.

The extent of the physiological fallout from this experience is greater than anyone but my wife, Lesli, knows. But I have learned to embrace it. For through it, God has chosen to reveal more of himself. And because of this, I wouldn't undo a bit of it.

Today, the lingering effect of this episode is undeniable. But it has taught me that my sufficiency is now in Him and not in my own ability.

Second, God's way of preparing our hearts for a move of his Spirit within us is to prompt us to invest unequaled time in his Word.

The first time God had me cloaked in his Word for more than an hour or so was at the tail end of my 2nd three-month period of stillness, having broken my wrist, which put me out of service in my current occupation.

Toward the end of my recovery, I decided it would be good to have a therapeutic week at my parent's cottage about 450 miles north of Indianapolis.

As I began my trek, riding my 1982 Honda Silverwing up to Northern Michigan for a few days of examining introspection about how the Lord may like me to communicate what he had been teaching me, I hit play on Max McLean's audio recording of the Bible.

Never before had I been so completely saturated in God's Word. The experience changed me.

In what ended up being an unexpectedly short 3 or 4 day round trip, God had taken me on a whirl-wind tour through the history of my spiritual ancestors—from Genesis 1:1 through what seemed at the time to be the relatively cool waters of the Psalms and Proverbs and beyond. I had been given a precious gift.

I learned more of God's character in 16 to 18 hours of scriptural emersion than I had absorbed in 40 plus years of self-disciplined readings. For the first time, I experienced the living, breathing nature of God's words to us. I would never have guessed I could feel like a kid in a candy shop as I skipped through the likes of Numbers, Deuteronomy and Judges...but I did.

In short, God met me over those 900 miles. I don't think it is too great a conclusion to say that the groundwork was laid for an awakening to the Holy Spirit, long having lived inside me, as a result of what has become an ongoing practice of bathing my soul in his Biblical texts.

And I'm not alone. Roger Basick, host of Moody Radio's *Music Through the Night*, informed me that George Mueller's[16] most effective work was accomplished between the ages of 71 to 92 while he was reading through the Bible four times each year!

Mark Hamby, of Lamplighter Publishing, makes this practical recommendation: Before turning on the TV, practice reading first. 2 Timothy 2:21 says, *"Therefore, if anyone cleanses himself from what is dishonorable, he will be a vessel for honorable use, set apart as holy, useful to the master of the house, ready for every good work."*

And in spending time in the Word, I've learned to not always worry about deeply studying what I'm reading at every turn; it is a first great step to just obediently deliver the Word into our souls. In the very least, the Spirit living inside you is being fed. He will appreciate your act of obedience. This practice *will be* a difference-maker.

> *My word that comes from My mouth*
> *will not return to Me empty,*
> *but it will accomplish what I please*
> *and will prosper in what I send it to do.* – **Isaiah 55:11** (HCSB)

Having said this, herein lay a danger as well–and we must contemplate this sure thing; there is no one-two punch, no formula through which the Spirit of God is obligated to be awakened within us. God knows best how to reduce us individually. Our simply being available and nourishing the ground for his tilling is a great place to start. And once we are delivered to the place where the Spirit has used our stillness and his Word as preambles to the main work he has in mind, having helped us attain to the end of ourselves while realizing we have nothing worthy of contribution apart from him, we can finally, in his time, be seized by the Spirit of God.

So let's put the wraps on this introduction with some of the Truths which point us to the great irony of our glorious freedom

---

[16] http://www.desiringgod.org/biographies/george-muellers-strategy-for-showing-god

through enslavement in Christ. It *begins* with our growing in the knowledge, wisdom and fear of the LORD.

> ***Desire without knowledge is not good—***
> how much more will ***hasty feet miss*** the way! – **Proverbs 19:2**

> *Wisdom rests in the heart of him **who has understanding**,*
> *But what is in the heart of fools is made known.* – **Proverbs 14:33**

> *The fear of the* LORD *is the beginning of wisdom,*
> *and **knowledge of the Holy One is understanding**.* – **Proverbs 9:10**

> ***Apply your heart to instruction and your ears to words of knowledge.*** – **Proverbs 23:12**

> [NIV]
> 1 My son, if you accept my words
>   and store up my commands within you,
> 2 turning your ear to wisdom
>   and applying your heart to understanding—
> 3 indeed, if you call out for insight
>   and cry aloud for understanding,
> 4 and if you look for it as for silver
>   and search for it as for hidden treasure,
> 5 then you will understand the fear of the Lord
>   and find the knowledge of God. – **Proverbs 2:1-5**

> [The Message]
> 1-5 Good friend, take to heart what I'm telling you;
>   collect my counsels and guard them with your life.
> Tune your ears to the world of Wisdom;
>   set your heart on a life of Understanding.
> That's right—if you make Insight your priority,
>   and won't take no for an answer,
> Searching for it like a prospector panning for gold,
>   like an adventurer on a treasure hunt,
> Believe me, before you know it Fear-of-God will be yours;
>   you'll have come upon the Knowledge of God. – **Proverbs 2:1-5**

This book is my attempt to trace the pathway of God's jealous pursuit of my life. The journey is far from over, but I'm excited about what lay ahead.

What Samuel Kaboo Morris[17] said about himself I have found true of me as well: I have a thick head.

You see, the things described in this passage from Proverbs, though I'd attempted to *achieve* such a heart attitude in the past, now characterize my pursuit of him because He has helped me grasp some new and critically important things about myself as a believer and what happened that day at Calvary 2000 years ago.

I will be trying to describe this throughout this book. But thanks be to God, I can finally say these verses really and truly describe the base desires of my heart.

I am fully aware that I could not have done this on my own—not in three and one-half decades of walking as a Christian. So praise be to God for his gift. May his mercy and grace continue to go before both you and me. For if he doesn't continue to make less of us and more of himself in our lives, we are without hope to begin and continue to live a Spirit-filled life...a life truly *Set Free*.

While only God can plot the points we are to travel on our pathway into deeper fellowship with him, we know where to begin—a heart filled with remorse for our self-will, self-trust and pride. A heart bled of everything *except* that which our Lord wants from us begins with a repentance so deep and genuine we could never manufacture it or come to it on our own.

"Repentance," writes Bonhoeffer, "means turning away from *one's own work* to the mercy of God."[18]

There is no merciful release for the clearing of our heart's wayward separation from a holy God without it being *His* release. Repentance is all we can offer. We cannot earn God's favor. It is *He* who calls. And it must be He who does all the work. For our part, we must be ready, listening, willing, preparing the way for His still, quiet voice to be heard. And, in His time, He will do that which He desires to be done in us—that, through our death, His plans may become alive in us.

And so looking back now, though very much feeling as though I am still, and knowing I will always be in the midst of the process of being made new, my first conclusion is that **I had settled for too little**.

---

[17] http://www.taylor.edu/about/heritage/samuel-morris/the-samuel-morris-story.shtml

[18] Bonhoeffer's sermon for Repentance, Sunday, November 19, 1933

PART I

WE ARE OUR OWN HANDICAP

CHAPTERS 1-11

SETTLING

Chapter 1

Settling for Too Little – The Role of Faith

"What a tragedy it has been that in our time we are taught to believe in him and accept him–and to seek him no more."[19] – A. W. Tozer

This book is my attempt to encourage us to seek Jesus *beyond* acceptance; to *continue* seeking Him and to stop settling for so little.

In my Christian walk, I had *settled* for a cerebral comprehension of the historic facts on which my faith had been based. Likewise, it was along this same continuum that most of my spiritual growth for the next thirty-five years was based–in the cerebral.

Doing so robbed from me a quest for an experiential faith. But make no mistake, I was okay with that...a bar tragically, and surely to

---

[19] Tozer, The Crucified Life

Jesus' aching heart for me, far too low. I didn't know any better. I have come to believe this is a disease from which many of us suffer.

Mine was a faith sufficiently delivered from the Spirit which allowed me to believe I had been forgiven my sins and saved unto eternal life. I believed Jesus died, rose and saved me, but I hadn't felt a need to go any further than a cognitive apprehension of such knowledge.

Had I been pressed, I would have told you that while experiential or tangible evidences of my walk with Christ would have been encouraging, such neediness was mostly for those lacking in faith—or for the charismatic church. Anyway, to *seek* such substantiation for my salvation would only have been a crutch, tantamount to my saying that what the Lord had impressed upon me for a life saved from hell and redeemed for heaven was insufficient! Besides, it's not like I felt I was missing anything—so why search for something more?

Whether because I have never been a doubting Thomas or because I have an undersized intellect, one thing is sure: mine was an underdeveloped Christian life. But again, I didn't know it.

By way of illustration, my faith was not unlike the fact that Columbus sailed the ocean—an entry of data into the knowledge bank. I am grateful Columbus further exposed this piece of real estate to the developing world, and personally benefit from the rich and blessed heritage of America.

Similarly, I have been grateful for my faith in Christ. The work he did on my behalf was a fact of history for which I *was* very grateful. But such cerebral knowledge of God can only lead to a limited exchange with him.

> You cannot know God like you know the multiplication tables or Morse Code.... However, when Paul said, "that I may know him," Philippians chapter 3 verse 10, he did not mean intellectually but experientially.... The best unregenerate man can do is know *about* God.... We can think of his attributes and rejoice in his grace, but the unregenerate can only do it as an academic exercise. But it is only in a heart, quickened by the Holy Spirit, that God can really be known.[20]

There's nothing wrong with a Christian life characterized by a thoughtful quest of his attributes and a deeply grateful heart which rejoices in his grace. Nothing wrong, that is, unless you're bothered by

---

[20] Tozer, The Crucified Life; Chapter 12

the fact that a relationship with God under such limited, academic parameters is incomplete and underdeveloped.

But I *wasn't* bothered.

Even though my walk with Jesus was mostly cognitive, I cannot imagine what my life would have been like to this point without him—even while operating under such Spirit-limiting conditions. He has been my hope through many a day, week, month and year! And throughout my Christian life, I have even been the recipient of well timed, God-arranged convictions and other proceedings that have undeniably pointed to God's moving hand in my life.

But, for the Spirit's purposes and desires for us as new creations, I had been missing something; my past *faith* had not represented the entirety of what He had *planned for us* as new creations in Him. He desires infinitely more...a more we begin to grasp when we become not more, but less content.

I now see that verses 3-5 in Proverbs 2 are not only for those in need of salvation, but also for us who have been redeemed—that our lives would be filled with a Spirit-driven *progression* characterized by the reduction of our old Adam in lieu of a supernatural expansion of our new man.

> *Indeed, if you call out for insight and cry aloud for understanding, and if you look for it as for silver and search for it as for hidden treasure, then you will understand the fear of the Lord and find the knowledge of God.* **– Proverbs 2:3-5**

Even still, it will never be our effort that will prove the ultimate difference-maker in our knowing God more deeply. Rather, such is only achievable through a revelatory move of the Spirit of God in our hearts and minds. Ours is a merely preparatory role.

I had known these and other similar passages of Truth, but as if only with my old composition, enlightened just enough to trust in it; to trust in something I could never see or actually perceive of if left completely to myself. And certainly that *is* a miracle in itself! Thank God for his willingness to enlighten our hearts enough to trust in him in such an initial way.

But the pity is that I didn't command a need for a more visceral faith—believing that such a need could only come from a *lack* of faith and our adversary! How could I ever tell the Almighty that what He'd given *me* wasn't enough? Do you follow me? Can you relate?

I was what Tozer calls, in chapter 13 of The Crucified Life, an underdeveloped Christian.

I could not get at the idea of truly attaining fellowship with God. I could intellectually grow and grow in familiarity with his Word, but I had not come to an understanding that even the Scriptures themselves, by themselves, have a limited role.

The Word is purposed to point us to God himself. The Scriptures will not in themselves generate fellowship with God. Fellowship with the Almighty comes only through a supernatural intermingling of his Spirit with our spirit. A bursting of the Holy Spirit onto the scene of our lives is the beginning of our knowing God, not to be confused with knowing *about* God.

My **faith** was merely a **willful belief.** By definition, it could have looked like this in a Webster's Dictionary by Greg:

Faith [feyth]:
noun – a cognitive, willful acceptance of or in a thing; having no need or desire of confirmation; accompanied by no experience of fact that would lead one to have absolute confidence

But God desires our walk with him become *more* than this kind of faith! He would that, over time, our *faith* become *belief* and, eventually, an absolute *confidence*. He, as Proverbs 18:24 conveys, who sticks closer than a brother desires an intimate, *active*, positively personal experience which instills within us an unshakable confidence.

Let's be clear that this Proverbs 2:3-5 pursuit of God is one that points us toward a tangible, experiential faith and should not to be confused with an intellectual pursuit purposed to determine Christ's divinity, historicity and the like—in an apologetics sort of way. This, too, would represent a low bar of spiritual expectation. Such research can be done sufficiently without a supernatural illumination.

How many people do you know who believe in God and that Jesus was a real figure of history, but cannot cross the line of demarcation to becoming a child of God through Jesus?

Really, one could claim *that* isn't faith at all, but merely the act of an historian. It's merely evaluative. An intellectual pursuit to convince oneself of Christ's validity *can* merely be a study of historic evidences—like a detective doing his due diligence.

This, of course, is fine in our post-modern, Holy Spirit aside, Christianity. For such is merely an intellectual pursuit for the sole purpose of "having a ready defense of the hope within." **But to have to seek the non-empirical to satisfaction, that's a different matter** altogether. And it is a need for THIS kind of pursuit, of non-empirical, supernatural-based knowledge and understanding that I thought was all wrong–and lacked faith. You know...took one to the weird side.

I saw my faith as so purely a holy act of God that I believed it would be much like thumbing my nose at him were I to *seek* ways to have my faith substantiated. Surely, I thought, the weakness displayed in needing something more would itself be displeasing to God.

I thought if I needed a supernatural, personal acquisition of knowledge for a successful daily life in Christ, I would be scorning his grace in my life. I would be, in effect, telling the God of the Universe that what He'd given me for my salvation and ensuing life of faith wasn't enough. After all, I am the created and not the creator, right? I am the subject, not the authoritor. Therefore, the faith given me was to be something for which I was unquestionably grateful–end of story.

Thus, my spiritual bar was kept dreadfully low. And in doing so, I never hungered for supernatural revelation to satisfy and substantiate my faith. All the while, God's deep desire was that I seek and learn of him in that very way–personally, satisfyingly!

In conclusion of this matter, then, I had not been urged to **need** a revelatory, soulish confirmation of my faith.

Because I had bought into a definition of faith as a cognitive, willful acceptance of or in a thing, I had thanked God all my life for the mustard seed of faith that *had been sufficient* for me. I had determined I was, and would forever be content therein.

Oh, the boredom of it all. How shortsighted.

It was like I had short-sheeted (ask a junior high student what that means if you don't know) my own spiritual life–and never knew it. I had curled myself into an embryonic life in the Spirit–and desired that it be that way. I thought that not *needing* to stretch my arms and legs out towards the edges of the bed was honoring the God who had bought my life.

But the nature of my spiritual contentment was terribly short-sighted and uninformed.

Chapter 2

It Doesn't Have To Be This Way

But things have changed.

Only through a pressing and pleading with the Spirit of God to take on my **faith** has it become **belief**–a belief which, over time and experience, has become an absolutely dominating and unshakable **confidence**.

I am certain God wants us to become ambassadors fully compelled and usable. I am utterly convinced God desires to reveal to us all we need so that we can become his unshakable confidants in the battle.

This kind of faith is more like a **complete trust**, coming both from the Spirit's personal interaction with us and through his revelation to our soul by means of the Word, leading to an undeniable, unrelenting and overpowering compulsion to hit the floor in a desperate state as the created clay at the disposal of a mighty God. Through occurrences in our lives that regularly point to God's movement on our behalf in our physical world, **our faith becomes an all-consuming assurance that affects the desires of one's heart!**

What's more, I have come to realize that God actually pleads with us to *seek* such substantiation. For crying out loud, why did Jesus tell the disciples to stay put until the Holy Spirit was sent if he didn't want them to have an emotional, subjective, kick in the pants substantiation that he is alive and well, that he is their authoritative power and that he is who he claims to be in relation to us, his beloved?

Let's look again. What do *you* think?

> ² *turning your ear to wisdom*
>   *and applying your heart to understanding—*
> ³ *indeed, if you call out for insight*
>   *and cry aloud for understanding,*
> ⁴ *and if you look for it as for silver*
>   *and search for it as for hidden treasure,*
> ⁵ *then you will understand the fear of the Lord*
>   *and find the knowledge of God.* – **Proverbs 2:2-5**

Does God want us to have a strong, personal, viscerally experiential knowledge of him? Absolutely.

Ask, He says.

Seek, He says.

Knock, He says (Matt 7:7-8).

And no, I don't believe these verses are asking us to seek for such understanding and knowledge to merely pacify our human plane of intellectual curiosity or belief–the type of cerebral pursuit of him I'd mentioned earlier. No, I believe this passage demands a deeply searching, interpersonal quest for the tangible Spirit of God who dwells within us.

But sadly, for most of us self-assertive, confident American suburban types, God's Spirit tragically lies quietly within us– underappreciated and unrequested, safely in the corner of our low bar lives.

PAUSE to PONDER

- Does *your* faith need substantiation to grow into an *unshakeable* belief?
- Would seeing God's hand in your personal life increase your confidence in him?
- When your children obey you as a father or mother, does your heart soften toward them? Does this increase or decrease communion?

Chapter 3

An Increased Appetite

But what about God's perspective?

Maybe God also doesn't want our post-salvation walk with His Son to be strictly based in the world's definition of faith at all...a belief in something without being able to substantiate it empirically! Maybe if we understood that *He desires* that we raise our bar of expectation, our appetite for such would increase.

Certainly the *first* step in our spiritual journey, accepting Christ as our substitute for the penalty of sin, is of faith alone–having maybe had no tangible or empirical evidence to which we could point that may have led us into initial surrender.

But thereafter, is our walk with Jesus faith alone? Or, as Hebrews 12:2 says, does our journey become a continual progression of upward *trust* through personal experiences gained with the Holy Spirit?

At this point, because we have experience with the author and perfector of our faith to *validate* that which was previously faith alone, I no longer think our faith is strictly "a belief not based on proof."

Think of it this way. *Prior to conversion*, faith would be trusting in an initial hypothesis that God *could* save us from our sin through Jesus. *But after conversion* and the indwelling of the Spirit of God, our previous faith should now be substantiated through the Holy Spirit's ministry to our spirit. And as we acquire knowledge from the Spirit of God within, we say our "faith" grows.

But more accurately, I would propose that what is growing is actually our *substantiated knowledge of* what has been happening within us!

Beautifully after conversion into God's family, the ministry of the Holy Spirit begins to transform our **faith into belief**. And as we live actively and obediently with the Spirit, we find that our belief bank becomes less about faith and more about the knowledge of what is.

It is when we look at the life of a mature, lifelong seeker of God that we say, "What a life of faith".

But if asked, that person would likely tell us that *faith* played a critical role early on, but as God proved faithful and as the Spirit showed Himself trustworthy of all that was revealed to him, *knowledge and confidence grew*. And that body of experience became so large, so confidence building, so overwhelming that his life became one characterized more by *belief* than faith.

Why is this?

It is because *faith* is an acceptance of something *un*seen or *un*substantiated.

Chapter 4

Stopping at Faith is Lazy

So why the splitting of hairs between faith and belief?

It is because too many of us cross the threshold of faith and stop there! Then, on the intellectual side, we add to our unsubstantiated faith a few dashes of biblical factoid and...we're good.

Somewhere along the way we have missed that God wants to *take us over*—not merely be our eternal insurance plan with zero deductible and a good declarations page.

God gifts us with *faith* to help us approach the *starting* gate. But only if our appetite is increased for an in-breaking and active work of the Spirit in our lives can we begin experiencing God in such a way that our faith can turn into an unshakable *belief* in our God. And this is what He desires for us.

So what about you? Is your relationship with Christ still living on faith alone? Or, having lived many months or years in deep communion with God's Spirit, all the while witnessing His movement in and through your life in very personal, subjective, deeply emotional ways, can you say that your walk with God has moved *from* faith *into* a substantiated belief?

Yes, a maturing walk with God under the guidance and tutorship of the Spirit necessarily progresses into a substantiated, subjective and personal enlightenment into known facts of occurrence. I may not be able to subjectively and sufficiently explain to another person how I know my relationship with God through Jesus is absolutely and factually real, but I *know* it just the same.

So why live a blind, settling faith when the Spirit of God was given us to TAKE US OVER?

Our walk with Christ is intended to be a beautiful dance between *both* an intellectual understanding of who we are as believers in Christ, **and** a growing perception of the Spirit's guidance, insight and indwelling power!

For those of us with a more conservative spiritual upbringing, there is a tendency to lean almost exclusively on the cerebral confidences we find in the Word. In such cases, the Lord wants to awaken us to the difference-making power available through a life in the Spirit.

For others, it may be that their spiritual life has been so heavily weighted on the experiential aspects of spirituality that their walks don't have sufficient theological rootedness. Such doctrinal insufficiency can lead to a relationship with Christ which looks and feels like a rollercoaster.

It is important we find the stabilizing equilibrium that meets midway between these two polar extremes. The academic and supernatural realities of our new life in Christ are equally important for a dynamic life in Christ.

And so through all of this having become evident to me, I have come to understand we are not asked to have a faith that is blind trust at all. Rather, God wants to reveal himself to us so much that he made a way for his very Spirit to *live inside us*, and to make us new in ways and in areas we know we are completely incapable of altering on our own.

But this journey from faith to belief does not come cheap—for there are things God must do in us that may seem unpleasant at the time. But we aren't left alone; his Spirit will help us through our dismantling. He will require sacrifice, for we know that he who loses his life for Christ's sake will find life.

But...there *is* that losing part.

He searches the hearts of willing men and women with intentionality—for the purpose of making incisions and removals; there is much that needs to be cut out of us. But as ones he has adopted and grafted into his very own life, we should rejoice in his dismantling and disciplining work—it is a sign of our sonship in him.

> [5] *And have you forgotten the encouraging words God spoke to you as his children? He said, "My child, don't make light of the Lord's discipline, and don't give up when he corrects you.*

> *⁶ For the Lord disciplines those he loves,*
> *and he punishes each one he accepts as his child."*
>
> *⁷ As you endure this divine discipline, remember that God is treating you as his own children. Who ever heard of a child who is never disciplined by its father?*
> **- Hebrews 12:5-7 (NLT)**

Besides, there is no other way. It is the only road to freedom and wholeness.

I'm still in the process of trying to identify the path through which He has brought me recently, but what I do know is this; his releasing me into himself has come, in great measure, from his revealing a greater understanding of some key truths from His Word. These truths are at the heart of this book and will be covered in Part 3.

Some were things I had known cerebrally, but it took the Holy Spirit's work to reveal them to my soul. These deeper discoveries were the catalysts that brought about His pursuance of me to a point of broken surrender.

It comes to this; if you are not being made new in ways you *know* you couldn't change yourself through any amount of will power or self-discipline, if your heart is not measurably softening to the things of God, if there is no deep and abiding pleasure derived from time in his Word, you need to question whether you've settled for too low a bar in your walk with the Holy Spirit.

But here's the kicker! I have been searched, prodded, revealed to, broken and remade in a way **I had never allowed myself to even desire previously**. But this experience was never intended to be for a few. It was intended for us all—all who belong to Jesus.

But we have settled for a low bar of spiritual expectancy.

Chapter 5

The Role of Self-Saving Financials

In America, we fight an amazingly fragile and uphill battle for our faith.

First, though not a matter for discussion here so only a passing comment will have to do, we don't want to be let down as a byproduct of placing our complete trust in God – lest he not *come through* as we desire. But second, and more to our point here, we seldom come to a place where we are uncomfortable enough to even *desire* more.

When we're physically uncomfortable or a bit emotionally needy, what do we do? **We spend money in our possession to appease our desires, regaining a satisfactory level of comfort.** And we move on.

In doing so, we, in the least case, quench the Spirit without knowing it–leading to ineffectual lives in the Spirit; in the worst case, we fall into sinful patterns of complacency leading to spiritual deadness.

As we see many times throughout the history of our faith, Nehemiah summarizes this human propensity well.

> [28] *"But as soon as they were at rest, they again did what was evil in your sight. Then you abandoned them to the hand of their enemies so that they ruled over them. And when they cried out to you again, you heard from heaven, and in your compassion you delivered them time after time.*
> **– Nehemiah 9:28**

On our own, we become spiritually complacent when prosperous. This propensity is less a character flaw than a natural predisposition for those of us with skin on.

Prosperity has a way of bringing us to a place of self-confidence and self-trust. It's in our DNA.

"Look what I have accomplished," we say.

This all too quickly turns us into spiritual midgets.

This spiritual self-life then leads us into a place of spiritual complacency. And God being a jealous God, abandons us to our own demise–that we would yet again recognize our insufficiency without Him in order that we would once more, like the stoutly disciplined Israelites, return to Him with all our heart.

But, I'm afraid in America and in other places where we have the ability to self-medicate with earthly indulgences, we continually salve God's chastening discomfort with something less than himself. Thus, we end up living terribly uninspiring lives.

Now a note of caution; I know it is *possible* for some to live with great financial wherewithal, and still live centered and deeply obedient lives in Christ. But that number is *small*. It is smaller than we think.

It is a hard thing, Jesus tells us, to have much provision and still enter, let alone walk deeply in, the Kingdom purposes most dear to God's heart. If not so, why did He refrain from providing for himself all the comforts his world had to offer? He refrained because it would have been a distraction to his call. He did so, I believe, because it kept him dependent, leaning and trusting in his Father alone for comfort.

Would it have been wrong for Jesus to have had a place to call home as he walked in his adult ministry–a place to have a straw mattress and a cotton-stuffed pillow? No. But he *chose* to forgo these things (Matt. 8:20, Luke 9:58). We have to look at that seriously.

And if we claim to want to walk with Jesus, following Him as He bids us to do, we have to be *willing* to do without the vast and continual physical comforts our world offers *if doing so* sharpens our ability to walk humbly with Him.

Most of us mortals living lives of ease, entertained with the things our horizontal world values, are *distracted by them* more often than are we driven by them into deep brokenness, surrender and an awareness of our utter depravity, lostness and neediness apart from Christ.

Isaiah 1:2-4 should give us pause. Remember, these words were being spoken to a people who had known God...but were now a stench in the nostrils of the Almighty because they had become reliant upon their own wherewithal.

> *² Hear me, you heavens! Listen, earth!*
>   *For the Lord has spoken:*
> *"I reared children and brought them up,*
>   *but they have rebelled against me.*
>
> *³ The ox knows its master,*
>   *the donkey its owner's manger,*
>   *but Israel does not know,*
>   *my people do not understand."*
>
> *⁴ Woe to the sinful nation,*
>   *a people whose guilt is great,*
>   *a brood of evildoers,*
>   *children given to corruption!*
> *They have forsaken the Lord;*
>   *they have spurned the Holy One of Israel*
>   *and turned their backs on him.*
>   — Isaiah 1:2-4

In receipt of much blessing, they again and again turned their eyes away from God, having been entangled by their prosperity and achievement amongst the nations. Are we much different?

Ezekiel, in Chapter 7, was given this for "the end." His vision begins by setting the stage this way in the first 4 verses:

> *The word of the Lord came to me: "Son of man, this is what the Sovereign Lord says to the land of Israel: 'The end! The end has come upon the four corners of the land! The end is now upon you, and I will unleash my anger against you. I will judge you according to your conduct and repay you for all your detestable practices. I will not look on you with pity; I will not spare you....'"*
>   — Ezekiel 7:1-4a

Then, in the heart of the Lord's accusations is this about what will *not* be able to save them. Not only that, but it completely turns the table as they literally detest their wealth, desiring only to dispose of it:

> *"They will throw their silver into the streets, and their gold will be treated as an unclean thing. Their silver and gold will not be able to deliver them in the day of the Lord's wrath. It will not satisfy their hunger or fill their stomachs, for it has caused them to stumble into sin."*
>   — Ezekiel 7:19

It is not a small thing to the Lord that we use our money and things to save ourselves. It is evident from this passage that the Israelites were confident in their trinkets. Over and over again in their wealth and gain, they sinned and turned. Do we really think we are any less susceptible?

Mark 10:17-30 has more to say to us American, self-saving suburbanites than we may like to admit.

When Jesus tells his disciples it is easier for a camel to go through the eye of a needle than for someone who is rich to enter into the Kingdom of God, I believe he's referring to those of us who are self-savers. He is referring to us who have the possessions, the riches, the capacity within our own realm of influence to make ourselves comfortable, to solve our own problems—*at least to our low bar of satisfaction*.

After all, when we can turn so readily to our material world or our personal hang-ups for comfort, why would we turn for comfort to that which we don't humanly understand so well, that which is ethereal—to the Spirit of God? It is not in the natural man to do so.

PAUSE to PONDER

- Does your dependence upon God increase when your money runs short? If so, why is this?
- Is the reverse of the above true in your life?
- Does coming to God with greater frequency and intensity when your ability to self-resource is diminishing indicate you love God's gifts more than you love Him?
- Can you quench the movement of the Holy Spirit in your life by self-resourcing with your money?

Chapter 6

Isn't Being Grateful Enough?

Properly assessing our self-saving tendencies is especially difficult when we follow our self-saving with eyes and lips heavenward, accompanied by a *genuinely* grateful heart that says, "Thank you, Lord, for your provision."

But in doing so, we are frequently fooling ourselves, for we have given God thanks for what *we* have done ourselves in actuality–in our own strength and pursuance.

I am not saying we are wrong for being grateful. Certainly not. I am just saying that our honest and sincere gratitude is mostly for the blessings of comfort, provision and a peaceful life of our own practical making and undertaking.

Is such a life of comfort God's undertaking or what we assume he desires for us given our culture's lead?

All I am saying is that when we have such a comfortable society, imbued with God's *assumed* blessing, we are actually in a very difficult position if we have interest in a deeply surrendered and passionate fellowship with the Holy Spirit.

This difficult position of surrendering all in a society that so values its comfort is one we come by quite naturally. John Piper, in his convicting book *Don't Waste Your Life*, points out that we are wired by nature to love the same toys that the world loves. He says,

> I start to fit in. I start to love what others love. I start to call earth, home. Before you know it, I'm calling luxuries needs, and using my money just the way unbelievers do. I begin to forget the war. I don't think much about people perishing. Missions and unreached peoples drop out of my mind. I stop dreaming about the triumphs of

grace. I sink into a secular mindset that looks first at what man can do, not what God can do. It is a terrible sickness.[21]

Were we to put Jesus' illustration of a camel going through the eye of a needle into today's modern vernacular, we could say, as does Keller in chapter 11 of King's Cross, we have "a snowball's chance."

While Jesus is talking about a wealthy, self-saving, unbeliever's chances of entering the Kingdom, I don't think it's too much a stretch to relate it to the challenge we have in pursuing a passionate and life-changing walk with the Holy Spirit. **On our own, in our willful, workman-like effort, we don't have a snowball's chance—no matter how hard WE try to get more of the Spirit's guidance, presence and relationship.**

Such workman-like effort is the wrong way around the problem. Instead, we must *lay down* our workman-like effort of self-solving and self-saving.

We must stop living the way unbelievers do.

We must stop calling this earth home.

We must DIE, become limp to our self-effort, and finally admit **we just don't have it!**

Oh, and here's a news flash for us Type-A personalities; try as we may, we cannot come to this admission on our own.

Self-saving through our financial wherewithal must be viewed for what it is—a form of idolatry.

The Ten Commandments begins with three warnings against idolatry. Idolatry, of course, is the attempt to erect an allegiance higher than God.

To whom, or what, do we turn first when in physical need—our wallet or our Lord?

You may say, "Greg, that's a silly question. If I'm out of bananas, milk and cereal, or am in need of Tylenol to take the edge off, I think you're being a little hypercritical to say that in doing so we are being idolatrous."

I do see your point. But my emphasis here is not to equate using the ten-dollar bill in your pocket to purchase the next morning's Maxwell House coffee with an act of idolatry. Rather, I want us to ask

---

[21] John Piper, Don't Waste Your Life; Chapter 6

ourselves how often our needs have to be met with something *other than* a trip to the grocery store, our workplace for another paycheck, the local medical facility, the loan officer's office for that car purchase, a visit to Google, or via a quick phone call?

When compared to the world as a whole, our society is still rather unique when it comes to how it is we can so easily meet our own needs. And I'm not sure we're the better for it.

Today we need to hear again that God alone is worthy of our undying reliance, worship and obedience.

As Richard Foster says in his work called Freedom of Simplicity, "the idolatry of affluence is rampant." And affluent we are. He goes on, "There is no greater need today than the freedom to lay down the heavy burden of getting ahead."[22]

We work more in order to solve more…ourselves. But, we say, we are surely not *worshipping* the things our society provides us in our admitted lives of ease.

And this may well be the case. But here comes the rub.

All of us feel that we are in complete control of the way in which we self-save with what we possess. We aren't coveting what we do not have, but are grateful for what we do have, right?

"The problem," again articulates Foster, "is that we, like the alcoholic, are unable to recognize the disease once we have been engulfed by it. Only by the help of others are we able to detect the inner spirit that places wealth above God."[23]

And we must come to a point where we fear the idolatrous place of living self-saving lives in a society where we are seldom driven to our knees out of a desperation for much of anything. And when things become our life's salve, our priority to seek God in his care for us is extinguished. And the moment things we provide for ourselves take priority, radical obedience to an effectual walk in the Spirit becomes impossible.

When we continually regain our contentment equilibrium with our own wherewithal, we quench the Spirit. And when our self-sufficiency becomes our primary crutch, we dry up, or maybe never do get to a point where we get off the ground spiritually.

Foster puts his thoughts this way.

> Jesus…saw the wearisome burden upon those who had gotten riches and were trying to hold onto them. He knew the cancerous

---

[22] Foster, Freedom of Simplicity; Chapter 2, Page 20
[23] Foster, Freedom of Simplicity; Chapter 2, Page 20

nature of wealth and often warned of its dangers. He spoke of the "deceitfulness of riches" (Matt. 13:22). Riches are deceitful precisely because they lead us to trust in them, and Jesus saw that trap and the spiritual destructiveness which attends it. This was the burden that bore down upon the rich young ruler. Not only did he have great possessions, but more significantly, the great possessions had him. Of all oppressions, his was the most spiritually debilitating.[24]

And on the very same topic, Platt weighs in as well this way.

> The reality is, most of us in our culture and in the American church simply don't believe Jesus on this one. We just don't believe that our wealth can be a barrier to entering the Kingdom of God. We are fine with thinking of affluence, comfort, and material possessions as blessings, but they cannot be barriers.
>
> We think the way the world thinks – that wealth is always to our advantage.
>
> But Jesus is saying the exact opposite (Matt 19:21, Mark 10:21, Luke 18:22). He is saying that wealth can be a dangerous obstacle. That's why Paul says in I Timothy 6:6, "Godliness with contentment is great gain."
>
> In the context of this passage, contentment is described as having food and clothing–having the necessities of life provided for. Put this together with verse 9,...and [we find that] those who desire to be rich and acquire more than the necessities of life [food and clothing] are in danger of being plunged into ruin and destruction.
>
> This passage begs the question. Am I willing to live a life that is content with food and clothing, having the basic necessities of my life provided for, or do I want more? Do I want a bigger house, a nicer car or better clothes? Do I want to indulge in more and more luxuries in my life?[25]

PAUSE to PONDER

- To what or whom do you turn first when in physical need, your wallet or your Lord? (Be honest. Think practically.)
- Is your wealth (and if you are reading this book, you are wealthy) an obstacle to your dependence upon God?

---

[24] Foster, Freedom of Simplicity; Chapter 3, Page 39
[25] Platt, Radical; Chapter 6 (BTW, read this entire chapter)

Chapter 7

Exalting the Glory of Christ, Our Purpose

The objective here is not to reduce our reliance on abundance merely for the sake of living simply, for being good stewards of our finances, or for the sake of bringing a masochistic manner of discipline into our lives for the purpose of becoming tougher. No.

The purpose is that we position ourselves so that our hearts can be increasingly receptive to the voice of God in our lives without excessive distraction, clutter, and a pre-occupation with the things of this world.

The purpose of limiting our self-preserving impulse to bring resolution to our discomfort is so that our souls, when living in some degree of discomfort, may become more sensitive to the movement of the Spirit in our lives. And I think the purpose is also to consciously deny ourselves the habit of using our wealth to return to that equilibrium of comfort.

From what are we robbing ourselves when we refuse to live lives of reduction or denial?

What are we missing in our predictable habit to self-save financially? We're missing an abandoned life like Lisa's.

> "For months" says Lisa, "I've been listening to the Word and banging my head against the wall, trying to reconcile my life with what the Gospel demands. I've been trying to find some comfortable alternative between my life now and the radical idea of selling everything I own and leaving the comfortable life to take the Gospel to the world. But I've realized there is no comfortable alternative. Risking it all is the only option.

So I'm selling my stuff on the internet, and trying to pay off my debt so I can give as much as possible. In order to pay off that debt, I really am going to have to sell almost everything I have except the shirt off my back, and maybe a spare. I can't wait to see what happens from here. I'm totally unprepared, totally inadequate, totally scared. But I'm ready. Bring it on."[26]

Now this may seem extreme to some of us, but the reality is that this woman's actions correspond far more with Jesus' words in Mark 10 than with the actions of those of us who sit back and live the default life of the American dream, financially saving and sheltering ourselves from need of almost any kind.

But Jesus didn't mean it's a sin to be rich.

It is not that all individual rich people are bad. Nor is it true that all individual poor people are good. Neither was Jesus saying we should be careful not to fall into greed, but rather being generous from time to time, give of our comforts to those in need.

No, as Timothy Keller says, Jesus was saying there is something *radically* wrong with all of us. And money has a particular power to blind us to it. We use it to regain our comfort. And in so much as this is the case, money has the power to deceive us of our true spiritual state. And we need a gracious, miraculous intervention from God to see it.

And this kind of vision is impossible without God—without the illumination of the Holy Spirit, without a miracle…without grace.

But all this said, the point is not to be obedient in stewarding our possessions well or even helping others in need. The point, as Platt says, is to exalt the Glory of Christ as we express the Gospel of Christ through the radical generosity of our lives.

Where your treasure is, there your heart will be also (Matt 6:21, Luke 12:34). And so the way we use (not only view) our money is a barometer of our present spiritual condition.

Moreover, the way we use our money and possessions is an indicator of how often we live in light of what we know to be our eternal destination. The mark of Christ-followers should be that we are living heavenward. Our treasures should be spent there. The only way we can struggle with this kind of living is if we have not yet fully come to the conclusion that we have already died with Christ. More on this later.

---

[26] Platt, Radical; Chapter 6

Now on another level, so as not to be too hard on ourselves, we must recognize this important bit of reality. On our own, we are neither capable of escaping this inclination toward self-saving, nor are we able to truly surrender the leanings of the human will until a way is made clear for the Spirit to move in and through us freely.

"The fact is, we can urge, cajole, shove and push one another to loath self-sufficiency or discover simplicity, but in doing so we can find it all quite destructive." These objectives," continues Foster, "are just another anxiety-laden burden until people have experienced God's gracious power to provide them with daily bread. Only as kingdom power breaks in are we free to live in trust."[27]

And with that, we are pointed to a broader truth of our human condition; a condition which nearly daily drives me floor-ward.

We cannot save ourselves.

And in this state, we can only plead with the Holy Spirit to save us from ourselves–to give us the ability to properly assess our condition as helpless and hopeless wanderers apart from our being given completely and daily into His hands.

No amount of money or possession can save us from this condition. But freedom *from* it is a must on our journey into who Christ desires us to be.

---

[27] Foster, Freedom of Simplicity; Chapter 3, Page 54

Chapter 8

We Are Far Too Easily Pleased – Our Bar is Too Low

Now at the risk of cornering this whole idea one too many times, I feel compelled to put vice-like clarity to this whole matter of our settling for too little in our sensitivity to, and our lack of a love affair with, the Holy Spirit who could set us ablaze but lies dormant within. And it goes back to one of the first sentences of this book when I asked the following question:

> "How *does* a forty-six-year-old man, having lived with Jesus as his Savior for thirty-five of those years, discover something so new, so revolutionary about his identity in Christ that he feels as if he's been born again, AGAIN?"

In short, I believe **we are far too easily pleased**.

This may sound greedy, but when it comes to your ambitions for God's infilling and your expectations of God in your life, you need to want seconds at the banquet table of spiritual expectations. When it comes to God, you need to be like Oliver Twist and say, "Please, sir, I want some more."

If God gave Elisha a double portion of Elijah's spirit, then why not you? God is looking for the person who says to him, "I want double of that. I will surrender whatever is required–just raise my bar of expectation of you, O God."

We need to want more than what our culture has convinced us Christianity should look like.

"Our desires," as C.S. Lewis preached in a 1941 sermon, "are not too strong, but too weak. We are half-hearted creatures, fooling about with drink and sex and ambition when infinite joy is offered us, like an ignorant child who wants to go on making mud pies in a slum because he cannot imagine what is meant by the offer of a holiday at the sea. We are far too easily pleased."[28]

The prophet Jeremiah put it like this:

> *My people have exchanged their glory for that which does not profit. Be appalled, O heavens, at this; be shocked, be utterly desolate," declares the LORD; "for my people have committed two evils: they have forsaken me, the fountain of living waters, and hewed out cisterns for themselves, broken cisterns that can hold no water.*
> – Jeremiah 2:11b-13 (ESV)

By this we learn the heavens are *appalled* and *shocked* when we give up too soon on our quest for *real* pleasure – our glory in Christ, settling instead for broken cisterns. Oh, the pity of it.

Our self-saving, solutions oriented, suburban lifestyles of relative ease have softened us and made us look around at the rest of the world and believe there is nowhere to go but down. Seeing what the world has to offer, and possessing most of it ourselves, *we settle*.

We forget we are no longer strangers of what *used to be for us* the mysterious promise of God. Rather, since we have partaken in his promise, we should be strangers of this world (Ephesians 2:1-6).

Are we?

We *forget*, among other things, we are smack dab in the middle of a raging war for the souls of men (I Peter 5:8); for it is our postmodern lives of horizontal distraction and preoccupation that lull us to sleep. We are altogether unaware of and estranged from the continual and catastrophic loss of eternal life all around us. I don't think we have *lost* a wartime mentality as ones enlisted into the ranks of King Jesus. Rather, I think we may never have gained it.

> We are at war—whether the stocks are falling or climbing, whether the terrorists are hitting or hiding, whether we are healthy or sick. Both pleasure and pain are laced with poison, ready to kill us with the diseases of pride or despair. The repeated biblical warning to be alert fits the wartime image. And I need this warning every day.[29]

---

[28] C.S. Lewis, The Weight of Glory
[29] Piper, Don't Waste Your Life; Chapter 6

Satan and his ilk are promulgating upon the post-modern Christian a silencing stench of self. And in our trance, we merrily live good lives, and keep our noses clean while filling our days with what is appropriate, kind, and today–tolerant.

According to John Piper,

> Clean noses and quality family time is not life. Oh how many lives are wasted by people who believe that the Christian life means simply avoiding badness and providing for the family. So there is no adultery, no stealing, no killing, no embezzlement, no fraud–just lots of hard work during the day, and lots of TV and PG-13 videos in the evening–during quality family time. And lots of fun stuff on the weekend, woven around church, mostly. This is life for millions of people. Wasted life. We were created for more...far more.[30]

Just reading that quote again aches my heart, puts a small lump in my throat and moistens my eyes. I believe this way of living, for the Christian, is a symptom of an unbroken life.

For once our souls are sufficiently broken by whom and what we are in the midst of our low-bar-of-expectation lives, we will be incapable of living out our days on the fence.

Oh God, if this is us, please help us recognize that we are merely existing rather than living as supernatural misfits, aliens and strangers in this place we used to call our home.

If we're completely honest, many of us would rather blend into the scenery than become radically given over and enslaved to Christ– for there is danger there.

By blending in, we can stealth along undetected. In so doing, we can preserve our comfortable state. A little discomfort or inconvenience worked into our schedule is doable. But losing control– completely losing control of our *own* lives? Now that's a bit over the top, don't you think? That is hardly prudent behavior.

Yes, in our lukewarmth, we are completely off the radar of the adversary. And all of hell likes it that way. So do we. Why, after all, should we dangerously ingest too much Light of Life–that we would knowingly become a flashing blip on Satan's radar? How reckless!

Yes, reckless *if* we are still trying to preserve rather than lose ourselves (Matthew 10:38-39, 16:25, Mark 8:34-35, Luke 9:23-24, John 12:24-26).

---

[30] Piper, Don't Waste Your Life

But when we walk in self-preservation, the chains that once had us sharing Satan's eternal destiny will never be replaced with chains of enslavement to the One who purchased and ransomed us! Instead, our lives reflect Casting Crown's interrogation-by-lyric from their song, Somewhere In The Middle, when they ponder the question;

> Just how close can I get, Lord,
> To my surrender,
> Without losing *all* control?

In Billy Graham's book, The Reason For My Hope, he says this. I'd like to bold print the **entire** quote, but I'll spare you that visual irritation.

> Many people who think about becoming Christians ask, 'What's in it for me? How can I benefit?' If the answer is only to keep you from hell, you haven't considered the cost of living for Christ on earth.
>
> The right question is not, 'What's in it for me?' But rather, 'Is Christ in me?'
>
> That very idea is unsettling for many because it means forfeiting control. It means the Lord Jesus Christ will come into your life and reform, conform and transform you into an obedient follower. If that is not your desire, you have every reason to question whether or not you have been saved. Most people are not willing to take their hands off their lives to that extent.
>
> But this is Christ's offer. When you acknowledge your sin and ask for forgiveness, he cleanses you from the sin that has entangled you and kept you estranged from him. Immorality, pride, selfishness–it is all sin just the same.
>
> The great sacrificial work of the Lord Jesus was accomplished for you. For him to save you and then leave you to clean up your life would be impossible. So the Lord Jesus *moves in* and *takes up residence* in your life. That means, things are *going* to change.[31]

Too often, our lives do not show that we are running a race to break a *different* tape (I Corinthians 6:20, 7:23, 9:26, Hebrews 12:1, Luke 14:26-27).

---

[31] Billy Graham, The Reason For My Hope

Our lives as followers of Jesus should sometimes make us look like seriously counter-cultural weirdos in the eyes of the world, like ones who just don't fit in—ones who just cannot adjust to our earthly culture.

Do we not have the stomach for this new life in Christ?

The Spirit who lives within us desires to awaken, nourish and then fan into flame a holy discontent of his choosing—one tailor made for us. *We have been called with **purpose**!*

> When we're rescued from something, we are also saved for something…. We are saved from our sins by a free gift of grace, something that only God can do in us and that we cannot manufacture ourselves. But that gift of grace involves the gift of a new heart, new desires, new longings. …So we yearn for him. We want him so much that we abandon everything else to experience him. This is the only proper response to the revelation of God in the gospel.[32]

PAUSE to PONDER

- Have you ever pulled a spiritual Oliver Twist?
- What can you learn from 2 Kings 2:1-14 about the heart of God for those who relentlessly pursue him for more? Did God grant Elisha the desire of his God-fearing, obedient and sold-out heart?
- What holy discontent is God placing on your heart these days through which He is prepared to give you more?

---

[32] Graham, The Reason For My Hope

Chapter 9

A Cost-Benefit Analysis

Yes, God has saved us for something—new desires, new longings, for he has given us a new heart (Ezekiel 36:26).

Do we not think his master plan, having knit us together from the foundations of the earth, has placed us here individually for such a time as this?

God has saved us *for* something so overwhelming that, if discovered, we would lose sight of ourselves as we run headlong into it without regard for our own safety. We would make decisions that appear utterly absurd to an onlooking world. It would become apparent that our confidence and security is purposely not anchored in what this temporary home has to offer.

But time is growing short. The battle has come to our shores, fellow Christian. Satan knows the stakes. Do you?

Are you willing to become useful to God?

Are you willing to ask the Savior of your soul to bring to light whatever things there may be living within that are preventing you from living an undivided life?

What are you holding onto that you refuse to trade for God's glory?

Too often, I wonder if we look at becoming a true and undivided disciple of Jesus as something we may add to our arsenal so that we can become more instructive and useful to God. Really?

Do we *really* think God is somehow waiting around to see if we're going to give him a bigger slice of ourselves so he can impact the world? Do we really think He needs us at all to accomplish his ways? Do we really think he's just holding his breath, hoping against hope that we offer ourselves more unreservedly so his plans can go forward?

We would never say it that way, but the way we sit back and make decisions about whether we're going to follow God wholeheartedly, pursuing absolute death to ourselves as following Jesus requires, it's as if we're thinking of doing so only after evaluating how much the additional percentage of being given over will cost us.

If the cost-benefit analysis seems to tip in our favor, then we wade in a bit–until the discomfort of such abandonment becomes perceptively irrational, too costly to our family or the ramifications seem to cost us too much security.

Where have we gone wrong? How have we Christians gotten to the place where this self-determination is even tolerable?

Indeed, the cost of being a disciple of Jesus *is* great. But the cost of non-discipleship is even greater. And the cost of our non-discipleship, while being great for those yet outside the Kingdom of God, is even greater for us as believers. And this is the part we miss! While the cost of not taking Jesus seriously is immense for those who are hungering for the Truth in our spheres of influence, the cost of non-discipleship is not paid solely by those outside the Kingdom. **It is paid by us as well.**

Here is what I mean. Follow me here.

When Jesus *told* the rich man to abandon his possessions and give to the poor, have you ever really caught the second half of Jesus' invitation? It is this second half we fail to find comfort in trusting into– in no small measure because we don't feel we can control the payoff.

In the first chapter of his callout book, Radical, David Platt helps communicate what we're missing when we fail to become fully committed followers of Jesus. I will now quote extensively from this section of his book.

> *Go sell everything you have and give to the poor, and you will have treasure in heaven.* If we are not careful, we can misconstrue these radical statements from Jesus in the gospels and begin to think that He does not want the best for us. But he does.
>
> Jesus was not trying to strip this man of all his pleasure. Instead, he was offering him the satisfaction of *eternal* treasure. Jesus was saying, it will be better not just for the poor but for you too when you abandon the stuff you are holding onto.

We see the same thing over in Matthew, chapter 13. There Jesus tells his disciples; *the Kingdom of Heaven is like treasure hidden in a field. When a man found it, he hid it again. And then in his joy, went and sold all he had and bought that field.*

I love this picture. Imagine walking in a field and stumbling upon a treasure that is more valuable than anything else you could work for or find in this life. It is more valuable than all you have now or will ever have in the future. You look around and realize that no one else realizes the treasure is here, so you cover it up quickly and walk away, pretending you haven't seen anything.

You go into town and begin to sell off all your possessions to have enough money to buy that field. The world thinks you're crazy.

"What are you thinking?" your friends and family ask you.

You tell them, "I'm buying that field over there."

They look at you in disbelief. "That's a ridiculous investment" they say. "Why are you giving away everything you have?"

You respond, "I have a hunch." And you smile to yourself as you walk away.

You smile because you know! You know that in the end you are really not giving away anything at all. Instead you are gaining. Yes, you're abandoning everything you have, but you are also gaining more than you could ever have in any other way!

So with joy – with JOY, you sell it all. You abandon it *all*. Why? Because you have found something worth losing everything else for.

This is the picture of Jesus in the Gospel. He is something, someone worth losing everything for.

And if we walk away from the Jesus of the Gospel, we walk away from eternal riches. The cost of non-discipleship is profoundly greater for us than the cost of discipleship. For when we abandon the trinkets of this world and respond to the radical invitation of Jesus, we discover the infinite treasure of knowing and experiencing Him.[33]

---

[33] Platt, Radical; Chapter 1

What I have begun to find, credit and glory to God alone because of my inability to find Truth on my own, is that if you were to take all of the heavenly treasures away from this cost-benefit analysis, I would *still gladly* trade all I have for the simple pleasure of knowing and experiencing Him while in this body of flesh.

When the Maker of your soul begins to reveal himself to you, there is no greater joy than to know he is wrecking you and killing you off so that he can take up greater residence in your soul. I am nearing the place where I would trade just about anything for this.

But the question for each of us individually is whether or not we actually believe Jesus is worth it. Is Jesus worth trading it all in for? Too often, we ask ourselves whether we can, in effect, have our cake and eat it too. We say,

> *"He isn't actually asking that we rescind possession of things He has already given us. No, that would seem counter-productive. Rather, he is showing us in the scriptures that he is concerned about the heart. Yes, it's the heart. After all, what we have been given we do recognize to be a blessing from his hand."*

I think it's that way for us much of the time.

And so while we may say that we believe he is worth giving it all up for, we are also quick to remind ourselves that the comforts of this world don't necessarily *have to be* forgone in order to also follow Jesus with all our hearts. This is true. In theory.

In the end though, at the pinch point of decision, if God is asking that we remove some or all of the encumbrances of this world that *could* take away from how he may choose to reveal himself to us, do we fall short on the follow-through by determining that we can give all our heart, soul, mind and strength to our Lord while, at the same time, holding loosely *(we would say)* to the trinkets and comforts of this life?

Do we find ourselves willing to, in fishing terms, bait the hook of intention, grab the line with our thumb, and even cock the reel back behind our head—while listening *terribly intently* and *assumptively* for the call to *not* cast the pole forward, sending our bait sailing into the waves of the unknown?

It's as if we assume all God will ask for is our *willingness*—not our follow-through.

Do we see this kind of half-intentioned positioning in the faith life of Abraham as he prepared to take the knife back for its plunge into his most cherished promise from God? I think not. I don't think, for Abraham, there was this "listening terribly intently and assumptively for the call to *not* cast the knife into his son."

So, getting back to my earlier point, here's our danger.

By recognizing God as the source of our trinkets, we believe this *is*, to some degree, stewarding them wisely.

But, alas, we hold on.

"Still," we say, "my heart *is* grateful and I *am* giving God thanks–genuine thanks for my trinkets. And, therefore, it's all good, right?"

And somehow in this process, our conscience is salved and we are satisfied–content with our low bar of expectation, seldom really hungering for more of him.

PAUSE to PONDER

- Is placing too high a value on comfort, security or trinkets dividing your loyalties between heaven and earth?
- What comfort or convenience of self-determined 'right' are you willing to give up in order to raise the bar on your pursuit of God?
- I dare you to text a friend or mentor your answer to the previous question.

Chapter 10

Which Do You Despise?

Truth be told, though, we'd rather have about half of Him and half of the world. We *can* have *both*, right?

Where *is* that dividing line for you and Jesus?

Yours won't be where mine is, and mine won't be where yours is. But here's one thing we do know.

> *No one can serve two masters. Either you will hate the one and love the other, or you will be devoted to the one and despise the other. You cannot serve both God and money.* – **Matthew 6:24**

So which do you despise? To which are you devoted?

It appears we *cannot* have them both.

But in America, if I hate my stuff and what money can buy, and rid myself of it all in lieu of seeking the Lord Jesus first, second and third, then how am I to get to work without a car? How is putting my family out on the street, living out in the elements without shelter and needlessly endangering the health and safety of my wife and children, caring for and loving my family?

Well, in our culture, we may *not* be asked to become John the Baptist! We may also not be asked to become a millionaire. Odds are, we are going to be somewhere in between. Exactly *where* we are to live in that spectrum is going to be a matter of personal sensitivity to the Holy Spirit in each of our lives.

But our desire to obey our call had *better be* weightier than what we incorrectly *perceive* to be leaving behind. If not, and the Lord Jesus knows the heart, the Spirit may chase us down; this is seldom comfortable...or convenient. Would you rather come clean with what the Lord already knows or have him hunt you down?

Here I must take a brief, but hard left hook from the fairway and into the rough. I'm going to ask you a probing question I have been asking myself for the past year or two. If the Spirit of God is *not* living actively within you such that your daily life is perceptively impacted by his fellowship and guidance, could it be that you're still living life alone, quenching the Spirit regularly—even daily?

> This seems to be the condition of many Christians today. They are willing to get rid of some things in their lives, and God comes and fills them as far as he can. But until they are willing to give up everything, and put everything on the altar as it were, God cannot fill their entire lives.
>
> One of the strange things about God is that he will come in as far as we allow him. I've often said that a Christian is as full of the Holy Spirit as he wants to be. We can beg to be filled with the Holy Spirit. We can talk about it. But until we are willing to empty ourselves, we will never have the fullness of the Holy Spirit in our lives. God will fill as much of us as we allow him to fill.[34]

If the Spirit of God is *not* living actively within you such that your daily life is perceptively impacted by his fellowship and guidance, there are likely still too many of those 'self-hyphens' I mentioned earlier still alive and well within your daily experience.

You are saved, perhaps, but not dead.

But if you are serious about following Jesus and not quenching the work the Spirit would love to do in your life, Platt observes that at least two preconditions must exist.

> First, from the outset, you need to commit to believe whatever Jesus says in His Word.
>
> As a Christian, it would be a grave mistake to come to Jesus and say, 'Let me hear what you have to say, and then I'll decide whether or not I like it.' If you approach Jesus this way, you will never truly hear what he has to say. You have to say yes to the words of Jesus before you even hear them. And second, you need to commit to obey what you have heard.

---

[34] Tozer, The Crucified Life; Chapter 4

> The Gospel does not prompt you to mere reflection. The Gospel requires a response. In the process of hearing Jesus, you are prompted to take an honest look at your life, your family, and your church, and not just ask 'what is He saying,' but also ask 'what shall I do?'[35]

Please hear me here as we return now to where we may be individually called along this continuum of how we are to live with what we've been given.

Because we are called *individually*, and because the Holy Spirit lives in those of us who have placed our trust in Jesus Christ, we should know where we are being asked to live along this continuum. And this sweet spot of obedience may change from time to time. Be ready! But when He asks for our obedience, He probably isn't asking theoretically.

How American we are—how consumer minded.

Too often, our only assumption is that we should merely steward well what we have, not whether its possession in the first place has any bearing on our ability to identify with Christ.

We don't even ask the latter question, but presuppose every day that our fullness of life in Him can be found *in the midst of* possessing all we have earned by the sweat of our brow. And, therefore, we become attached to these things as items to which we have become entitled. After all, we earned them. We planned for them. We sacrificed for them. And now, at long last, the Lord has blessed us with them—and *we have them*!

Therefore, we know God wouldn't ask for them back—for he has given them *to* us, right?

But for what purpose are we given things?

Would God be so cruel as to provide you with things for which you've labored, and then ask for them back? Really?

If this line of thinking enters your mind, then you may be missing the point.

What if he has given you trinkets so that you can turn them back over as a declaration of a *greater* love—of him?

Actually, how much *less* costly could it possibly be for you to give up the things you have? If you really believe your things were never yours in the first place, but his for your borrowing, then how could he be better setting you up for success in your relationship with him than to ask for something back that isn't yours in the first place?

---

[35] Platt, Radical; Chapter 1

Do you follow me?

This, then, should be of no real cost to you at all.

If I'm standing on the street corner and Jesus comes along and gives me a million dollars, along with free and clean titles to a car and a house, how difficult would it be to, *sixty seconds later,* turn right back around and give them all back to him?

"Do you love me more than these I am giving you?" he asks.

It would likely be easy to say "yes" to that question, proving it to him by returning them back into his care–without having even benefitted from them in the first place.

Likely, considering how my tight budget would have been able to go so much further, I would have spent many future moments revisiting what *might have been* were I to have been able to *keep* those things. There may even be some "awe shucks" moments from which I'd have a hard time fleeing mentally and emotionally.

But what if he permits me to borrow them for a while? Maybe for five years, or ten?

How much more difficult would it be, in the course of time, to turn around and give it all back to him at *that* point, after having become accustomed to their earth-side benefit? For now, this is a rhetorical question.

And then, also, why do we so frequently look at our Christian walk with a payoff in mind? We do this most of the time. Admit it.

If I give up some stuff, or for that matter sell all I have to follow Jesus, then…. You finish the sentence.

Certainly, most of us wouldn't finish it with anything *less than* some sort of payoff *in this life*. A job we'll enjoy, a convergence of circumstances that will redound positively upon us, our children's health, the reaping of a great harvest of souls, and so on. This is what we expect to get in return for our "sacrifice."

But either God is worthy of all or he is not. If we are looking for how He may bless us *in this life*, other than through deeper relationship and identification with him, then we are still lost and seeking after that which cannot satisfy.

C'MON MAN!

Consider most all of Jesus' disciples. Here's how it looked for them: Give up all you have and follow me. Then, you'll be able to be spoken of hatefully, imprisoned frequently, rejected by your loved ones, driven out of your previous places of worship, spat upon, tortured, and, among other things, martyred at the end of it all. Insert here the closing curtain and lovely orchestral theme song. The

End...well, earth-side anyway. And all this as thanks for giving it all up to follow Jesus.

So, on a much lesser scale presently, *would* he ever give us things in order for us to turn around and give them back to him—maybe even recklessly?

This is *not* a theoretical question, but a practical one. One that some of us may be asked to deliver upon. I say *some* of us because, remember, we are called individually.

Your call is not mine, nor mine yours. What you may be asked to deliver upon may not be a trinket, but a person. What you may be asked to deliver back to him may not be a person, but an attitude.

You see, the Spirit of God knows you individually. He knows what you cherish. He knows what makes *you* tick. He knows those things onto which you lean instead of Him alone.

But one thing is sure for us all. When the Spirit of God asks for our loyalty and begins to do His work within us, there will be nothing too costly to turn over into his care. Tangibly. Worshipfully. Obediently.

And make no mistake, you will be asked to give things up. However, this with no sense of loss but of overflowing joy—of absolute gain! **And there is no sadness to be found in the exchange.**

So here is the crux of the matter in summation to these last few paragraphs. Again from Platt's book, Radical:

> Do you and I really believe that Jesus is so good, so satisfying, and so rewarding, that we will leave all we have, and all we own, and all we are in order to find our fullness in Him? Do you and I believe Him enough to obey him and follow Him wherever He leads—even when the crowds in our culture, and maybe in our churches, turn the other way?[36]
>
> ...with the best of intentions, we have actually turned away from Jesus. We have, in many areas, blindly and unknowingly, embraced values and ideas that are common in our culture, but are antithetical to the gospel He taught. Here we stand amid an American dream dominated by self-advancement, self-esteem and self-sufficiency. ...We need to return with urgency to a biblical gospel because the cost of not doing so is great for our lives, our families, our churches and the world around us.[37]

---

[36] Platt, Radical; Chapter 1
[37] Platt, Radical; Chapter 1

Personally, I have to admit that the more I listen, the more I learn, and the more the Spirit enables the old me to be left behind, the more questions I have.

The process sometimes seems so slow, and my flesh so strong. But every week that passes, I see more and more disconnects between the Christ of Scripture and the Christianity that has characterized my life and the church in America.

I have so far to go, but I want desperately to know Him. I want to experience Him. I want my family to undergo the freedom that will come from abandoning those things onto which we may cling for comfort in order to leave room for the Spirit to do His work in us.

And I want to one day be able to honestly say that I'm willing and ready to risk it all for Him.

I guess the point of this whole idea of our self-saving efforts and our bar of expectation in our walks with Jesus being far too low is that it just appears to me in too many ways that we are, as new creations, *far* too comfortable here on planet earth.

After being reborn and recreated as new men and women, we either fall quickly back into the warm blanket of our entitled life of ease, or maybe–just maybe, we were never sufficiently discipled into our newness in the first place.

Either way, too many of us are walking in the body of a forgiven dead man–we *refuse* to let loose of what God has buried! Our old Adam *has been* done away with–killed off by the Cross. But our new man, the one resurrected with Christ, is not electively converging *into* Christ, and we are shunning our own victory because we are afraid to give up control.

We are, as Casting Crowns surmises from the same song quoted earlier, Somewhere In The Middle...

>Fearless warriors in a picket fence,
>>Reckless abandon wrapped in common sense,
>
>Deep-water faith in the shallow end,
>>And we are caught in the middle.
>
>With eyes wide open to the differences,
>>The God we want and the God who is,
>
>But will we trade our dreams for his,
>>Or are we caught in the middle?

Instead, we live as though *this were* our home. We have pulled shut our eyelids over the supernatural eyes given us when we became children of God, and have continually quenched Him with our low bar of expectation and our love of the world.

Perhaps part of our problem is that we feel we must be content with our lives. We think we are being, as Paul requests that we be, satisfied with what we have–thus honoring and bringing glory to God.

But Paul is speaking of being content with the worldly comforts and provisions in our borrowing possession. He is not talking about our being satisfied in our relationship with God! Our Lord's heartbreak is NOT that our desire for something more is too strong, but too weak!

I believe the Lord's concern is more about the things that *have* begun to satisfy our hearts than the idea that our souls are unsatisfied.

A soul that pants after the living God (Psalm 42:1-2), to be read that it isn't satisfied with what it has, will certainly not be condemned. No, our bar of expectation is *not* too high, but too low. Just resting in our Christian zone of goodness has just got to break God's heart.

As John Piper surmises,

> "No one will ever want to say to the Lord of the universe, five minutes after death, 'I spent every night playing games and watching clean TV with my family because I love them so much.' I think the Lord will say, 'That did not make me look like a treasure in your town. You should have done something besides provide for yourself and your family. And TV, as you should have known, was not a good way to nurture your family–or your own soul.'"[38]

Jesus rebuked his disciples with words we could easily apply here. See Luke chapter 6, verses 32-34 and Matthew chapter 5, verse 47.

Even sinners work hard, avoid gross sin, watch TV at night, and do fun stuff on the weekend. What more are you doing than the others? Says Piper,

> We have settled for a home, a family, a few friends, a job, a television, a microwave oven, an occasional night out, a yearly vacation, and perhaps a new personal computer. We have accustomed ourselves to such meager, short-lived pleasures that our capacity for joy has shriveled.[39]

And in like manner, our sensitivity to the Spirit has shriveled.

---

[38] Piper, Don't Waste Your Life; Page 120
[39] Piper, Desiring God

Our desire for a life passionately pursuing what the Lord has for us while yet on this side of heaven has shriveled—or may never have grown up. Many cannot imagine what is meant by "a holiday at the sea" – a life empowered and enlivened by the awakened power of the Spirit of God in their lives.

Shall we again visit C.S. Lewis' take?

> The crazy irony of our human condition is that God has put us within sight of the Himalayas of his glory in Jesus Christ [through deep fellowship with the Holy Spirit], but we have chosen to pull down the shades of our chalet and show slides of Buck Hill... We are content to go on making mud pies in the slums because we cannot imagine what is meant by the offer of a holiday at the sea.[40]

Steven Curtis Chapman wrote the lyrics to his song, See The Glory, to bring home this same point of frustration.

> So what is this thing I see
> Going on inside of me
> When it comes to the Grace of God
> Sometimes it's like
>
> I'm playing Gameboy standing in the middle of the Grand Canyon
> I'm eating candy sitting at a gourmet feast
> I'm wading in a puddle when I could be swimming in the ocean
>
> Tell me what's the deal with me, Wake up and see the Glory
> Every star in the sky tells His story
> And every breeze is singing His song
> All of creation is imploring (hey)
> Come see this grand phenomenon
>
> The wonder of His Grace
> Should take my breath away
> I miss so many things
> When I'm content with
> ...playing Gameboy standing in the middle of the Grand Canyon
> I'm eating candy sitting at a gourmet feast
> I'm wading in a puddle when I could be swimming in the ocean
>
> Tell me what's the deal with me, wake up and see the Glory

---

[40] C.S. Lewis, The Weight of Glory

Chapter 11

Improving Our Vision

If the failed expansion of our vision for a life lived victoriously and beyond our wildest imaginations is a result of our inability to grasp *how* we could ever possess such victory, then I'm afraid we may simply be lacking an appreciation for the source of our strength.

Our eyesight is so poor.

If the Holy Spirit were to expose us to a Holy Discontent *(see Hybels' book by that name)*, the sad reality is it may die a quick death because we are so leashed to the shackles of our very tangible American Dream culture.

The fact is, it is *hard* to escape the American Dream of prosperity, comfort, self-satisfying work and well-earned recreation and rest.

But on the other hand, if a Holy Discontent were to become strong enough, and we are gifted by the Spirit to be sufficiently wrecked and ripped from our comfort zone, such can actually move us from the American Dream and into a dream of *God's* choosing–for the times in which He has us living.

You say, "Greg, I understand there is more. But I am insufficient to conjure up such newness of vision because I am so limited."

But you're only partially right–you just have the tense of the verb all wrong. You *were* limited!

WAKE. UP. PEOPLE.

You have been given all you need to partake in Christ's overwhelmingly powerful victory in your life! Have you not been born into a newness of life in Him?

Which of these statements is true of you?
- a. My God is not capable, or
- b. I have not been born into newness?

If you believe you are not capable of attaining to a newness of vision for the precious life God has given you to live on this planet, then one of the above statements is true of you. Or just maybe neither is true and you just need to educate yourself about what *is* true of you as God's child! If so, this is why you are reading this book. It is for this purpose this book was written–to educate Christians about what is true of us as God's children!

What does 2 Peter 1:3-4 mean if it is not pointing to the fact that **you have what it** takes within–not on your own, but through the power of the Spirit of the God living within you?

> [3] ***His divine power has given us everything we need*** *for a godly life through our knowledge of him who called us by his own glory and goodness.* [4] *Through these he has given us his very great and precious promises, so that* ***through them you may participate in the divine nature, having escaped the corruption in the world caused by evil desires.*** *– 2 Peter 1:3-4*

My goodness, read that again! This passage is FULL of victory! Which of these three truths of this scripture passage are you going to deny and claim to be a lie, if you dare?

1. **We have everything we need for a godly life through His divine power!** Is this one you want to refute with God?

    Did the Holy Spirit blow it when communicating this one to Peter?

    If we are completely surrendered to the power of the divine living *inside* us, we have access to everything we need for victorious living–it is *his* power doing the work, not yours brother and sister.

    We MUST stop habitually picking up our old man in lieu of surrendering to our newness IN CHRIST!

2. Or maybe this truth from the second half of verse 2 makes you uncomfortable. **...through our knowledge of him who called us by his own glory and goodness!**

Ok, so if you are lacking in knowledge, what's up with that? Do you not know where to go for that knowledge?

BATHE in the "sharper than any two-edged sword" Word of the Living God, my friend! It is through a knowledge of HIM that we gain, then possess and finally claim ownership of this divine power.

If you want to strip God of glory and goodness, then remain ignorant of his Word–stay out of the scriptures which bring understanding. *Or,* a better recommendation is that you could engage your circumstances, relationships and the world around you in victory by gaining in wisdom and knowledge of the tool you carry around with you 24/7...the Spirit of the Living God!

3. Perhaps *this* is the part you want to leave behind, that **through them** (meaning his promises) **you may participate *in the divine nature, having escaped the corruption in the world* caused by evil desires.**

There it is! Do you want to participate in the divine nature or do you want to live in the power of the dead man of flesh inherited after the nature of that which is dust–a nature of sin, death, darkness, and ignorance of that which is right?

The triune, personal, all powerful God has told you that YOU HAVE ESCAPED THE CORRUPTION OF THE WORLD! Why, oh why, continue wallowing in it when you don't have to?

God says that the new nature within you has given you full rights to participation in *the* divine nature. You *are to be* free from the evil desires of the world. If our hearts are set in Him, our old desires no longer have victory over us.

If there is trouble here for you, it is possible there is a problem in your life with surrender. But why, oh why should we not surrender ALL OF WHAT WE CARRY AROUND that was born of an old, defeated, now dead man? Where's the joy in *that*? Where's the appeal in *that*?

There is tremendous freedom, joy and victory that can only come from a brokenhearted surrender of our lives into the Cross of Christ which has already done *all* the work!

Indeed, it is the Word of God which breaks the spell of counterfeit pleasures. Let me say it again, **it is the Word which breaks the power of counterfeit pleasures.**

And as we listen to the Spirit of God while in his Word, we can recognize how it is that we can be made new—prepared for a life lived dangerously with the presence of God.

What about Isaiah?

When, like Isaiah, we have a personal encounter with God, we are changed forever. The counterfeit pleasures of this world pale by comparison when God finds us willingly living palms up...positioning ourselves for God's movement in our lives. What God did for Isaiah at the leading edge of *his* call, God can do for us.

Check out Isaiah's commissioning experience in the first 8 verses of Chapter 6:

> *¹ In the year that King Uzziah died, I saw the Lord, high and exalted, seated on a throne; and the train of his robe filled the temple. ² Above him were seraphim, each with six wings: With two wings they covered their faces, with two they covered their feet, and with two they were flying. ³ And they were calling to one another:*
>
> > *"Holy, holy, holy is the Lord Almighty;*
> > *the whole earth is full of his glory."*
>
> *⁴ At the sound of their voices the doorposts and thresholds shook and the temple was filled with smoke. ⁵ "Woe to me!" I cried. "I am ruined! For I am a man of unclean lips, and I live among a people of unclean lips, and my eyes have seen the King, the Lord Almighty." ⁶ Then one of the seraphim flew to me with a live coal in his hand, which he had taken with tongs from the altar. ⁷ With it he touched my mouth and said, "See, this has touched your lips; your guilt is taken away and your sin atoned for." ⁸ Then I heard the voice of the Lord saying, "Whom shall I send? And who will go for us?" And I said, "Here am I. Send me!"*
> > – Isaiah 6:1-8

What a picture of redemptive change through God's power and undoing in Isaiah's life. His experience resulted in a newness of duty and call.

Isaiah didn't have the benefit of the Holy Spirit entering him as do we today. His experience was, one could say, a pre-Christ substitute experience. Christ had not yet been situated at God's right hand, so the Holy Spirit had not yet been made available to Isaiah in the same way He is today.

But through this pre-Christ experience, Isaiah knew about and deeply sensed his guilt and sin. And he didn't know how to be made right...just that he had been "undone."

So God took care of that—the seraphim flying to him with a live coal—touching, purifying and redeeming him in one swift moment. And *he was made new*! **Isaiah got it**. He knew what it meant to have all things new, old things passing away. And a new mission consumed his life.

In the same way, *we* need to be *undone*. It is a prerequisite without which we cannot be fully effective in hearing and executing our spiritual call.

Our undoing can only happen through a personal revelation from God in our lives. And an informed theology of who we are as Christians can help set the stage. Our being undone can awaken the sense of who we are—and who God is relative to us. It *can* break us. Our being undone through an understanding of accurate theology can humble us. And it can give us newness of life, boldness and purpose.

So while we will deal with this in more detail later, it is my strong belief that when we become both academically *and* emotionally connected with an accurate theology of God, we, like Isaiah, will have such a "woe is me" experience—one uniquely crafted for us by the hand of the Spirit. We will know that we are ruined, that we are men and women of unclean lips.

And just as Isaiah was made clean and commissioned by the seraphim's hot coals, our hot coal experience can begin with a real apprehension of the work done by our Lord Jesus through his shed blood, and victory gained us on the Cross.

But in what way might this benefit us? And how can Jesus' triumph live itself out in *our* lives?

It is the objective of Part III in this book to help us gain this apprehension.

But before we go there, we have some cobblestone paths over which to travel together. I say cobblestone because the next two sections are not to be skimmed through at 70 mph with the cruise set. Instead, ask the Holy Spirit to help you personally reflect on the observations I am making about many of us who may have become a bit too attached to the *American* Christian life.

In these pages, I will propose what I believe is largely true about us as life-long, American Christians; our longings still find their roots in what this earth side life has to offer. And insomuch as this is the case, we settle for the crumbs falling from the banquet table that was intended for us–a feast of intimate, ever-deepening fellowship with our Redeemer.

Thus, the following lyric from the song *Slumber*, by NEEDTOBREATHE.

> All these victims stand in line for
> Crumbs that fall from the table just enough to get by
> All the while your invitation
> Wake on up from your slumber baby, open up your eyes
> Wake on up from your slumber baby, open up your eyes

May what follows continue to lead us into wholeness, and may our satisfaction with the dry crumbs of Spirit-less living become a thing of the past. Oh that we would position ourselves to let the Spirit open our eyes. This positioning is the intended purpose of the next two sections. Are you ready for the cobblestone?

PAUSE to PONDER

- Carve out five minutes right now. The world will wait. If you are out of time, return here when you have it – before continuing on. Take a deep breath and quiet your mind and spirit. Ask God to speak to you through his Word.
- Read 2 Peter 1:3-4 out loud once each minute. Talk to God about a different facet of this passage each time.
- Ask God to forgive you for ever believing you are impotent in this life as his child, or that you don't have what it takes, in Christ, to live a victorious Christian life.

CHAPTERS 12-17

HOLDING ON

Chapter 12

Saved But Never Dying

Or do you not know that your body is a temple of the Holy Spirit within you, whom you have from God? You are not your own, for you were bought with a price. So glorify God in your body. – **I Corinthians 6:19-20** (ESV)

    I think most of us believe we would stand in line for an Isaiah experience of our own! However, being in the midst of the worshipping heavenly host, and experiencing the full measure of God's holiness while everything around us was blowing up may find us deeply regretting what we *thought* we might enjoy. Thankfully, our guilt and sin has been atoned for through the Cross of Christ–rather than our having to take a live coal to the lips. I mean, who really wants to be "undone" like *that*?

    But as one who has received the new nature *of* Christ, I want you to begin reflecting upon what is really expected of you as a new creation *in* Christ. If the Holy Spirit of God is living within you, you must realize the implications—you are no longer our own. This awakening to the Holy Spirit is the only way to begin walking a new road.

Once Isaiah experienced God firsthand, and had been cleansed by his healing touch, the only response was complete and utter surrender. "Here am I, send me," he said. His life was never to be the same.

Can you relate to this at all? If not, perhaps you have not fully understood the price paid for you. If old things are not passing away, perhaps you have embraced a Christianity that did not actually include Christ at all. Or, assuming you have given your life to Jesus, maybe you are lacking a true comprehension that the One who died for you has also *taken up residence in* you to take you over.

You see, when you have made the discovery of the fact that you are the dwelling place of God, then a full surrender of yourself to God must follow. When once God gifts you with a visceral apprehension of the fact that *you are the temple of God*, you will immediately, like Isaiah, acknowledge that you are not your own.

And this will not be an intellectual conclusion, but a weighty, humbling, subjective onset that should drive you to your knees and into submission. And dedication of yourself entirely to his cause (consecration, if you will) will compulsively follow such revelation.

The difference between victorious Christians and defeated ones is *not* that some have the Spirit while others do not, but that some *know* his indwelling and others do not. Do not confuse knowing *about* his indwelling and *knowing* it. Subsequently, some recognize the divine ownership of their lives while others are still their own masters.

A fresh illumination, not of something mystical or new to the world, but a fresh, personal illumination of existing Truth from God seems to be the first step to a personal awakening of the Holy Spirit in our lives; consecration, the dedication of ourselves entirely to his cause, is the second. This was Isaiah's experience. It should be ours as well.

Such consecration is a compulsory response much like an if-then statement. **If** we gain a real understanding that we are the temple of God, **then** our compulsion, our natural response, will be surrender.

A day must come in our lives, as definite as the day of our conversion, when we give up *all right to ourselves* and submit to the absolute Lordship of Jesus Christ. There may be a practical issue raised by God to test the authenticity of our consecration, but whether or not that be so, there must be a day when, without reservation, we surrender everything to him—ourselves, our families, our possessions, our business and our time. All we are and have becomes his, to be used entirely at his disposal.

From that day, we are no longer our own masters, only stewards.

Not until the Lordship of Christ is a settled thing in our hearts can the Spirit really operate effectively in us. With rare exception, He will not direct our lives effectually until all control of what we once thought was ours is committed to him. If we do not give him absolute authority in our lives, he *can be* present, but he *cannot be* powerful. The power of the Spirit is stayed.

But, you say, this is a difficult thing—this giving up, this surrendering of *everything*.

Yes, following Christ *is* a risky duty. This is especially so when we understand that he is asking for our very lives.

Do we really understand that he is asking that we give up the control of our most cherished things? What else could he mean when saying, "If you don't carry your cross and come after me you cannot be mine?" This is heady stuff. It makes us look inward. It compels us to ask, "Am I his?"

What we're being taught in Matthew 16:24, Mark 8:34, Luke 9:23 and more specifically in Luke 14:33 is that things are not to have us. Christ is to have us. I may have a few things...but they're all his.

As Corrie Ten Boom put it, "I have learned to hold everything loosely because it hurts when he pries open my hands and takes things from me."

I like the way one man put it when he called this process of complete surrender, "Purchasing the Pearl of Great Price."

> "I want this pearl. How much is it?"
> "Well," the seller says, "it's very expensive."
> "But, how much?" we ask.
> "Well, a very large amount."
> "Do you think I could buy it?"
> "Oh, of course, anyone can buy it."
> "But, didn't you say it was very expensive?"
> "Yes."
> "Well, how much is it?"
> "Everything you have," says the seller.
> [We make up our mind] "All right, I'll buy it," we say.
> "Well, what do you have?" the seller wants to know. "Let's write it down."
> "Well, I have ten thousand dollars in the bank."
> "Good – ten thousand dollars. What else?"

"That's all. That is all I have. Well, …I have a few dollars here in my pocket."

"How much?"

[We start digging.] "Well, let's see—thirty, forty, sixty, eighty, a hundred, a hundred twenty dollars."

"That's fine. What else do you have?"

"Well, nothing. That's all."

"Where do you live?" [He's still probing.]

"In my house. Yes, I have a house."

"The house, too, then." He writes that down.

"You mean I have to live in my camper?"

"You have a camper? That, too. What else?"

"I'll have to sleep in my car!"

"You have a car?"

"Two of them."

"Both become mine, both cars. What else?"

"Well, you already have my money, my house, my camper, my cars. What more do you want?"

"Are you alone in this world?"

"No I have a wife and two children….."

"Oh, yes, your wife and children, too. What else?"

"I have nothing left! I am left alone now."

[Suddenly the seller exclaims,]

"Oh, I almost forgot! You yourself, too! Everything becomes mine—wife, children, house, money, cars—and you too."

[And then he goes on.]

"Now listen—I will allow you to use all these things for the time being. But don't forget that they are mine, just as you are. And whenever I need any of them you must give them up, because now I am the owner."[41]

NOW THAT'S THE WAY TO LIVE! It means whatever I have is on loan from my Savior. And I do not bow down and worship before it. I worship *Him*! And *He* gives me a direction in life that makes it fulfilling and satisfying. None of the other things are going to satisfy me. Only He can satisfy.

And only when we come to the place that it is all his, and we see that He loans it to us regularly on a day by day basis, can we live freely and joyfully with open palms.

Are we saying there's no struggle in this kind of living? No, we're never once told this kind of living would be easy. But it is He, our Lord Jesus, who has already counted the cost for us. It is not we who must

---

[41] Chuck Swindoll, Insight for Living, May 9, 2014

count the cost! The cost has been counted...and paid for. It is only ours to live into it–into his release of our very lives.

What has so come home to the depths of my being is the fact that as long as we are trying to do anything, he can do nothing. Mark illustrates this point.

> *Jesus said to them, A prophet is not without honor except in his own town, among his relatives and in his own home. ⁵ He **could not do any miracles there**, except lay his hands on a few sick people and heal them. ⁶ He was amazed at their lack of faith.* — **Mark 6:4-6**

Here, Jesus was, as the text says, *incapable of*–or at least unwilling to do, the miraculous because of the capacity we as people possess to quench the Spirit's ability to work. The importance of our obedience and attention to holiness as his children is equally demonstrated in God's instruction to Abraham in Genesis 17: 1-2 when he reminds him to "...walk before me, and be blameless, so that I may...."

Oh Church, please get this! *We* get in the way with our sinful inability to render fully unto him. And I don't think this is only done by those who deny Christ or are obstinately in conflict with him, but also by those of us who claim him as Savior but refuse to surrender unto Him everything.

It is because of our *trying* to *do* and *be* "good" that we fail and fail and fail. God wants to demonstrate to us that we can do **nothing at all**–and until that is fully recognized in all honesty and introspection, our despair and disillusion will never cease.

In his book, The Normal Christian Life, Watchman Nee shared this from a consultation with a brother in Christ who was trying to struggle into victory.

> The gentleman said, "I do not know why I am so weak."
>
> "The trouble with you," Nee said, "is that you are weak enough not to do the will of God, but you are not weak enough to keep out of things altogether."

2 Corinthians 12:9-10 helps us recall how it is *not* in our effort but Christ's that allows God's power to be alive within us.

> *But he said to me, "My grace is sufficient for you, for my power is made perfect in weakness." Therefore I will boast all the more gladly about my weaknesses, so that Christ's power may rest on*

> me. That is why, for Christ's sake, I delight in weaknesses, in insults, in hardships, in persecutions, in difficulties. For when I am weak, then I am strong.

Nee continues,

> You are still not weak enough. When you are reduced to *utter* weakness, and are persuaded you can do nothing whatever, *then* God will do everything.

To this I personally shout, "Yes!" For this has become my experience. We all *need* to come to the point where we say, as Nee writes, "Lord, I am unable to do anything for thee, but I trust thee to do everything in me." *

---

* Do not misunderstand this to mean we have no responsibility whatever for obedience through self-discipline. The last two pages in Chapter 51 will bring this into clear focus later.

Chapter 13

Self-Assertion

There is another concern that lies at the very heart of how it is we quench the active move of the Spirit in our lives. Further distancing us from experiencing the movement of the Spirit's hand in our lives is our **self-assertion.** In short, it stinketh.

Rather than waiting on God's arrangements for our lives, we formulate our own plans. Then, we ask his blessing on our terrific bit of calculation.

While we may grasp that we have moved through the death of our old Adam and into a new life in Christ, we must also learn what it means for us to *refuse to move* apart from him. For when we do move apart from him, and make no mistake we *are* capable of it, we are living in our old, mortal, controlling flesh.

God *so* wants to do the pruning work of the vinedresser, but we are *so* inexperienced at living in the Spirit.

We find it so difficult to be patient *(ref: Chapter 14–Waiting Expectantly)*. We know well how to move and do, but we are foreigners to the idea of letting the Spirit make the first move. We know that our initial salvation (justification) secured through Christ's sacrifice on our behalf is ours without any work on our part, but we think that our ongoing growth into becoming Christ's disciples (sanctification) is dependent upon our own efforts.

In Watchman Nee's words...

> We know that we can receive forgiveness only by entire reliance on the Lord, yet we believe we can obtain deliverance by doing something ourselves. We fear that if we do nothing, nothing will

happen. After salvation, the old habit of doing reasserts itself and we begin our old self-efforts again. Then, God's Word comes afresh to us. "It is finished." (John 19:30) He has done everything on the cross for our forgiveness, and He will do everything in us for our deliverance. In both cases, He is the doer. It is God that worketh in you.[42]

Then, as well, as Watchman Nee conveys in chapter 12 of his book, The Normal Christian Life, every day we must be learning these two lessons; a rising up of the life of this One who lives inside us and desires to use our bodies and souls, and a checking and a handing over to death of that other soul-life[43]....the life of the flesh which will never stop fighting for control until its earth-side breath is gone.

These two processes go on all the time and we must get used to it, embrace it. For God is seeking the fully developed life of his Son *in* us in order to manifest himself *through* us.

Paul says: "We which live are always delivered unto death for Jesus' sake, that the life also of Jesus may be manifested in our mortal flesh" (2 Cor. 4:11 KJV).

What does this verse mean? It simply means, says Nee, that:

> I will not take any action without relying on God. I will find no sufficiency in myself. I will not take any step just because I have the power to do so.[44]

> ...Even though I have that inherited power within me, I will not go ahead solely because I 'own it' in myself. Rather, I will put no reliance in myself.

> I think when we begin to be sensitized to our being given over, we learn so much more about how dark, how lacking in God's light we really are in ourselves. We all know ourselves in measure, but many times we don't truly *tremble* at ourselves.[45]

I remember the first time God gave me a subjective and personal peek into my utter darkness, my complete waywardness and helplessness to bring anything good to him in myself, separate from

---

[42] Watchman Nee, The Normal Christian Life: Chapter 9
[43] Watchman Nee, The Normal Christian Life; Chapter 12, Page 150
[44] Nee, The Normal Christian Life; Pages 150-151
[45] Nee, The Normal Christian Life; Page 151

Him. You are never the same after He does you this favor. It, I feel, is the starting point for a newly awakened fear of God within.

But in our practical living out of life, we fool ourselves. As a matter of courtesy to God, we may say things like: "If the Lord does not want it, I cannot do it." We know, intellectually, that the Word says we can do nothing of real value without him. "But in reality," suggests Nee, "our sub-conscious thought is that *really we can do it quite well ourselves*, even if God does not ask us to do it nor empower us for it."

Too often, confident in the abilities he has given us, we have been caused to act, to think, to decide, to have power, regardless of Him. "**Many of us Christians today are men with over-developed souls. We have grown too big in ourselves. When we are in that condition, it is possible for the life of the Son of God in us to be confined and crowded almost out of action.**"[46]

As the sky is blue, I can so relate to this ability we have to move onward on our own, perceiving it to be forward. By way of a corresponding and helpful illustration, Watchman Nee tells the story of the following.

> Once I met a young brother–young, that is to say, in years, but who had learned a good deal of the Lord. God had brought him through much tribulation to gain that knowledge of himself *[that he had at times been moving largely in the strength of his own, carnal equipment while believing he was moving in obedience to God's compulsion]*.
>
> As I was talking with him I said, "Brother, what has the Lord really been teaching you these days?"
>
> He replied, "Only one thing: that I can do nothing apart from Him."
>
> "Do you really mean," I asked, "that you can do *nothing*?"
>
> "Well, no," he said. "I *can* do many things! In fact that has been just my trouble. Oh, you know, I have always been so confident in myself. I know I am well able to do lots of things."
>
> So I asked him, "What then do you mean when you say you can do nothing apart from Him?"

---

[46] Nee, The Normal Christian Life; Page 151

He answered, "The Lord has shown me that I *can* do anything, but that *he* has said, 'Apart from me ye can do nothing.' So it comes to this, that everything I have done and can do apart from him *is nothing!*"[47]

And we, too, have to come to that valuation. I don't mean to say we cannot do a lot of things—we can. We can schedule and execute meetings, we can build churches, we can go to the ends of the earth and found missions, and we can seem to bear fruit; but remember that the Lord's word is: "Every plant which my heavenly Father planted not, shall be rooted up" (Matthew 15:13 KJV).

God is the only legitimate Originator in the universe (Gen. 1:1), and his Holy Spirit is the only legitimate initiator in our hearts. Anything you and I plan and set into motion without Him has the taint of the flesh upon it, and it will never reach the realm of the Spirit— however earnestly we seek God's blessing on it. It may last for years, and then we may think we will adjust here and improve there and maybe make it into a better instrument, but it cannot be done.[48]

I'm now at a point where I really want time and activity invested into things that are of maximum eternal consequence *according to the Lord*...not according to my estimation of value. What about you?

PAUSE to PONDER

- Take time right now to humbly as God if your soul has become overdeveloped by its outer garment of flesh.
- If you are willing, ask God to root up anything in your life which He has not planted.
- Are you willing to let God use whatever means necessary to root up what isn't gaining nourishment from himself, The Vine? If so, tell him so.

---

[47] Nee, The Normal Christian Life; Page 154
[48] Content from Nee, The Normal Christian Life; Page 154-155

Chapter 14

Waiting Expectantly

Using the cognitive skills of my natural man, outside the compulsion of the Spirit's guidance, I simply cannot decipher that which is temporal from that which He deems to be *something*.

Just yesterday, I came across a beautiful snapshot of this principle, found in the first three verses of Psalm 40.

> 1 **I** *waited patiently for the Lord;*
> **he** *turned to me and heard my cry.*
> 2 **He** *lifted me out of the slimy pit, out of the mud and mire;*
> **he** *set my feet on a rock and gave me a firm place to stand.*
> 3 **He** *put a new song in my mouth, a hymn of praise to our God.*
> **Many will** *see and fear the Lord and* **put their trust in him.**

David's experience *could be* ours were we to daily walk in the Spirit, increasingly dying to the flesh of our old man. In this passage, David's experience begins with what? *Patience. More specifically, patience for the Lord to move.*

But we so refuse to wait because we believe we are called to move, MOVE, **MOVE!** And, thus, we do so…in our *self*-empowered, *self*-asserted, *self*-confidence. Like the bull in the proverbial china shop, we hammer through too much of life without staying our sledge.

As an aside, I wonder if David wrote this psalm sometime after his confrontation with Nabal. The circumstances surrounding the story revealed to us in I Samuel 25 seem to be fodder for a lesson God wanted to teach David along these lines; namely, that it is frequently not in our best interest to "strap on our sword" in order to *be* our own solution.

Not only did God teach David that He was sufficiently able to bring about a right solution without David's taking every matter into his own hands (I Samuel 25:27-38), but he also both saved David from regret *and* brought blessing into his life in the person of his wife-to-be, Abagail, as part of the lesson. What a story...read it!

Ok, back to Psalm 40. *If we but wait on God*, we won't miss the blessing He may be anxious to deliver into our lives. Again, here's the storyline:

> **I** wait patiently.
> **You** turn to me and hear.
> **You** lift me out.
> **You** firmly set my feet.
> **You** put a song in my mouth.
> Many see, fear and trust in you!

What part of this process is ours? Haha, yes! **We merely WAIT - and it is GOD who does the work.**

I so fear we really don't believe He intends to live his life through us SUPERNATURALLY! We are so earth bound, so what-is-tangible bound that very few of us ever believe He intends to move supernaturally in and through us for his purposes.

We THINK we're out of the way when we come to some conclusion and then ask the Lord to bless it...to put a stop to it if He so desires. But in doing so, we have too often moved first in our natural man—refusing to wait on what we haven't experienced...God's supernatural lead. This is the Father's plan for us, that all glory, honor, credit and praise be his, not claimable by us in any fashion.

But we REFUSE to remain under his umbrella, coming out into storms of our own choosing—when all along he has placed the umbrella over us for protection; He intends that we wait...not until the skies clear and all obstacles are moved, but until the path is lighted—before our feet hit the ground.

So it comes to this: origin determines destination, and what was "of the flesh" originally will never be made spiritual by any amount of "improvement."

That which is born of the flesh is flesh, and it will never be otherwise. Anything for which we are sufficient in ourselves is "nothing" in God's estimate, and we have to accept his estimate and write it down as nothing. "The flesh profiteth nothing." It is only what comes from above that will abide.

We cannot see this simply by being told it. God must teach us what is meant, by putting his finger on something he sees and saying: "This is natural; this has its origin in the old creation, and did not originate with Me; this cannot abide." Until he does so, we may agree in principle, but we can never really *see* it. We may assent to, and even enjoy, this teaching that the flesh profiteth nothing, but until we set free the Spirit in our lives to do such operative work, we will never truly loathe ourselves.

> *Oh that we would learn to see time as you do, Father.*
>
> We fear that this short life must be filled with doing...NOW. We must not, we think, allow ourselves to be accused of slothfulness.
>
> But in doing so, we miss it. We miss *your* movement—because *we* move FIRST. Forgive us, Holy Spirit.
>
> We DO desire to let *you* be Lord, but we feel we see what can be done to effect a given situation forward with our physical eyes and off we go, walking in our own solution—one that may, more often than we know, be lacking in patient, purposeful, watchful anticipation of what you have in store for us.
>
> It is an alert awareness of your Spirit's movement we need...and this not of ourselves. **Please help us escape our eyesight, Lord Jesus!**
>
> Oh God, please be merciful to show us your hand, and strengthen our faith, that it would truly evolve into subjective confidence. We are a weak and pitiful people. Forgive us. DO keep us out of the way, that we may see and marvel in your greatness.

Chapter 15

Erasing us

What I more and more feel the need of in myself, and what I believe as His children we all need to seek from God, is a real revelation of ourselves. I do not mean we should be forever looking within and asking: "Now, is this my fleshly soul or is it spirit?" That will never get us anywhere; it is darkness.

No, Scripture shows us how the saints were brought to self-knowledge. It seems to consistently be a result of his choosing to break into our consciousness through an illumination of his light; and that light *is* God himself.

Isaiah, Ezekiel, Daniel, Peter, Paul, John: all came to a knowledge of themselves because the Lord flashed *himself* upon them, and that flash brought revelation and deep conviction. (Isa. 6:5; Ezek. 1:28; Dan. 10:8; Luke 22:61-62; Acts 9:3-5; Rev. 1:17.)

Now we cannot anticipate, nor should we seek, an experience exactly like any of these men. For to do so would only be another self-assertion, would it not? But at some point, in the Spirit's own way and as an instrument of his timing in each of our lives, I do believe he wants to arrest our attention through a revelation, an opening of our spiritual eyes, which will so make us aware of the extent of our treason before God, that we will never be the same. And I am coming to see *this* as the beginning of our undoing (Proverbs 1:7a).

We can never know the hatefulness of sin or the treachery of our self-nature until there is that flash of God upon us, call it what you may.

I speak not of a sensation, but of an inward illumination of the Lord himself through his Word. Such an in-breaking of divine light does for us what doctrine alone can never do.

Now I know we most pragmatic of believers are putting up our guard with the previous sentence. But please, read on.

We conservative evangelicals are, to be sure, well versed in our doctrines—not a bad thing in itself. In fact, being well-versed in an accurate theology is a *crucial* thing. I have already and will continue to argue this very point. However, we may lack an openness to that which doesn't strictly fit into the realm of the verifiably academic.

I'm afraid because we so live by Jesus' words that "ye shall not put the Lord your God to the test," we miss out on another equally existent realm of what is *completely natural* to God, but unseen to us given the limited perception of the flesh. The antagonist in us cautions, "Who are *we* to even so much as anticipate the possibility of some subjective, personal, supernatural markings on our lives?"

I'll tell you who we are. We are children of the One True God who went to ultimate lengths to secure us as his instruments in a desperately needy and very broken world!

But we have unknowingly fitted ourselves with a spiritual version of NASCAR's restrictor plate. We have limited ourselves to only a portion of what is ours through Jesus' glorification and placement at the Father's right hand.

Now in all fairness, our hesitancy to let the Lord remove our self-limiting restrictor plate is understandable. We back off from the supernatural work of the Holy Spirit because we cannot explain it—it doesn't "make sense." It's easier to just hit the panic button, stamp it charismatic, and live a life steeped in the cognition of the academic side of the Word alone.

But in doing so, we are effectively refusing to be awoken to the very Person of God himself *living inside* us.

We are, in this matter, victims ourselves of our post-modern, earth-bound, if you cannot scientifically verify it, it must not be, culture. We freak out about anything that could give off even a whiff of a subjective experience from God. We see a red light *and proceedeth not*—not even with caution.

As a result, we are missing out on much of what God *intended* for us to experience as part of a *normal* Christian life.

Why would Jesus have asked the disciples to 'stay put' until the Helper comes if he didn't intend for our lives to be lived in, and characterized by, access to his supernatural, attention grabbing in-breaking into our lives?

But without experiencing Christ in this way, we will be neither sufficiently reduced ourselves nor lifted up in Him to walk obediently in the Light.

The Holy Spirit *is* our Light. He is our interpreter of the living Word. When we read the Scriptures, our life in him brings revelation. This is the natural experience of a Christian. Illumination may not come to us all at once, but gradually; **but His work in us will search the depths of our being until we see ourselves in the light of God, and all our self-confidence will be gone.**

Without a supernatural exchange, there is no dividing asunder of joints and marrow. Instead, our journey becomes to us only a set of religious teachings. But when the radiant work of the Spirit is freed to live actively within us, we begin to know fear and trembling as we recognize the corruption of our nature, the hatefulness of self, and the real threat we are to the work of God in our soul.

All I'm saying here is that God's breadth of blessing and desire for us as new creations in Him *must not be* subject to the limitations of our old man. If so, we will never subjectively and emotionally own a difference-making fear of our great God.

> Oh God, we must pause here again to ask that your Word pierce our hearts, minds and souls.
>
> Through your Word, destroy any self-sufficiency we feel we need for some sense of control.
>
> Please, Spirit, as your Word unfolds in our lives, wreck us to a point that we are eager to live a life *free* from control. Help us lose control that you may freely take up *your* cause in our life.
>
> For if our life is just that—ours, then we've not been given over to you. But if we have become yours, then please help us *lose control* of the life you have already purchased and rightly own. Erase us, that you can write a story of your choosing for your glory. Amen.

Chapter 16

Releasing – God Waits On Us?

The next logical step after recognizing the need to stop holding onto your life is to discover how to let it go. I have so far to go, and the Lord has so much surgical work yet to do on me, but what has begun to break my heart is when I see other brothers and sisters in Christ living in pain or challenge, trying desperately to solve matters in their lives to no avail–or to no real progress.

We, even under the cover of much prayer, continue to practically exert our own will, discipline, and terrifically dedicated and even heroic effort without realizing we will never win the battles of this life in that way.

It is not just a refusal on our part to release ourselves into the power that will solve the deepest matters of our lives. Rather, I believe our dilemma comes in our inability to fully realize that *WE are NOT CAPABLE OF* the solution. We can know we don't have what it takes, but until we are convinced to *let go*, we will only find that we have become an even greater source of dread to ourselves.

This reminds me of something I saw the other day in my parent's garage–where dad keeps everything and disposes of nothing. I saw a pink post-it note affixed to the front of an old, green baseball cap. The post-it read what must have been the result of an especially trying set of expectations on a long "to do" list.

My guess is that after my dad had gathered himself for perspective, he walked into the house to greet mom, hat on his head with the post-it revealing three simple words, "I Am Mortal."

As I stood there alone in their garage, it made me laugh *out loud*! I think it was dad's way of reminding mom that he is *not* capable of all solutions.

I believe God feels great sadness as he observes the path of our life prior to our *final* release as followers. And observe he does–because that is all we have really given him the freedom to do.

If we have not yet reached a place where we have come to the very end of ourselves, his work in us is quenched and his operative desires will be on hold.

Our problem is that when we reach the end of our rope, we DO tie a knot–*and hold on*. God so desperately wants us to *lose* our grip on that knot. He's continually calling us to LET GO! Regrettably, we think it is honoring our Lord when we REFUSE to let go–as if he is going to doll out heavenly reward points for how effectively we used the asset of our stubborn pride–a toughness we conjure up *in our own fleshly strength*.

Do we really believe that God is going to gain praise from our lives while we demonstrate to him a great inner strength to "pull ourselves up from the boot straps?"

No! This is not the way of our Lord. This is not the way of a Christian life realized in Christ. Our ability to walk in the strength, wisdom and energy of the Spirit of God only edges its way into our experience when we are utterly convinced that letting GO of that knot is our *only* hope! This is what He has called us to–the letting go.

An illustration I read may help us understand this from God's perspective. Watchman Nee shares this from a personal experience he had while traveling overseas.

> I was once staying in a place in China with some twenty other brothers.
>
> There was inadequate provision for bathing in the home where we stayed so we went for a daily plunge in the river. On one occasion, a brother got a cramp in his leg, and I suddenly saw he was sinking fast. So I motioned to another brother who was an expert swimmer to hasten to his rescue. But to my astonishment, he made no move!
>
> Growing desperate, I cried out, don't you see the man is drowning? And the other brothers, about as agitated as I was,

shouted vigorously too. But our good swimmer still did not move. Calm and collected, he remained just where he was–apparently postponing the unwelcome task.

In the meantime, the voice of the poor drowning brother grew fainter and his efforts, feebler. In my heart I said, I *hate* that man. Think of his letting a brother drown before his very eyes and not going to the rescue.

But when the man was *actually sinking*, with a few swift strokes, the swimmer was at his side and both were safely ashore.

Nevertheless, when I got an opportunity, I aired my views. I have never seen any Christian who loved his life quite as much as you do, I said. Think of the distress you would have saved that brother if you had considered yourself a little less and him a little more. But the swimmer, I soon discovered, knew his business better than I did.

Had I gone earlier, he said, he would have clutched me so fast that both of us would have gone under. A drowning man cannot be saved until he is utterly exhausted and ceases to make the slightest effort to save himself.[49]

Do you see the point? When we give up the case, then God will take it up. He is waiting until we are at the end of our resources and *can do nothing more for ourselves.*

God has condemned all that is of the old creation in us–and assigned it to the cross! The flesh profits *nothing* (John 6:63). We can give ascent to this, but until the Spirit reveals this to us subjectively through the conditions of our life, we will never really *see* this. Instead, we will still think we can profit ourselves and the Lord in some way.

Rather, God has declared our flesh to be fit only for death. So why do we continue to hold onto that knot of control when all seems to be spinning out of control? In one word, sin. But in a broader sense, I believe it is because we do not utterly trust in God's provision on our behalf.

PAUSE to PONDER

- Ask God if you trust yourself more than you trust Him.

---

[49] Nee, The Normal Christian Life; Page 110

Chapter 17

If/Then...

If we truly believe our flesh profits us in no way, *then* we will confirm God's verdict by abandoning all fleshly efforts to earn him. There is, in fact, no greater way we can earn a more favorable standing with God than has already been provided us through the all-sufficient work of the Son.

Our every attempt to do God's will through our old man is a denial of his declaration in the cross that we are utterly powerless to do so. To think we can do anything to give ourselves a favorable disposition before God is a misunderstanding on the one hand of the demands God places on us, and on the other hand on the source of supply.

We see the Law and think we must meet its claims. But we need to remember that though the law in itself is right in its demands, it will be all wrong if it is applied to the wrong 'person.'

Here's what I mean.

Paul demonstrates this point precisely in Romans 7. In this passage, he tells us of how he had tried to meet the claims of God's law himself. His trying to do so was the cause of his trouble. The repeated use of the little word "I" in this chapter gives a clue to the failure. "The good which I would, I do not. But the evil which I would not, that I practice" (Romans 7:19 ASV).

There is a fundamental misconception in our mind. Like Paul, we think God is asking *us* to keep the law. So of course, we try to do so, whereas God is requiring of us no such thing.

What is the result? Far from doing what pleases God, he and we find ourselves doing what displeases him. In our very efforts to do the will of God, we, like Paul, do the very opposite of what we know to be his will.

But our new man, covered by the complete fulfillment of the Law in Christ, can live in the reality of the Law's claims having been satisfied! Glory be to God for his great and awesome plan for our redemption! And I think this may have been the precise point of this passage.

By continuing to live in our old Adam, we are choosing to live in self-defeating enslavement. God has purchased us but we have not given ourselves fully to him.

Don't we realize we are not our own? Do we not realize that the old man has *no* ability to live victoriously? C'mon, man! What then does I Corinthians 7:23 mean if not what it says—*God paid a high price for you, so don't be enslaved by the world.*

What a quandary, then, in which we find ourselves. We *cannot but* be slaves to the world *in our flesh*. But it is impossible to be anything but a slave to the flesh without the indwelling power of the Holy Spirit, awakened, willing and active in our souls! Nothing we can do or be in ourselves can effect a righteous life. As Paul writes to Titus,

> *He saved us, not because of righteous things we had done, but because of his mercy. He saved us through the washing of rebirth and renewal by the Holy Spirit.* **– Titus 3:5**

Our flesh must be completely denied its self-reliant life for us to have *any* authority over the world and its ways. For in our self-reliance, we lose.

But there is good news! We have access to the way of this death to self—we just don't understand it to be so! And thank God this book doesn't begin and end with Part I. If so, I would be compelled to direct you to a physician who could provide you with some numbing medication or anti-depressants.

But as we soldier on together in later chapters, we will make a very practical and essential discovery; namely, how it is we can win our battle with the tenacious tendencies of our old man.

I just regret it took me so long to see the insufficiency of myself in this life.

For most all my life, until 12:27am on May 6, 2012, I only cerebrally understood the whole idea that, as Paul says in 2 Corinthians 5:17, *"if anyone is in Christ, the new creation has come: The old has gone, the new is here!"*

I knew the words. I absolutely trusted God whole-heartedly that if he said I was new, then I was new. But I never for one instant felt the *need* or *right* to *really grasp* what that meant! I just accepted it with what I understood to be *faith*, a simple matter of fact–a fact I didn't need to cerebrally comprehend.

I didn't even give a thought to the *idea* that there was something more to grasp in such a verse. What more could there be?

But things have changed.

Are you ready for more than the crumbs falling from the Father's banquet table of relationship and rebirth? As Will Reagan's lyrics from the song Colorful convey, are you at a place in your life where you are ready for your Savior, Father and Maker to truly and experientially become the God of new and sovereign life restarted, remaking, changing the desperation of your heart as his son or daughter?

Our hearts can only long for what the Holy Spirit desires if *we* are *out of the way*. But how do we do this?

The bad news is that *we* cannot. We *cannot* remove *ourselves* from the scene of action.

The good news is that *He* can. The purpose of what comes next in Part II is to assist us in setting the table of our hearts.

PAUSE to PONDER

- What does it mean that the claims of God's Law over your life have been fully met in Christ?
- Read, and then rejoice with Paul in Romans 7:24-25a.
- If, in Jesus, all wrath and guilt has been met in the eyes of God the Father, what does this mean for you when Satan points to the shortcomings of your flesh to 'remind you' that you stand condemned?

PART II

TRANSITIONING TO TRUTH

CHAPTERS 18-35

THE COMPONENTS OF TRANSITIONING TO TRUTH

Chapter 18

A Personal Turn

So far, in Part I, we have mostly reviewed what ails us. I have tried to convey what has burdened my heart pertaining to our condition as Christians—as ones still clinging to this world, and, thus, quenching the active work of the Holy Spirit in our lives. Now we will try to slowly merge into what, for me, became the solution for the still wayward condition of my redeemed soul.

If you deeply desire a Spirit-enlivened walk with God, there are some prerequisites I believe must be met.

The next eighteen short chapters of Part II represent my attempt to visit some of these preconditions. Perhaps it can serve as a setup for what will come next in the book. And likely because of my thick-headedness, I only realized the Lord had brought me through such prerequisites after he was deeply into his surgical work on my spirit.

Here is where this writing will take a more personal turn. And along with it, an honest confession of concern–one which nearly kept me from writing this book.

I am nervous about taking what has been a very personal journey and making it public. Nonetheless, I'm going to do it because it is part of what the Lord seems to have asked me to do. So here we go.

This next short section is more an anecdotal, internal argument I have already been attempting to express as I have pondered how I could possibly share the exceptional things the Spirit has chosen to bring into my life. I will simply expose you to what I have been thinking.

For months, what has been happening has been so experiential that I have been unable to trace its development. Certainly, I know when it began–what kindled its awakening in my soul. But I hadn't been able to trace back through the *how* of it...until just the other day.

The process has been most holy and rooted in a new understanding of truths revealed to me in His Word. But my fear has been that the catalysts God used in my life may not be the same as that which He would choose to use in another believer's life. And thus, any attempt to document it could actually misguide others, thinking their process toward a greater illumination of life in Christ would have to somehow be patterned after what **I** have experienced.

Were this to happen to you, the reader, causing greater striving in your soul rather than the release into Christ this book is intended to bring about, I would be heart-broken. Therefore, going forward, I reconstruct where the Lord Jesus has led me with the caveat that follows–intended for your consideration.

We are all searched and found by the Spirit uniquely.

Nonetheless, given our vastly different makeup as individuals, we can know that while our experiences will be different, if timed and led by the Spirit, *they will all effect to the same end*.

Our common destination will be one which possesses similar characteristics–things which bear the true markings of God; these being to be overtaken by the Holy Spirit, reduced to dust and ashes in ourselves, made more aware of his grace and mercy in our lives, and to be more tenderly surrendered to the relationship he longs to cultivate within us.

I now point this attempt to the Lord as I recount how great he has become to me through a series of circumstances, brought on by his willingness to be found, as I began to seek him with an intensity of his own doing. This, therefore, is his story, not mine.

Interesting to me, though, was how the path my soul had traveled was becoming undeniably important. **I was longing to grasp a discernable path of progress I could put into words.**

It was as if I wanted to express my gratitude to God for what he had done by being able to stand back and point to something concrete and say, "Look what you've done, Lord! I praise you!"

And, was there a way we could somehow construct a framework to which others could relate, and that the Lord may be willing to use for the purpose of impacting others' lives?

I remember deeply desiring that what the Lord was doing in me would be affected in the lives of my family members...into the lives of all believers who, like me, had lived without such holy discontent and Spirit-awareness.

I remember thinking about how the lives of my kids and grandkids would be so much more passionate, obedient, dangerous, meaningful, deeply soulish, surrendered, heaven-sighted and eternal in scope were the Holy Spirit to be freed up to do his work in their lives.

In a nutshell, the ability to point those who already belong to Christ to such a newly surrendered life in the Spirit became a cry of my heart.

And this *not* for the sake of pursuing an experience, but rather that other believers who have also walked a conservative, tolerant and resigned Christian half-life would have their eyes opened just enough to the spiritual realm that they would be compelled to enlist themselves as unreserved, radical, counter-cultural slaves to God.

I know such an experience with the Living God cannot be duplicated through a formula or technique. Yet, it is my prayer that the pathway the Lord used to reveal himself would find its mark; that going forward together we may prepare in you an opening for the Spirit to do his work.

Chapter 19

The Holy Spirit Experience

Let's face it, we are created experiential beings. I am sorry to say I have had to come to this realization diagnostically. If God did not want us to be experiential, then he would never have created within us that quality.

Why would he create us with qualities from the beginning, saying "it" was all good, but then down the road, tell us to squash, reduce, in fact exterminate any desire we may have to be experientially connected to Him? That makes no sense!

Nonetheless, coming from a more pragmatic than what I thought to be 'unreasonable' background, the intangible aspects of what the Holy Spirit was doing inside me scared me a bit. But not anymore!

I remember I began to feel out of control. Yet I knew what God was revealing to me was nothing more or less than that which was intended for me—for us all—from the day of Jesus' return to the Father.

But why have I missed out on such an intimate, enlightened, active, two-way communicative walk with the Holy Spirit all my life when I, all along, absolutely belonged to Christ?

In years past, I remember the likes of Bill Bright concerning me with what seemed to be his out of proportion focus on the role of, and being given over to, the Holy Spirit. Now however, as I assess things, I am not so sure he was off base. In fact, I'm confident he was right on target!

He, and others, understood our human need for subjective, real experience in our walk with Christ. But for me, unless I could place my finger on it, it was a spooky, misguided focus for the weak among us—or, in the least, for those of us believers who don't possess sufficient belief without such an experiential crutch to back it all up.

Boy was I wrong.

By contrast, I was primarily living a *self*-empowered life of discipline continually held together by an act of the will. But God never intended our post-resurrection walk with Jesus to be that way. His active, perceptible walk with us through the power of the Holy Spirit was part of the new covenant deal!

What did Paul say to this effect? While, in 2 Timothy 3:5 he's talking about those who may be false teachers or believers who are not believers at all, I have to ask the question to myself as well; "Am I denying the power of the cross and the power of the indwelling Spirit of God if I live only in a state informed by that which is intellectually perceptible?" Am I actually living with the same illness as that of our young people–that being a worldview which informs my personhood based solely on that which I can touch, taste, feel, hear or see?[50]

I think the Lord finally just got tired of my living on 50% of that which he'd already given me! So WHAM...He broke in. And my world has been turned upside down.

And so while I am really ok with not having to place *all* of what I've been experiencing into a framework perceptible by the flesh, there is now something finally coming which could be helpful in communicating what has been happening. It's more like an anatomy of how truth works its way into our lives for lasting impact and God's glory.

I am perceiving that this path, which seemed to have come to a head and transpired inside of a 2-4 day period, has not been unlike that which we undergo when first accepting Jesus as our Savior. And for most of us who haven't yet been able to successfully release into the LORDSHIP of Jesus in ALL ASPECTS of our lives, *perhaps* there is another exchange that needs to happen between ourselves and God.

Now a word of clarification. I am *not* saying we are in need of *receiving* the Holy Spirit. No, that exchange happened the very moment we accepted Christ into our lives as the Sufficient One for the forgiveness of our sins. The New Testament is clear on this issue–that Jesus' ministry would be one through which he would become real to us, his children, through the indwelling of the Holy Spirit. Trusting in Christ indwells us with the Holy Spirit of God. Nothing we do relieves

---

[50] Here, a shameless plug for my curriculum within the Truth Will Survive Us Project for Christian parents of pre-teen and teenage students called, *Kingdom or Culture*.

us of this fellowship. It may be a cold and nearly dead fellowship, but he, the Holy Spirit, is still there.

What I *am* saying is that if we are unable to carry ourselves through this life adequately to honor Christ, then we likely have a knowledge and power shortage...one restricted primarily by our flesh's willful and still sin-laden need for control. In such a state, I am convinced we are only saved—*not* given over.

And while the power of God lies within, we are disquieting Him through a lukewarm, self-preserving life. There *is* a difference between possessing the Holy Spirit of God through our profession of faith, and being *led* and *controlled* by the Holy Spirit, having been given over completely to his authority in our lives.

We will revisit this idea shortly as we query ourselves about whether we may have "an ownership problem."

PAUSE to PONDER

- If you are ready, ask God to help you identify anything in your life that, in your self-preservation, may be restricting the free-flow of his Spirit within you.
- Give God permission to break, and then mend your heart, as he touches anything he wishes that is keeping him from full, backstage access to your life.

Chapter 20

A Traceable Pathway

Now on to the point of there being a traceable pathway for that which happened to me when the Lord brought to bear the catalyst of his choosing in May of 2012.

The truths[51] which the Spirit allowed to come crashing into spiritual awareness were truths which, as a long-time believer, had previously entered and then dead-headed in my intellect. It was critically important stuff having to do with who I am as a believer and a new creation—and what happened that day at Calvary 2000 years ago.

The book of Romans and its theological underpinnings regarding our sins, our sin problem and how the blood, the cross and the Holy Spirit each play a crucial role in our delivery from the bondage of our old man were about to take center stage.

These distinctions were the catalysts of God's choosing I mentioned earlier. And Watchman Nee's treatment of Romans in his

---

[51] When I speak of "Truth" from this point forward, I am referring to scriptural, biblical Truth...truths taught us by Paul and others which have their foundation in the inerrant Word of God and which are pinned to the nature and character of God. One can refer to Truth as the whole of scripture, to God himself - the very representation and embodiment of Truth, or to elements of his Word which become newly enlightened to our soul once the Holy Spirit brings such illumination for our edification or a deeper walk with Him. So by Truth, I'm not talking about truths like the world is round, a baseball will fall to the ground when you drop it from your hand, and the like. These kinds of "truth" obviously do not bring significant impact into one's life.

book, The Normal Christian Life, was what the Lord used to begin to bring these truths to light in a way I alone had not grasped.

Though some of Nee's writings may be a bit of a stretch for theological *absolutism*, most of this book is rock solid, brutally honest, and doesn't dodge real barriers we have to our faith.

What Nee's handling of Romans brought to light was as perspective altering for my walk as a follower of Jesus as anything I had read outside of the scriptures themselves. This book, rooted in the Truths of the scriptures, was the catalyst of God's choosing to awaken within me something from which I am yet to recover. And I pray I never do.

Here's as traceable a pathway I can render regarding what happened to me on a journey toward what I can only describe as *God's willingness* to awaken his Spirit within me.

I am still a bit hesitant to put an experience that has been so holy into a *process*; we too readily turn such things into techniques or formulas. But really, this pathway is less about *what* the Lord may use to draw us into a deeper knowledge of him, and more an evaluation of how enduring change comes to pass in our spiritual life.

And to my surprise, it has come as such a complete, seamless body just today as I prepared to write this section that I am actually somehow finding relief! Thank you, Lord. You are amazing. You have brought peace and much anticipated rest in having this pathway be somewhat tangible. How oddly wonderful.

Now please understand something here; this process I am about to explain is not safe. It will not permit a stagnant life anchored in what is comfortable. But you can trust the Spirit of God to tenderly walk alongside you if you are willing to comply.

It would seem the Holy Spirit will be willing to camp out on these first nine phases until he has eliminated everything that hinders his command of our lives.

We do not want to rush this operation. It is one of the most holy things that can ever happen to us in this life. It is heart wrenching. It is difficult. It is humbling. It is intimate. It will utterly break you—it must. And as the Spirit begins to surgically clear away the clutter of those things onto which we hold, this process [He] begins to set us free.

Only God knows what clutters our individual lives—we cannot detect most of it ourselves. But I beg of you to *let go of each piece of baggage* he brings to your consciousness. He likely won't ask you to let go of more than one at a time.

His operative work is like the peeling away of the layers on an onion. He must tear from us one sense of sufficiency, pride, ownership, control or entitlement at a time. And although there will be sorrow, I have found what Paul teaches us through his letter to the Corinthian church to be true; Godly sorrow brings repentance that leads to salvation and leaves no regret, but worldly sorrow brings death (2 Cor. 7:10).

This peeling away may take months...or years. But if you are willing, he will sufficiently break and empty you of everything that hinders his *absolute* authority in your life.

Do not play games with God.

If there is any willful sin pattern or addiction in your life, you had better be ready to give it up and let him root it out. Don't waste God's time. His work will continue until one of two things happens; either you will balk at something you are unwilling to release—at which point the process will stall out, or He will become Lord.

If you let him establish himself in your life as Lord, then in God's time, *you...become useful.* Thereafter, he can walk you into phases 10 and 11. And Life really begins!

Here is how it went down for me, *each stage bringing about the next as a natural progression—over time.* Phases 1 through 9 were repeatedly visited for several months, as if in a loop, before we broke out into the final two phases. Only the Holy Spirit can bring us to and through each step of this work of enlightenment. So here it is—pasted directly from my scratches on another document. *(For a more detailed account, secure the audio version of Set Free at* www.audible.com.*)*

1. **Truth Received**—brought awareness. **Led to understanding.**
2. **Truth Understood**—brought awe & gratitude. **Led to knowledge.**
3. **Knowledge**—brought contemplation of and meditation upon the new Truth. **Led to belief.**
4. **Belief**—brought confidence in a new reality. **Led to willing, almost compulsory release.**
5. **Release**—brought introspective and accurate view of depravity, a direct result of the Holy Spirit's freedom to move—finally! **Led to humility.**
6. **Humility**—brought an accurate view of myself. **Led to brokenness.**
7. **Brokenness**—brought deep sorrow & soulish regret, but interestingly no shame before God. **Led to repentance.**
8. **Repentance**—brought freedom, newness, joy, peace, rest. **Led to joyful & eager surrender.**

9. **Surrender**–brought strength, passion and confidence. And once enough clutter had been removed, <u>**Led to** unreserved trust & newness of **purpose**.</u>

---

10. **Newness of Purpose** – brought clarity and perspective to all things temporal and earthbound. <u>**Led to** reclamation of God's calling</u>.
11. **Calling** – brought utter dependence on the Holy Spirit. <u>**Led to** a hunger for **Truth**.</u> And the Spirit then delivers a **new Truth** into our consciousness, bringing awareness…which as we seek the Lord's clarity on such Truth, leads to **Understanding**…and he begins to teach us anew in another area of his choosing!

This is as near a pathway I can put into print which represents what happens within us when, generically speaking, God reveals to us a truth catalyst of his choosing–something that awakens within us an illumination of that which needs to change in response to reading, being taught, reflecting upon, or digesting **his Word**…THE source of Truth.

Chapter 21

Who Am I?

Now on a more personal level again, which sometimes makes this seem less like a book and something more like a journal, what has convinced me to undertake this writing is the hope that the Lord Jesus might be willing to use it for the purpose of drawing other lifelong Christians into deeper fellowship with himself.

I cannot describe the extent to which I feel ill-equipped to do this because I have so come to realize I am nothing and He is everything. I find myself struggling to find words that can express the inadequacy I feel to even deliver what I am writing. Moreover, I am reminded in countless ways every day that I am still in the midst of this journey myself, and will struggle forward alongside you until we are together made perfect in Christ's presence.

Only as I regularly review what the book of Romans teaches is true of us *in* Christ am I made bold enough to bring anything to the table of discussion.

My earnest prayer has been that God would use these ruminations for the purpose of helping to exchange other Christian's cerebral spiritual walk for one set ablaze by His Spirit. I know what the Spirit used to kick start my heart, but I don't know if God will choose to bring those same truths (in Part III) to the fore of other Christian's spiritual awareness for the sake of a more broad-based spiritual revival. I guess time will tell.

In my more vulnerable moments of doubt, Satan has attempted to shoot down the idea of writing this book with more varieties of the *'but who am I'* question than I can tell you.

"Why not just tell people to read Watchman Nee's book?" is the adversary's favorite refrain. Or, "Why not just tell people to spend more time in the book of Romans. It's already been written! Plus, it is the Holy Spirit who translates truth into people's experience."

But doing so would never cauterize my bleeding heart on the question posed in the first sentence of the Introduction–let alone pacify its answer. In spite of my personal weaknesses, and there are many, one sure thing makes me press on; there is a spiritual sickness in most of our well-intentioned, Christian hearts. Its impact dysfunctions our fellowship with and restricts our ability to bring glory to God–the dual purposes of our existence. And it matters less who addresses its plague-like impact than *that* it be addressed.

The problem doesn't lie in our church leadership, the structural or programming preferences of our weekend services, or the level of teaching available to us on any given Sunday.

Having personally been infected with the virus responsible for at least part of this illness for too many years, I could no longer keep my discontent on the matter to myself.

As stated earlier in a concise quote from Watchman Nee, the problem is best stated as follows:

> **"Many of us Christians today are men with over-developed souls. We have grown too big in ourselves. When we are in that condition, it is possible for the life of the Son of God in us to be confined and crowded almost out of action."**[52]

And there is only one answer. The Spirit of God must be set free to lay claim to our hearts and to arrest *from* us *his* rightful place as Lord.

Our desperate prayer should be, "Oh God, don't put a lid on my life because of a self-confidence that crowds you out and keeps me from recognizing my desperate need for you. Don't put a lid on our life together because of my inability to understand and know your Word. Don't put a lid on my life because of my lack of belief. Don't put a lid on my life because of my inability to perceive of something that is grieving your heart, estranging myself from you and quenching your Spirit's mobility within me."

Giving credit where it is due, we *are* cerebrally well-versed in the Word and goodhearted. But many of us are relatively powerless,

---

[52] Nee, The Normal Christian Life; Page 151

lukewarm Christians, living hard-working, effort-filled lives—without the supernatural power of the Spirit to assist us.[53]

Oh, how it mourns my heart to know I am speaking about the life I had been living, and still could live were my soul left unattended, quenching the movement of the Spirit within. And again, we won't find the solution with any amount of institutional resolve.

Our estrangement from the Spirit living inside us will not be cured with committee meetings, strategy sessions, new initiatives resulting from church member polling data, clever marketing campaigns, better videography, a new logo, more leadership resolve, a bigger, more attention-grabbing flag for our satellite campus or anything else we can enact in *our* heroic effort.

Rather, we need to be crushed.

Our spiritual mediocrity will only be overcome when we lose our sense of adequacy and are individually struck with our true wretchedness before a Holy God.

We need revival. We need the Spirit of the Almighty God to flame us out.

Many whose eyesight is so very good from an earthly vantage point, have, like me, not been pulling from the sap of the Vine because we don't *know* the power of God. We know *about* the power of God, but we don't know it ourselves. We're like the decedents of Jacob, a generation who knows *about* the works of God, but who have not experienced such things themselves. In just two generations, they didn't even *know about* the works God had done for Israel! Where are we, I wonder, on that generational continuum?

But how *can* we gain in appreciation for our state of need? *How* can we be recipients of an in-breaking of God's authoritative power in our lives?

All I know is what God used as the catalyst in my life—and what has stricken a couple of others to awaken them to a newness in their walks with the Lord Jesus. And I am compelled to share it with anyone whom God would give pause to consider it.

But it is no special formula—and there never will be anything we can do to earn God's favor. It's purely a matter of having the deep truths of God's Word freed up to do their work in our souls; this is my attempt to recount what the Spirit used in my life.

---

[53] Notice I did not say theologically negligent or doctrinally incompetent.

Surely there are other Christians like me who have known *about* the truths Paul was struggling to make known to the believers of the early church *without having had the Holy Spirit pin their souls to the floor with those game-changing truths*.

It is one thing to know *about* spiritual truths; it is quite another to have the Spirit of God give you a *knowledge* and *understanding* of them. However, when he does you this favor, there is no turning back. You are never the same.

You and I both know many people who know *about* God. But if they really *knew* God, they would have no other reaction than to fall in surrender to his immeasurable grandeur and mercy and give their lives to him. I believe many of us fall into the same camp.

I finally came to agree with the Lord, that if He would allow me to retrace something of a discernible thread or pathway on which He has had us travel together, I was going to be willing to write it down. So now we have this book. And as we continue our transition toward the Truths from Romans which so altered my spiritual playing field, I want to ease into it with a few final clarifiers and loving admonitions.

Chapter 22

Clarifier: Man's Writings / God's Word

While one must be careful about placing too high an opinion upon the writings of men, there are substantial nuggets of truth pondered and communicated effectively by believers, born of their personal experiences with Jesus, which have proven to be exceedingly useful in my present journey.

As I look back, I can point with certainty to a few writings which God chose to use, circumstantially, in my life—books which may or may not necessarily be a critical part of the journey for another believer. Still, I believe *the results derived from these books* **represent necessary components** for any Christian's trek into a less predictable, less manageable relationship with God; these components should be understood to be comparative prerequisites when it comes to the Spirit's willingness and ability to move into deeper fellowship with us. These components are surely the very same things God has used since he began fellowshipping with and drawing people unto himself—things like an accurate reflection of our condition, sorrow and grief, repentance and humble surrender.

Some of the writings God used to kick start our new ground zero together are: Bill Hybels' *Holy Discontent*, Watchman Nee's *The Normal Christian Life*, and John Piper's *Don't Waste Your Life*.

And, while I'm sure this list will continue to grow into manuscripts such as Timothy Keller's book, *King's Cross*, which shares many commonalities with Nee's book, Platt's, *Radical*, which could run alongside Piper's book as a call to practical action, The Pursuit of Holiness—which I cannot read and listen to enough times through, by Jerry Bridges, and Tozer's amazing compilation *The Crucified Life* that has reinforced and legitimized what has been laid on my heart, I have to acknowledge these three books have been used in a miraculous and timely way by the Spirit of God as he has chased me down.

I am grateful beyond words for how God has used elements of these men's Christian walks **to help me gain in knowledge...a critical building block of strengthening what we call *faith*.**

But over the last couple years, as mentioned earlier in this writing, I have once again become convinced of something I have always known intellectually but lacked subjectively and experientially; *we open the floodgates to the revelation of our God and will begin to draw near to Him (and He to us) when we live in his Word.*

This practice is a most fundamental one. For it both nourishes our life with the Spirit of God living in each of us who have placed our trust in Jesus, and it gives us a benchmark of absolute Truth against which to hold the words and thoughts of man.

Many a man has been terribly misled while in the midst of a quest for answers in times of desperate need. Such need is the perfect fodder for inaccurate and very damaging "spiritual" teaching. And it is during such times that any number of experiential, opportunistic, unbiblical teachings, though maybe even well-meaning by their perpetrator, will present themselves to those in such dire need.

The miscalculation which leads to taking the wrong fork in the spiritual road comes when such a desperate need coincides with a lack of doctrinal knowledge or steadfast adherence to an accurate theology. It is at this crucial point the cry of our soul leads us to become vulnerable to any number of spiritual solutions. Sadly, much of the teaching in such cases not only leans too heavily into a reliance upon what a particular man, church or group is teaching–leading to Satan's deceptive trickery of the vulnerable, but it also stalls our *real* forward progress into true spiritual maturity. Good doctrine is irreplaceable.

"What doctrine does," said Tony Evans just today as I listened to his message on Moody Radio, "is serve as a filter for the soul in order to catch stuff that's trying to infiltrate into your life that doesn't work [belong there]"..."[and] when your life [is imbedded in sufficient] doctrine, when you understand the categories of truth that are in the Word of God, you may not know all the details, but you will know when 'something's just not right about that.'"[54]

---

[54] Message: The Strategy of Satan, Angels: Good, Bad and Ugly, Vol 2, Tony Evans (The Alternative). Brackets mine.

So, in conclusion to this matter of man's thoughts being held up against the light of God's Word, I don't see them in an adversarial but complimentary light.

Assuming man's thoughts have been tested and approved through the lens of God's Word, they can be used by the Spirit, capable of pointing our minds toward Truths discerned from Scripture. Still, we must remember that while the writings of men can lead to a comprehension of spiritual truths, their deductions are not a living organism as is the Word of God. Man's analyses and conclusions are only valuable in so much as they point us accurately to the Author and perfector of our faith.

That said, there is no doubt God has revealed Truths about Himself and his Word to men who are gifted to communicate such Truths in ways which draw other Christ-followers into a deeper fellowship with God through Jesus Christ.

So, in the end, of most critical import has been what the God of the universe has done *through* His Word and, by extension, through the internalization of His Truth. It has been a most amazing, humbling and introspective delivery *from* myself–a prerequisitive key to beginning a Spirit-filled life–a life set free!

PAUSE to PONDER
- To what or whom have you been turning for your primary spiritual insight?
- On whom do you place greater reliance for the delivery of truth to your mind, heart and soul, man's teaching or the Holy Spirit's illumination?

Chapter 23

Under the Influence: In Whose Spirit Are We Living?

Continuing our contemplative descent into "Destination Romans," awaiting us in Part III, we should freshly visit our soul's current resting place.

It has taken, I'm sorry to say, the better part of some 35 years after coming to Christ for me to really have it brought to my attention how utterly lifeless, hopelessly ill and completely void I am apart from Christ.

In a culture sick with grand estimations of our humanity, we Christians are not immune to thinking likewise. But thanks be to God alone, He is beginning to help me grasp there is *nothing* worth living for in our old man. How about you?

This is a difficult reality at which to arrive. And we cannot get there alone. **Only the Spirit of God living *dangerously* within us, having been given the absolute permission to freely wound us as *He* sees fit, can assist us in coming to such a place of accurate repugnance for the person we are when apart from the touch of our Savior.**

This must not be mistaken for a deep and sorrowful regret for the wretchedness of what I *do*—how I *act*. No, the problem lay deeper than that. **What I *do* is merely the output or production of what is wrong—*me*. It is *me*, the likeness of Adam, that is wrong to the very core...incapable of gaining full fellowship with the Holy Spirit *no matter what I try to do* to get into alignment with Him.**

It is one thing to intellectually acknowledge all this to be so; it is altogether another thing to subjectively, experientially have it revealed so that you *know* it to be so. It is in this latter place where the miraculous work of the Holy Spirit begins to deliver us from the limitations of ourselves. Once He begins to shine his incomparably pure light on our hopelessly wayward sickness, we have hope to gain better vision.

This point, for me, has been of such central importance, I must press the issue still further.

But before doing so, this one reminder.

I want to once again stress the indispensable role of the biblical texts for spiritual illumination. It is the discovery of, *and obedience to*, the truths found in God's Word that enables us to enjoy the relational infilling and subjective awareness of God which, all too frequently, resides dormant within us. He desires to reveal himself to us by his Spirit – something He longs to do in us **for his glory**.

But there are prerequisites to our being released into such a life-giving experience, and the beginning of such wonderful fellowship with the Holy Spirit. And through this process of our becoming *usable*, the Word must remain central. God's holy scripture has been, is currently, and will always be the living, breathing, life-giving words of our God, sharper than a double-edged sword and capable of operating to the most core depths only reachable by the Spirit of God (see Hebrews 4:12).

The exact purposes for such illumination in each of our lives are his alone, but I cannot help but believe it is, in the very least, to reveal and then give unto us the power and authority to carry out a central purpose for which He is uniquely calling us as we long to align ourselves with what He is doing in this world.

Now let's continue on with our first major hurdle to deep and abiding fellowship with, and a life capable of being controlled by, the Holy Spirit—this pivotal idea of our inability to sufficiently lay *ourselves* down for his use.

Though we believe we *are* given over, in our own power we are *not capable of* doing so. I am coming to believe we cannot release all of who we are until God makes this abundantly, experientially clear to us through what I can only explain as an illumination of such truth from His gracious, yet heavy hand.

This is not the same as a merely cerebral, intellectual acknowledgement of this truth. The experience of the intellect cuts only so deep...and not deeply enough.[55]

I am afraid what I see in most of us is that we are *still* trying to deliver ourselves into his hands *as an act of our will*. We can never do so to his satisfaction—or in a way to sufficiently provide for our deliverance and freedom. He can appreciate our effort, but it is insufficient in itself as a means to his being fully released to work his power in our lives.

If we continue holding onto even *one* thing earth side, whether person, place or thing, I am convinced we will not discover the Christian life God intended for us.

Daily we must ask ourselves, "What have I picked up from my old nature again *today* that could kick start another round of temporal baggage which could weigh me down?"

For me, one of the most challenging hills to climb was my being willing to most absolutely trust in his looking out for my earth-side interests...family members, finances, work opportunities and so on. And this was coupled with my still clinging refusal to grasp the utter and total depravity of my thinking that I had *anything* of value I could ever possess in my flesh which could be used as an offering for my Savior.

I love what William Temple said about our contribution in the direction of our righteousness outside of Christ:

> All is of God. The only thing of my very own which I contribute to my redemption is the sin from which I need to be redeemed.[56]

Until lately, I still really believed I had something—even one small thing that I, in my fleshly abilities, could turn around and offer my Jesus. In the very least, I figured I could bring *something* to the table which God could use. After all, He created me, right? Well, sort of.

---

[55] *But, ironically, the subjective experience of the depth of our depravity and insufficiency before God is usually reached through our knowledge – knowledge of what he teaches us in his Word. For we cannot internalize that which we do not know! A theologically uninformed Christian **is lacking a knowledge of** that which the Spirit would often like to powerfully and subjectively bring to our experience. More on this later.*

[56] Quote taken from Platt, The Cross of Christ; Secret Church, Part 3

Chapter 24

Adam's Upper Hand

God created Adam...and Eve. And as such, *they* were made in His image in a way unlike any man since–myself included. *They* were *created* without the encumberment of sin. They were capable, in their flesh, to fully fellowship with God rightly. But only for a time did even *they* experience this.

Because sin entered the world through Adam, so I enter the world *filled to the brim* with the same (Romans 7:18). This means I was not born into this world as was Adam. By comparison, as such a sin-laden being from the very moment of conception, there has never been, is not currently, nor will there ever be anything good enough in myself (precisely **nothing**–did I say that already?) that could ever satisfy and please God...let alone enable Him to work with me "in the same room," so to speak.

Every member of the human race is born spiritually dead. And nothing you can do *on your own* can *ever* change that reality, pure and simple. This is not merely my theory about our condition; this is what our loving Creator tells us is true about us. There can be no visage of light or goodness in us that has not been placed there by God. We cannot even so much as *discover goodness* without the illumination of the Spirit of God.

David Platt writes this in chapter 2 of his book, *Radical*.

> This is the reality about humanity. We are each born with an evil, God-hating heart. Genesis 8:21 says that every inclination of man's heart is evil from childhood, and Jesus' words in Luke 11:13 assume that we know we are evil. Many people say, 'Well, I have always loved God,' but the reality is, no one has. We may have loved a god that we made up in our minds, but the God of the Bible, we hate.

> In our evil we rebel against God. We take the law of God, written in his Word and on our hearts, and we disobey it.[57]

In addition, once God has drawn us into a recognition of our desperate need for Him and we have placed our trust in Him for salvation, we still act like spiritually dead men, unregenerate in our lives of sin.

> We spurn our Creator's authority over us. God beckons storm clouds, and they come. He tells the wind to blow and the rain to fall, and they obey immediately. He speaks to the mountain, 'You go there,' and he says to the seas, 'You stop here,' and they do it. Everything in all creation responds in obedience to the Creator…until we get to you and me. We have the audacity to look God in the face and say, 'No.'
>
> …Ephesians 4:18 says that we are darkened in our understanding and our hearts are like stone. …According to 2 Corinthians 4:4, we can't even see Christ because of the depth of our spiritual blindness. …The Bible describes us as enemies of God and objects of his wrath.
>
> The gospel confronts us with the hopelessness of our sinful condition. But we don't like what we see of ourselves in the gospel, so we shrink back from it.[58]

But, though not trying to defend or make excuses for us, there are definite barriers to our being able to accurately grasp how utterly lifeless we are in our flesh before a perfect and demanding God.

For starters, our self-confidence likes to make its case with great tenacity.

How deeply does our self-confidence live within us? J.I. Packer believes our inability to be sufficiently *done with ourselves* may have to do with our insufficient grasp of the extent of the necessity for, and lavish endowment of, God's grace into our lives. I agree that our estimation of God's immeasurable grace into our lives is terribly lacking.

In Chapter 13 of his book, Knowing God, he says,

> There are four basic truths which the doctrine of grace presupposes. And, if they are not acknowledged in one's heart, clear faith in God's grace becomes impossible.[59]

---

[57] Platt, Radical; Chapter 2, Page 30
[58] Platt, Radical; Chapter 2, Pages 30, 31

His first point is particularly poignant and illustrative in this matter of our seeming inability to grasp that there is truly no good thing living within us apart from God. In it, Packer talks about what he calls the *moral ill-desert of man*. He says,

> Modern men and women, conscious of their tremendous scientific achievements in recent years, naturally are inclined to a high opinion of themselves. They view material wealth, as in any case, more important than moral character. And in the moral realm, they are resolutely kind to themselves, treating small virtues as compensating for great vices–and refusing to take seriously the idea that, morally speaking, there is nothing much wrong with them. They tend to dismiss a bad conscience in themselves, as in others, as an unhealthy psychological freak, a sign of disease and mental aberration rather than an index of moral reality.
>
> For modern men and women are convinced that, despite all their little peccadillo: drinking, gambling, reckless driving, sexual laxity, black and white lies, sharp practice in trading, dirty reading and what have you, they are at heart, thoroughly good folks.
>
> Then, as pagans do–and modern man's heart is pagan, make no mistake about that, they imagine God as a magnified image of themselves and assume that God shares his own complacency about himself.
>
> The thought of themselves as creatures fallen from God's image, rebels against God's rule, guilty and unclean in God's sight, fit only for God's condemnation, never enters their heads.[60]

Why is this? It is because we are naturally and compulsively inclined to move ourselves in the direction of a good conscience.

We are born with a conscience, if even tinged with an overestimation of ourselves, as another avenue for God's creation to be drawn to Himself! Why do we even possess an inclination to feel good or bad about ourselves? It is because God put that tendency within us. It is because there is right and wrong. And because God is holy, He cannot reside or partake with us without interceding on our behalf...which we know He did through the Blood of his Son.

---

[59] J.I. Packer; Knowing God; Chapter 13
[60] Packer; Knowing God; Chapter 13

Chapter 25

A Savior Saves; A Lord Owns

But even after giving up our mind, heart and will to the work of the Blood of Christ, this does not mean we have necessarily given our lives completely into his care! No, we have only accepted his gift of eternal life, having responded to the fact that he has blotted out our sins–thus, enabling us to be "with Him."

But does our response to the atoning work of his Blood make Him my LORD as well as my Savior?

Though saved from eternal separation from God and now, through his blood, capable of sharing the same abode, I can without a doubt yet continue living my life as if I still have something of worth in my old man which God can use.

But to do so denies the power of the cross. It denies the fact that God has put my old man to death with Him on the cross. Yet, in most cases, what is it I do? I carry around what I think to be the *best* of my *old* nature–my old Adam-like man, believing I can *still* somehow honor Him with it. And in doing so, we cannot live in obedience to God's calling for us as believers.

Our living this way demonstrates an uninformed theology as well as a deficiency in reverence–both for what has been exchanged on our behalf and for the sovereignty of God in our lives!

Perhaps just a moment here to further clarify what I mean about our lack of reverence for God and how it impacts a life of obedience–which directly impacts the move of the Holy Spirit in our lives.

One reason many Christians don't experience the power of the Spirit of God in their lives, though He actually dwells in their hearts, is that they lack reverence. And they lack reverence because they have not had the eyes of their heart, mind *and* spirit opened to the fact of his sovereignty and personal presence. The fact is there, but they have not seen it. Without reverence for God, we will not be inclined to obey him. And we will, by default, live powerless and ineffectual lives for God. Let me illustrate.

One of the most powerful and feared men in ancient history was Pharaoh. Why did Pharaoh repeatedly feel free to disobey God's command through Moses to release his people from their slavery in Egypt? Read the text:

> But Pharaoh said, "Who is the Lord, that I should obey his voice and let Israel go? I do not know the Lord, and moreover, I will not let Israel go." – **Exodus 5:2** (ESV)

Because Pharaoh did not respect God, he felt free to disobey. When people disregard God's sovereignty, there is no reverence in their hearts for him. Disobedience, then, becomes second nature.

Now let me reverse the equation. If irreverence produces disobedience, then surely reverence should promote obedience. Yes?

If we really *know* our Savior and what he has accomplished on our behalf, then we will be compelled to give up the tendencies of the old, dead man we too frequently drag along through this life. But because we don't really *know* our Savior and his requirements of us as his children, a lack of reverence leads to a lack of obedience–and a powerless, self-resourcing life is the outcome.

Now for the point of clarity, there are two issues at stake. It is important we separate them. The first is the awakening of our cerebral knowledge to the fact that the Spirit lives within us. The second is a subjective impression into the depths of our soul (encompassing our emotions and gut) only seared into us by the powerful working of the Spirit himself. Without *both* of these, we will find it difficult to give up ownership of our lives.

Firstly, if it is a matter of a theological understanding about whether the Spirit of God dwells within us as believers, this should be cleared up right now. Although we already touched on this briefly, we will reinforce it here.

The apostle Paul clearly taught that we receive the Holy Spirit the moment we receive Jesus Christ as our Savior. I Corinthians 12:13 declares, "For we were all baptized by one Spirit into one body—whether Jews or Greeks, slave or free—and we were all given the one Spirit to drink." Paul could not say that we all were baptized by one Spirit and all given one Spirit to drink if all the Corinthian believers didn't possess the Holy Spirit.

Romans 8:9 tells us that if a person does not possess the Holy Spirit, he or she does not belong to Christ: "You, however, are controlled not by the sinful nature but by the Spirit, if the Spirit of God lives in you. And if anyone does not have the Spirit of Christ, he does not belong to Christ." This is an even stronger indication of this truth as we learn that if a person does not have the Spirit, he does not even *belong to* Christ. Therefore, the possession of the Spirit is an identifying factor of the possession of salvation.

Ephesians 1:13-14 teaches us that the Holy Spirit is the seal of salvation for all those who believe: "Having believed, you were marked in him with a seal, the promised Holy Spirit, who is a deposit guaranteeing our inheritance until the redemption of those who are God's possession—to the praise of his glory."

Oh how I could bust my gut in exuberant joy just processing what these two verses communicate to us! Clearly, the Holy Spirit could not be the "seal of salvation" if He is not received at the moment *of* salvation.

These passages make it clear the Holy Spirit is *received* at the moment *of* salvation.

With that behind us, if all saved Christians possess the Holy Spirit of God, why is it that some are living victorious lives while others live in a state of constant defeat, powerlessness, or uninspiring fellowship with God?

The difference, as we've noted just above, is clearly *not* accounted for by the presence or absence of the Spirit (for He dwells in the heart of every child of God) but by this; some *recognize* what Jesus, all along, intended to be the *normal* impact of his indwelling, and others do not.

This, then, is the second issue at stake; we lack a subjective impression of God's movement into the depths of our soul—only seared into us by the unquenched presence of the Holy Spirit. This is not in any way an indictment, but a matter of timing on both ours and God's part—His timing in our lives.

While gaining a knowledge of accurate theology plays a critical part in establishing our growth into Christ, it is this emotional connectivity to these truths the Spirit desires to use in order for its message to become personally relevant and real to us. God did not create us with a capacity for emotion without reason. He desires that we *feel* the weight of our insufficiency apart from God while, at the same time, being experientially overcome by what God has wrought in us as ones redeemed, remade and empowered to live anew, hearts (to be read emotions) swelling in humble gratitude! Emotions are a powerful motivator, and God uses emotion to encourage our belief in Him and to propel us forward. We cannot reduce these things to the intellectual. Somehow denying an emotional response of our gratitude to God and our love for him repudiates what it means to be human!

But here's the point; until we recognize Jesus as Owner, He does not have free reign in our lives to do as He pleases. And one outgrowth of our refusal to surrender is this very real stifling of emotional impressions which *should* testify as an evidence of God's existence and relationship with us.

But none of this can happen as long as we're holding onto anything in this life more so than onto our God. In chapter 1 of I Samuel, we see Hannah coming to this point when Eli the priest affirms the cry of her heart for the blessing of a son, and then God delivers...**but only once He knows Hannah has given up ownership** of what would become her most precious of possessions—a son.

> *And she made a vow, saying, "O LORD Almighty, if you will only look upon your servant's misery and remember me, and not forget your servant but give her a son, then I will give him to the LORD for all the days of his life, and no razor will ever be used on his head." (vs. 11)*
>
> *Eli answered, "Go in peace, and may the God of Israel grant you what you have asked of him." (vs. 17)*
>
> *So in the course of time Hannah conceived and gave birth to a son. She named him Samuel, saying, "Because I asked the LORD for him." (vs. 20)*

Hannah was willing to give up all rights of ownership to a son were God to bless her with such. Perhaps if only we would become more accustomed to surrendering ownership of all that is most precious to us, we may stand the chance of receiving a rock-solid belief to rest in God's plans for us—even before He delivers the goods.

In Hannah's case, with this news from a man of God, she *"went away and ate something, and her face was no longer downcast."* Isn't that interesting? May our lives reflect a similar trust and rest in our Owner.

> We all desire this kind of Spirit-delivered rest, for a true revelation of the Spirit's indwelling will revolutionize the life of any Christian.[61]

Naturally, if given a choice, most of us would eagerly ask God for such an illumination, cutting to the depths of our emotion. But there is a problem. Gaining such will not be like plucking your favorite cereal from the shelves at the grocery store. Becoming conditioned for Truths which could carry with them life-altering, spiritual impact may take you to places you'd rather not visit. But if you are willing, I believe there are things you can do to precondition your heart for such illumination.

PAUSE to PONDER

- Do you think you live in sufficient reverence before God?
- Read Revelation, Chapter 19.
- How about now? Do you think you live in sufficient reverence before God?
- Is Jesus your Lord...or only your Savior?
- How does a servant properly respond to a request from a Master or Lord?
    a. With conditions, based upon the servant's own preference and convenience?
    b. Without controversy?

---

[61] *This begs the question, "**How** then can we experience a life-changing, perspective-altering recognition of the Spirit's indwelling?" The tough news is that we cannot do, find or earn this. Our options are limited. There is no formula but release. God is God. We are not. What we **do** know is what he tells us—that if we knock, the door will be opened to us. What we **do** know is that He will not give us a snake when we need bread, that He has purchased us with a great price, and that He desires our fellowship so much that Jesus died to gain it—rather than live forever without it. What we **do** know is that He desires to live through us and empower us supernaturally, differentiating us from the on-looking world, that His name be praised through our lives. But more on how God can choose to reveal himself anew to us later in this whole attempt to objectively acknowledge what God desires to do in and through us, the end goal being to possibly help lead other lifelong, but relatively supernaturally powerless Christians, into the discovery of his undeniably communal enlivening.*

Chapter 26

Spurring On Our Death

Though certainly not a prerequisite, lest we put God in a box, **it seems that the more deeply spiritual, operational incisions initiated by the Holy Spirit coincide with times when one has been veritably leashed** (sometimes physically, whether through injury, searing crisis or otherwise) **to such *foreign practices* as stillness, silence, and sincere meditation on the Truths of God and His Word.**

For our part, we label these times as "interruptions to our productivity." For the Spirit's part, He labels them as *opportunity*.

Oh, Christian friend, it is in such times our loving and gracious God is giving us a painful pause *intended* to spur on our death. And more often than not, we hate every minute of it.

All we can do is think about what isn't getting done. "Lord," we say, "what duties should I be carrying out right now which I am incapable of *doing* because of this cursed stillness?" All the while, the week, month or quarter year of relative incapacitation ticks away, pregnant with God's purpose for us, and...we miss it.

The One who gave his life to gain relationship with us is stilling us and calling our name—but we cannot hear him because we are too concerned with our self-importance. The ears of our heart and soul are stopped up with the temporal. And we fail the test.

I can nearly see all of heaven, from the angels pausing from their work to our great cloud of witnesses, holding their collective breath when we are stricken with such times of what we call "unproductive stillness"– and we fail to recognize that it was a time divinely ordered for our becoming into Christ.

Your time of involuntary stillness may not be as incapacitating as was Dr. Rich Edwards', but if gifted with such, I pray the outcome will be comparable. In his book, Not a Fan, Kyle Idleman tells this man's story. I'd like to recount it here.

> On February 10th, 2006, I was in control of my life and I liked the direction things were going. I had a thriving chiropractic practice, two sons and a devoted wife. On February 11th, everything changed.
>
> I was heading out to my hunting cabin where I planned to meet up with friends and hunt wild boar. As I drove along, I could see the effects from the severe drought we had been experiencing. Everything seemed to have dried up and died.
>
> By the time I had reached the road heading to the cabin, it was dark. As I turned, I missed the road and ended up in five feet of thick brush. I tried to free my truck by putting it in forward, then reverse repeatedly. The friction from that somehow ignited the brush. Within seconds, the truck was a large torch.
>
> I reached for the door handle to escape, but the electrical system burned out and I was locked inside. Seconds later, the window exploded. I don't really know what happened after that. I have no idea how I got out of the truck. The next thing I remember is walking down the road to the cabin telling myself over and over, "Don't stop. Keep going."
>
> When I reached the cabin, my friends thought I was wearing some kind of three-dimensional, leafy hunting outfit. But it wasn't camouflage. It was shredded, charred skin.
>
> A Medflight helicopter took me to a burn unit where I was told I wouldn't have much of a face left, and I would probably lose my sight as well as the use of my hands. God put an absolute halt on my life.
>
> I was so busy being successful, I was on such a fast track, that God was a part of my life, but he wasn't the most important part. He was not on the throne of my heart or at the center of my universe. I was at the center.
>
> I don't believe God caused the fire, but I believe God allowed it because he wanted to get my attention. Like a parent who tries to get through to a child, God grabbed me by the shoulders, sat me down and said, "I want you to listen to *me*."

That was the beginning of a spiritual awakening in my life. Over the next four years, the doctors amputated seven fingers. I couldn't use what was left of my hands for even the simplest of tasks, but the doctors said there was nothing more they could do. That's when my wife, Cindy, asked about the possibility of a hand transplant.

That began a time of waiting, testing and prayer. We spent countless hours reading the Bible and praying together. Finally, the day for my double hand transplant arrived. Twenty surgeons and three anesthesiologists took seventeen and a half hours to attach my new hands.

Many people have pointed out that it was a miracle I didn't die in the fire that day. That's true, but in a very real way, I did die in that fire. The man I was died that day, and God gave me a new life where I'm not in control but have turned the controls over to Him. I'm not in charge of my life anymore, but have submitted everything to Jesus.

These days my wife and I constantly pray to be used by God in any way he wants–to bring glory to himself. It may sound crazy, but I would rather have gone through all of this pain and suffering, and all of these challenges and have the relationship with Jesus that I have now, than continue down the path I was on before the accident without that relationship.[62]

May I ask you a question? Given the torrid pace of your life, how but through a time of your being dropped onto a bed of stillness can the voice of God be heard in your life? Likely, you are too busy to *hear* otherwise! How can He become your great Love if you're incessantly consumed with the affairs of this world? How but through incapacitation might you recognize how broken and dead you really are in your overly confident flesh?

Oh, how God sits, waiting, His figurative hands folded patiently. He does not want what we can *do* firstly. He wants us. Broken. Humbled. Tender. Delivered from ourselves. In times of quiet and lengthy *need*, the odds of our looking longingly (and long enough) heavenward, significantly rise; it is in these times we stand the best chance of understanding the delivering value of a complete death to self, without which we are destined to a life of relatively powerless self-exertion.

---

[62] Kyle Idleman, Not a Fan; Chapter 3

Left to ourselves and without giving up, we are like those Habakkuk prophesied about in Habakkuk 1:11 where he spoke of the Babylonians as "that ruthless and impetuous people....guilty people, **whose own strength is their God**." I don't think this is meant to be our encouragement to live likewise—in our own strength.

No, **our own strength**, if we desire a vibrant walk with the Spirit of God, **must be ruthlessly slayed**.

I know this is a tremendously counter-cultural message, but it is the only way. When, after all, did we start finding it important to live sensitively and tolerantly in line with the cultural persuasions of the day? Certainly this is not the picture we see when studying Jesus' life. Certainly this is not the picture we see when observing the lives of Shadrach, Meshach, and Abednego, the lives of Moses and Aaron, the life of Stephen, the life of the disciples, the life of Paul, and so on. **Instead, those surrendered to God live in *notable* contrast to their culture's modus operandi.**

But while our need is for self-abandonment, positioning us for a life empowered by the Spirit of the Living God who aches to be unleashed within us, we seldom find the time for the prerequisites God often uses for such positioning—stillness, silence and sincere meditation on the Truths of God and His Word.

Such practices do not naturally coexist at the breakneck speed of our hectic lives. Like it or not, the busyness of America and much of the developed world *thrills* our adversary. While Satan knows he cannot have our souls, he is ecstatic about the unexamined pace of our lives. For it is this hurried (dare I say frenzied) pace at which many of us well-meaning Christians lead our lives that aids and abets such a low bar of spiritual expectation.

Yes, our adversary *must* keep us away from lives of contemplation by incessantly filling our eyes, ears, minds and hearts with things that, at worst, please temporally and relatively, and, at best, occupy our time with spiritually neutral substance. *And while it would be difficult to point out what is **wrong** with our daily, weekly, monthly and, before we know it, yearly pursuits, it may be a better question to ask what is **right** with them.*

And so as a result of the "busy and good" commotion of our lives, we seldom ponder the proposition that our Christian walks were intended to be so much more than fire insurance—a journey relegated to the enjoyment of good music which lifts our eyes heavenward while possessing a gracious heart of thanksgiving to God for saving us from hell.

Were there a thematic declaration of prognosis for our spiritually shallow and weak living to which I could point, it would lie in the content of the single-sentence paragraph you just blew past.

PAUSE to PONDER
- How have you responded to painful experiences that have inhibited your busy and productive life?
- Have you ever considered the possibility that there may be more to these 'interruptions' than meets the human eye?
- If you are a Christian, and your omniscient and omnipotent God is love (I John 4:8), can you trust Him with your life? How about with the unexpected and painful circumstances that change your plans, even radically?

Chapter 27

An Ownership Problem

"Our problem today," says Dr. Tony Evans, "is we have Christians who want God to get them to heaven, but who do not want Him to *own* them on earth."[63]

God must have your permission to own your life. He already has a *right* to it because, as the Bible says in I Corinthians 6:19-20, if you belong to Jesus Christ, you are not your own–you were bought at a price...so honor God with your body. *But while He has a right to you, He will not take by force that which refuses to be surrendered to Him.* God works in our lives only in those places where we give him jurisdiction. The fact is, we have an amazing ability to keep God at bay in our lives.

In Revelation 3, Jesus is writing to the Church in Sardis a warning we should take seriously in our Christian culture today. He says He knows their deeds; they have a reputation of being alive but are really dead!

Do you think if the membership of the Church in Sardis had been polled, they would have agreed that they were a dead congregation? But they did so many good things! Perhaps they were at church every Sabbath, gave generously, were people of integrity in the community, walked the second mile, turned their stricken cheeks when wronged, kept their commitments, gave a few shekels to the beggar at the gate, and so on.

---

[63] **Adonai–The Owner of All,** *a sermon message by Tony Evans from his radio broadcast, The Alternative (Aired on or around April 15, 2013)*

Jesus says he knew their deeds—so they must have looked pretty good to the world. They had a great reputation! But Jesus says even though they had a sterling reputation for being spiritually alive, really, they were dead!

What? How could this be? Weren't they making much of God by the way they lived their lives?

Apparently, while having a relationship with God, they refused to be OWNED BY Him. Apparently giving out of their abundance, giving of their time, and doing a multitude of good things wasn't making Christ look like the eternal treasure He demanded of them. Had they been completely given over to God, then God would not only have been their Jehovah, the one they recognized as God, but He would also have been their Adonai—their **Master**, their **Owner**...truly their **Lord**.

In 2 Timothy 3:5, the Bible warns us there will be terrible times in the last days when men will not love what is good. They will be lovers of their earthly surroundings and comforts, but not lovers of God—having a form of godliness but denying its power. These are indicators of an unsurrendered life.

And if Revelation 3:1-6 tells us anything, it reveals that even believers can carry around the nameplate yet deny its power. Therefore, know that if God does not OWN you, He is unlikely to powerfully intervene in the daily experiences of your life.

Our holy and just God will seldom be compelled to reveal Himself to you when you yourself are sabotaging the power of his Spirit in your life through patterns of willful disobedience, sinful habits, inattentiveness to his Word, selfish living, refusal to give up the reins of control on your family members, an imbalanced affection for material things or otherwise. Again, all barometers of an unsurrendered life. As Tony Evans says in his message, *Adonai—The Owner of All*, "God doesn't just want to be **in** your life, He wants to OWN your life."

What Dr. Evans seems to be saying is that is it possible for us to merely carry around the nameplate of Christian. And because it is important for us to differentiate between a life *purchased by* God and a life *owned or possessed by* God, I want to linger on this for a bit. Do not confuse the two.

You say, "Greg, how could someone purchase something, and *not* possess or own it? Doesn't the one who purchased the item become its rightful owner? It would create quite a stir were I to purchase a hammer at the hardware store only to find the store manager demanding that *he* maintain possession of *my* hammer for safe keeping. I purchased the hammer so it is mine! I cannot use what I have purchased unless it is *in my possession!*" you might say. And that is precisely the point.

You see, you may have purchased an item, thereby being the item's rightful owner, but until that item is actually delivered into your hands, you cannot *use* it, eat it, or take it home with you. Until the item you purchased is actually *in your hands for use*, merely being its rightful owner won't do you any good, will it?

In the very same way, as Christians, while we *have been purchased* by God, on our part having accepted the purchase price paid by Jesus, I am afraid much of the time we fail to deliver that which He now owns into his hands—namely, our life.

Again, were I to sell my motorcycle on eBay to a man in Georgia, having received full payment, the motorcycle would be his—not figuratively, but literally. It would be his. In due time, the title would be delivered to his house and he would be its outright owner. I would, in no way, be able to lay claim to that which no longer belongs to me.

But if the motorcycle is still sitting in *my* garage, it is not useful to the one who purchased, and duly owns, what *used to be* my motorcycle. Only upon *delivering it into the hands of the new owner* can it be of actual use to him. Only *then* can the new owner use it to run to the store for a gallon of milk, take his son for a ride, or change its oil.

Our relationship with God can be much the same. It may be true that He purchased us, but if we merely sign ourselves over to Him *on the signature line*, drawing eternity in his presence as the only ramification of his purchase while refusing to deliver *ourselves to him for use*, we have only completed half of the *intended* transaction God purposed for our life. A *completed* transaction could have led to a **normal** Christian life as God planned it to be lived post-Christ!

What does God have in you and me? I pray He has something more than ones saved as by fire. Are you living your Christian life on the periphery of his powerful infilling because *you* have constructed a life in your *own* strength? Do you know with absolute confidence that such a life will withstand the Refiner's Fire?

Do you remember Billy Graham's thoughts I quoted earlier?

> If that is not your desire [having the Lord Jesus Christ come into your life and reform, conform and transform you into an obedient follower], you have every reason to question whether or not you have been saved.

How sad it will be for such a man, having missed out on what a life built up by what the Spirit could have wrought. How much better it would be to live fully released into the Spirit's unreserved ownership of that which He purchased and already owns.

If I'm not completely given over to Him, then I cannot call him Lord–only Savior. Do you see the difference? It is important that you do! While He *may* own my life by right, not until I deliver it unconditionally into His hands will I begin to grasp the freedom and newness of life He has intended I be delivered **to**–through new life in Christ.

So the question begs to be directly addressed. Have you *delivered* the motorcycle of your life to God? Or have you sold yourself to Him to solve only the eternal destiny question, negotiating the *full* delivery of your life for a player to be named later?

Are you waiting for Him to forcefully take from you that which He has purchased? Don't count on his doing so. That is not His style.

Well what about delivering more than half way–say to Chattanooga, Tennessee? That would show pretty good intentions! How about that? Good enough? No. He wants us to electively deliver ourselves "all the way to Georgia."

Now don't get me wrong here. If you have trusted in Jesus as the all-sufficient One to remove from you the damnation your sin-laden soul deserves, He does *own* your life. Were God to find your expired, half-delivered body alongside a street in Chattanooga, soul ID number researched, God would rightfully have you delivered into his presence in heaven. You do, after all, belong to Him. There would be no other claim on your life but from your new owner.

Therefore, God may own your soul because He purchased it in agreement with your own free will–no one held a gun to your head when you gave up technical ownership of your life. But as I said to begin with, there is a radical difference between something being purchased by someone and that purchased item being given into the buyer's possession for *unreserved* use as its owner. What a pity to lose out on the Life He desires for us–if only we would but trust into His ownership.

So now back to where we started this. We want God to be everything *but* owner.

Adonai means you don't own.

The Bible says you came into this world naked and you're going to leave this world naked—because you own nothing. Everything is on loan. You are a borrower. So God expects you to recognize Him as Adonai.

There's only one response you give to Adonai, and that is surrender. It is surrender of your will to His will, your way to His way, yourself to Himself. And God will wait—until you give up ownership.

And the only way to truly give up ownership is for God to gift us with a revelation of how wretched we are. The Holy Spirit has to do a work in us so that we can see how necessary is our death—a death as close to literal as we can get without deceasing our physical bodies.

I think this is what NEEDTOBREATHE had in mind when they wrote the lyric to the song, Keep Your Eyes Open, that rings true this way; "Your chains will never fall until YOU do." And only *then* can we begin to experience the greatest of all ironies. Death produces Life.

> *How foolish! What you sow does not come to life unless it dies.*
> *— I Corinthians 15:36*

> *Very truly I tell you, unless a kernel of wheat falls to the ground and dies, it remains only a single seed. But if it dies, it produces many seeds.*
> *— John 12:24*

So to be the Lord of our life, God must put us into a place where we hold onto *nothing* for ourselves. THEN, Life in Him can begin. Fight this if you like, but know that in doing so you will be demonstrating your refusal to release into the hands you *claim* to trust.

Sadly, while death to self is what we need, we might not find it because we may have an ownership problem.

Until our love affair and deep fellowship with Christ becomes to us a greater treasure than our selfish and controlling nature, we will never experience the death of our old Adam. Said another way, until we fear quenching the Holy Spirit's abiding fellowship and power in our lives *more than* we love our flesh, we will never experience Life as Christ intended in our new man.

This being the case, we may now be getting to the bottom line; if you do not long for the indwelling fellowship of the Spirit *in a way that eclipses the compulsions of the flesh*, it is likely you have not yet experienced a depth of fellowship with God that casts out the proclivity to live within the confining walls of your willful and disobedient self-preservation.

And why might this be (let's see if you're getting this yet)?

It may be that there is still an ownership problem in your life. Cutting right to the chase, you love your sinful self-reliance more than you love your God.

PAUSE to PONDER

- Is it really possible for you, a mere mortal, to quench or resist the Holy Spirit, and thus God's movement in your life (Acts 7:51, I Thessalonians 5:19, Ephesians 4:30)?
- STOP! Take sixty seconds right now and ask the following question of yourself: Who...or what owns me (think practically)?
- Had you scheduled coffee with Jesus in order to get *his* take about you in response to the above question, what would He say?

Chapter 28

Transcendence & Time

When we see clearly, we realize our every attempt at self-preservation brings with it severe, earth-side limitations. Living within such self-imposed constraints, we will never transcend to fullness in Christ. Could it be that in our appetite for self-reliance and the compulsion we feel to control the variables in our life, we are only proving that we were, in Joe Stowell's words, built for transcendence?[64]

I say this because even when we feel we have reached some level of control, we are soon no longer satisfied with what our hands have wrought.

We know this about ourselves. It is a human condition. Just a little bit more_____. What is it for you today? Money, time, rest, work, entertainment, control, food, alcohol, friendship, power, health? We are, in fact, *built* to yearn for more.

We work to manipulate circumstances, people, decisions…just about anything we can so things will go well for us. But there's a problem with this tendency; we were built to yearn for something *greater than* what we can find ourselves.

If we are unwilling to *lose* ourselves into the only One who can help us transcend into the ultimate fulfillment of a personal and subjective experience with Himself, then our spiritual life will languish on in mediocrity, chained to our low bar of spiritual expectation.

But let's give ourselves a little break here! It may be that much of what we have been discussing has not previously been brought to your awareness with such naked aggression. For me, it took the Lord

---

[64] Phrase taken from Joe Stowell's message, The Word Became Flesh, originally delivered at a Moody Bible Institute student chapel

Jesus decades of patient pursuit before I slowed enough to go there. And even then it wasn't me, but *He* who did the bidding–and I still have *so* far to go. But what matters is where you and I go from here.

Practically speaking, *how* can we begin the journey toward transcending to a resting place of real relationship and fulfillment in Christ?

As mentioned earlier, I believe it is most frequently initiated during periods of involuntary stillness brought on by some level of incapacitation. In such times, God can break us down. It doesn't *have* to be this way. But more likely than not, and because you won't be broken any other way, this will most often be when the Spirit does his work. Our losing control can be a productive thing in the hands of a jealous God.

Without knowing you personally, I am going to take the liberty to presume something about you. The pace of your life keeps you so occupied that you are rarely able to identify with the involuntary stillness of which I speak.

I'd go so far as to say that keeping you busy with lots of *good things* is Satan's main line of passive attack on the growth of your soul. But in order for you to discover what stands in the way of your being fully delivered into the hands of the Spirit of God, it may be that the pace of your life *is the first thing* that has to change–*if*, that is, you want God to reveal how your dependence and confidence in self is quenching the movement of his Spirit in your life.

His stilling the pace of your life is usually not an easy road. It is a road that frequently brings hardship–whether financial, relational, physical or otherwise. But this is how the Lord breaks us. And, as you know, this was the avenue God chose to use in my life. He knew I could not digest the new, life-giving truths He had prepared for me from his Book of Life–truths which would lead to the first layers of surrender, *until* He had first slowed the pace of my life...to a crawl. At that pace, he could till the soil of my soul. At that pace, He would introduce me to the fact that my low bar of spiritual expectation was breaking his heart.

But the direction He would take us was one I would not have prescribed. He wanted to begin by substantiating my faith through his Word. He wanted to show me that my lack of reverence for how He had redeemed my life was a contributing factor in my bar of spiritual expectancy being so low. He was about to inform my faith.

Chapter 29

Informed Faith Facilitates Giving Up

I had no idea God really *wanted* to substantiate my faith!

Living an unsubstantiated faith life had me walking with God somewhat at arm's length–though I didn't know it. I had *no idea* what it was for the Spirit to open one's eyes to a subjective and intimate understanding of himself.

More to the point of what the Spirit used to gain ground in my soul, I never understood what Paul was so desperately trying to communicate in many of his letters to the burgeoning Church about the effect of the Blood and the Cross of Christ. Much of Paul's writing, and Romans in particular, is *filled* with evidence that he was terribly burdened about helping believers come not only to an intellectual, but also an experiential awareness of what *actually* transpired at Calvary by way of a complete remaking of our lives **in** Christ!

I think God's first order of business for ones He is preparing for a deeper understanding of himself is to rock us with a healthy fear of himself (as illustration, recall here Isaiah's experience from Isaiah 6:1-8 which we referenced at the end of Chapter 11). Once He tenderly and experientially reveals both who He is and who we are in relation to him, we will never again have to wonder about what it means to fear Him and reverence his presence.

> *The fear of the LORD is the beginning of wisdom, and the knowledge of the Holy One is understanding.* – **Proverbs 9:10**

God *wants* us to know we have a faith grounded in the intellect. But He more so wants us to *understand* the deep things of his Word. He wants us to have a grasp on why ours is a faith of reason. But He more so wants us to be overcome by its illumination into our lives. He wants these things to impact us every bit as much as did our first steps of trusting into him for our salvation. **But He wants us to *know* him more than we know a litany of facts *about* him.**

To be clear, I don't think God's Spirit is angling for us to advance in the apologetics of the scriptures as much as He desires that our spirit-being groan with such a deep understanding of him that it wrecks us.

What might He use in your life?

The journey of our beginning to *know* him is attributable to the interactive work of the Holy Spirit alone. It is a gift of God's grace. But far too often, we accept Christ into our lives through a series of seeking moments–and then discontinue the seeking, figuring that we have found the solution. Then, we live the rest of our Christian lives in gratitude for that one moment when we were saved from the eternal ramifications of our sinfulness.

In reality however, though not wanting to minimize our moment of salvation, we have only *entered* the race.

This morning while listening to the radio, I heard the story of a pastor who was imploring his congregation about the importance of *being one*. Right away, an outspoken 4-year old countered the pastor's plea this way. "I don't want to be one. I want to be five!"

If only we would be like that little boy, desperate to move on to greater maturity. Sadly, though, we all too often find ourselves content with *being one* in Christ.

> Today, we seek God and stop searching. Whereas the early saints sought God, found him, *and continued to seek more of him.*[65]

So what actually happens in that moment we say yes to Jesus? "We're saved from sin and are guaranteed heaven," you say. Wonderful. And both true. But why and how can that be so? Do we understand *that*?

We, to a great extent, do not. We just trust God for the supernatural reality that our sins are forgiven and that, as the Bible says, we're new people.

But we stop there–and that stoppage in our education preemptively destroys our ability to have a truly jaw-dropping revelation rock our world...one that is so awe-inspiring so as to

---

[65] Tozer, The Crucified Life; Chapter 4

compel us to pull our boats to the shore one final time and follow Him radically.

[Bear with me here for just one moment as I throw a little tantrum...]

> But radical is irrational. And irrationality in our world of prudence and groundedness continues to score highly on the annual "Top 10 Evils List" of the post-modern Christian.
>
> No, in order to best honor our Savior, being sure to steward our precious, irreplaceable talents in the most God-honoring way, our lives must be ones of planning, preparation, contingency thinking, plan-reviewing, focus grouping, re-preparation....and will you look at that, we're 50 years old and have *still* not learned to trust in the provision of the Spirit of God living inside us.
>
> All the while, He's waiting, watching, pondering our paths, waiting some more, wondering why we're so preoccupied with *our* thing that *His* thing has become something very different than He had in mind 2000 years ago when He first sent the Holy Spirit into the lives of believers.

And lest you think I'm never going to get back to my point, **it is the lack of a full understanding of who we *were* and *are* in Christ that may lead the chase in stalemating our spiritual growth, and has us failing to release all we are unto him.** We're too busy productively *using* our minds to lose them to Christ.

No wonder we cannot lay down our old Adam!

And so, in this way I had lived my Christian life without having acquired the deep, emotional connectivity that *should* accompany our understanding of what really occurred that day at Calvary.

It never occurred to me that my faith should be so informed.

I had *no clue* how an informed faith could revolutionize my walk with the Spirit of God. I had grasped that I was saved, but not sufficiently that I was new. I had accepted that I was new because Paul said I was new—but I didn't grasp what it really inferred onto my life.

I lacked the spiritual insight to see what such truths should really mean to a believer. In short, and overly simplified perhaps, I was theologically uninformed.

But even once informed, it would still only be through an *unquenched* Spirit of God that my heart, mind and soul could possibly lay hold of the intended impact of these truths. And I was 0-2! One, I was theologically uninformed, and two, I had lived my Christian life quenching the Spirit through the continued self-effort of my old man. Thank God his 0-2 pitch was a fastball down the heart of the plate, given me during a time of involuntary stillness–*when I was paying attention*.

While the first part is our learning something intellectually, it can only be *understood* when the second part comes into our experience– that being a revelation of the Spirit into our hearts. Without the second part, the first is of no value since it is only cerebral.

The interdependence of knowledge *(words on the page)* and understanding *(supernatural translation of a truth into our spirit)* is conveyed well in Tozer's words.

> The Church of Jesus Christ never runs on its head. The Church runs on its heart. The Holy Spirit never fills a man's head. The Holy Spirit fills his heart.[66]

---

[66] Tozer, The Crucified Life; Chapter 4

Chapter 30

Real Newness

I cannot explain it any other way but to say all of Scripture is new to me. It was when my faith became informed through the Truths we find in God's revelation to Paul in the book of Romans that the final clinging holds on my life were loosed–and I was most completely and utterly *broken*. It led to a brokenness only God could bring to bear through the Spirit.

For three and one-half decades, I had never *seen* how desperately I'd needed saving. And I think many of us lifelong Christians may struggle with this.

As a Christian, I was busy living victoriously and kicking like the dickens below the surface while swimming to and fro with great intentionality. But really it was *my* intentionality. It was a swim that kept my head well above the water, but it lacked in expectation. It lacked in inspiration. My spiritual bar was tragically low.

But then the Spirit began to reveal to my heart the realities of what we will study together in the ensuing chapters. And my newly informed faith led to a joyful and utterly complete surrender. I pray it may lead into a similar surrender for even one who may be led to read this book.

It led, interestingly, to a lack of fear of man. It led to the unlocking of the Word of God into my soul that I'd never experienced previously. It led to a fellowship with God through a continual walk with the Holy Spirit that is sweeter than anything I have ever experienced. It led to the Spirit's ability to uncover *specific* things from 30 years ago which He was healing within; things that were between He and me alone. I had never known their impact–but He revealed them to me, and I confessed and knew a forgiveness that made me fall in love with Jesus all over again. It led to a lively walk with the Spirit that has given me insight into things I could *never* have seen–things that have totally revolutionized the way I live, play, work, sleep and wake in the mornings.

Praise God, I became free–I mean really **free** for the first time in my life; free from *me*! But it was nothing I could ever have attained to. That exchange between me and my Jesus was nothing I could ever have worked harder to achieve. It was, and is continually, a work entirely born of the merciful, willing Holy Spirit of God.

There is no silver bullet of process or technique that unlocks this kind of freedom. I do, however, believe we can draw near to Him in a way that *enables* the Spirit to shine the light of absolute and surgical Truth into our soul. Therein we can be made low enough to finally and utterly release into Him. Then, we *are* his. *Then*, He becomes Owner! *Then*, He becomes Boss.

But this facilitation on our part begins with something that looks more like *release* than like pushing a right button or *doing* anything. We prepare the way for the Spirit of God by walking through but only one gate–and it is narrow. It is the same gate that brought us into relationship with God's Son in the first place on the day of our salvation. And it is wrapped up in one word. **Surrender.**

And still, lest we be fooled into believing we've arrived somewhere in our spiritual walk with the triune God, once the Holy Spirit has blessed us to *see and experience* some measure of surrender and newness in Christ, this does *not* mean our struggle with giving ourselves into His hands is over. For it is a daily, and sometimes moment-by-moment continuum of reckoning upon our having been completely spent of ourselves into His care (see 2 Corinthians 4:7, 10-11).

But here's the difference. For the first time, at that time, all our striving ceases. And cease it must, because we know that we know…that we *know* our old man is *finally* gone; he is lifeless, never to return again, removed completely from the scene of action. Oh this is a wonderful refrain! Words cannot describe it. Description fails me because it is a process that is so unreservedly not about us.

Oh God, please help the reader find a hunger for you not previously possessed, that such hunger may at least begin the process of driving him deep into a disownership of his life.

PAUSE to PONDER

- I'd like you to deeply think upon the following words and, *if you can mean them presently*, pray them aloud to God – knowing He is ready to set you free. But count the cost. Can you trust Him? Are you ready?

God, increase my hunger for you alone. I am sorry I have been settling for only the appetizers at the banquet table of our life together. Please forgive me. I'm not sure my stomach is ready for the main course, but I know you are a tender Shepherd, and you will not lead me anywhere we cannot travel together. Help me release the burden of owning my life; it is heavy and I am weary of carrying it. Take it up completely. I am utterly scared! But I am utterly ready because greater are you who is in me than he who has convinced me to continue carrying my life without you. Here I am, take what you own. Have your way in me. Amen.

- If you are not yet ready to lay it all down, don't worry about it. Keep seeking Jesus and continue listening to the Holy Spirit as you prayerfully read on. In his time, He will increase within you a confidence such that you will know when it *is* your time. Come back to this page when God has done this work in you.

[Consider using the rest of this page to write down every fear that comes to mind when it comes to the letting go of your life. Then, ask him to carry your fears until they are gone.]

Chapter 31

An Informed Theology – Narrowing the Focus

If, however, there *are* times when we actually pause long enough for the Spirit of God to teach us deep, spiritual truths, the impact of such times can change our lives forever.

Once God was merciful enough to help me escape the murky fog of self and my tendency toward a confidence in the willful disciplines of the flesh, He was more than ready to gift me with a singular truth so powerful that it would literally awaken my soul.

If you are a lifelong Christian and, if being completely honest, feel you are lumbering through life relying on the abilities of the flesh to keep you afloat in your walk with Christ, then perhaps it is time to ask God whether your bar of expectation of the Holy Spirit within you is too low. Amongst the most dangerous things we carry as believers is a partial death—one that is just weak enough to be of no real value to the world, but not yet weak enough to be of real value to the Spirit. And so we live out our days somewhere...in the middle.

The Casting Crowns song I have referenced twice before, addresses this very common struggle. Let's review the lyrics again in our current light. Thoughtfully read each line of the lyrics below, knowing this is *not* a song about the glories of our being sanctified or being in the process of becoming into Christ. Rather it is about our inability to die completely; and in so doing, becoming weak enough to be under the command of the Spirit.

> Somewhere between the hot and the cold
> Somewhere between the new and the old
> Somewhere between who I am and who I used to be
> Somewhere in the middle, you'll find me

> Somewhere between the wrong and the right
> Somewhere between the darkness and the light
> Somewhere between who I was and who You're making me
> Somewhere in the middle, you'll find me
>
> Just how close can I get, Lord, to my surrender without losing all control
>
> Fearless warriors in a picket fence, reckless abandon wrapped in common sense
> Deep water faith in the shallow end and we are caught in the middle
> With eyes wide open to the differences, the God we want and the God who is
> But will we trade our dreams for His or are we caught in the middle
>
> Somewhere between my heart and my hands
> Somewhere between my faith and my plans
> Somewhere between the safety of the boat and the crashing waves
>
> Somewhere between a whisper and a roar
> Somewhere between the altar and the door
> Somewhere between contented peace and always wanting more
> Somewhere in the middle You'll find me
>
> Just how close can I get, Lord, to my surrender without losing all control

And so there we live. We *desire* to be fully given over, but we find the talons that long to have *some* input, *some* veto power pertaining to the things of *our* life, to be rather tenacious. As Mark Hall's lyric illuminates, our problem is that we are good until—well, until we realize we must lose *all* control, *all* ownership, if we are to truly surrender. Now *that's* scary.

The solution has always been, and always will be, complete release of ourselves...utter self-renunciation. But praise be to God, we don't have a Father in heaven who asks us to surrender wholly without giving us ample reason to eagerly enter into such an arrangement!

While only God knows what key He may choose to use for the awakening of your soul for the purposes of surrender, for me the key was a revelation[67] of an accurate and informed theology of who I am in Christ. And once the Spirit graced me with a good, theological handle on Jesus, the dam was about to burst!

I trust there may be a thread of value along these lines in what follows for you as well so as to have impact on your life. This, along with recounting what the Spirit has done in my life for the purposes of heaven-directed gratitude, is the purpose of this entire writing; it composes the majority of what is to come.

Please know I have no intention in trying to script a road to spiritual fullness–especially since I will be right alongside as a student of my Lord for the cause of increasing in such fullness all the remaining days of my life. Only the Word of God can do this kind of work as we allow the Holy Spirit to lead us *into the Truths* He has purposed to reveal to us–in his time and through the circumstances of our lives.

One of the reasons this discourse has already been more than two years in its formation is because there is danger in systematizing an environment into which divine enlightenment may ensue. Moreover, when we do so, we fool ourselves into thinking we are setting specific conditions for and gaining understanding apart from the help of the Holy Spirit. But I so know there is nothing of truth or real value in anything we can create. Thus, my caution.

And on the mind's need to comprehend spiritual things, we should not always demand to have intellectually satisfying conclusions about everything spiritual. Ours are minds developed by God with gaps–gaps which cannot accurately and fully contain God's ways.

And yet even with this caveat, I press on. I press on because what He has taught me is, I have come to believe, of such central importance to our faith in Jesus as professing Christians, that as I look back I am as yet unsure how I had missed it. But sure enough, I *had* missed it–just as did much of the New Testament church back in the day Paul was busting his gut with attempts to teach such life-altering truths to the infant church.

Through extended periods of initially unwelcomed stillness, the Holy Spirit gifted me with time to quietly contemplate what, in part, he had revealed to other godly men through his Word. He affirmed

---

[67] *Don't get all weird on me here in response to my use of this word; by it I merely mean a disclosure of some Truth which already exists within the teachings of God's Word.*

these things in my spirit as well. These truths from the scriptures taught me about the purposes of his shed blood and the earth-shaking impact of what happened on the cross. The remaining chapters are my best attempt to convey what I have learned in hopes that its truth will also spur on the death of many a lifelong Christian.

As a single paragraph preview of things to come, let me introduce the following; the purpose of Jesus' redemptive act at Calvary was two-fold. And I think the two-part exchange God performed there, which ultimately leads us to a more victorious walk in the flesh, is one of which we know—really *know*, very little. Yet it is important that we grasp this because doing so carries with it such glorious implications![68]

Really *knowing* the fullness of the two-part exchange God performed for us through Jesus can, because of its core message for the salvation of our souls, condition within us an awakening to the access we believers have to the Holy Spirit.

In short, the extent of the victory given us in the cross goes beyond the work of the blood alone. The purpose of the blood was to give us access to the presence of God. The blood, while responsible for gaining our access into the presence of a perfect and holy God, is not, however, the agent that enables us to trust the Lord Jesus for every jot and tittle of our lives. No, this comes through the power of the *cross* on our flesh.

Thus, the blood and the cross play somewhat independent roles for our spiritual lives. When we grow in the knowledge and understanding of such truths, as I pray we will during our study of the chapters to come, our spiritual eyes begin to open and we are spontaneously led in the productive direction of becoming undone. From such a position, we better perceive the absolute depths of our insufficiency as people to strike the final death knell over the flesh that continues to rule over many of our lives.

But for life-giving, spiritual truths to work their way into our hearts so as to ignite within us a Spirit-filled Life, this prerequisite must become true of us; **God must completely cut us off from a will to live any element of our lives apart from Him.**

He must first help us grasp, intellectually and experientially, that we died in Him and are really and truly made new—not just

---

[68] But more than just knowing a truth, beginning the process of letting the Spirit reveal spiritual truths into your spirit can serve as a spark to ignite deep exchange. Doing so can open the floodgates of progression into a more contemplative posture before God.

illustratively or figuratively, but actually! And since death is a tough thing for us, we have the scriptures to help us desire the death which brings freedom.

Let's ask the Father to increase our thirst for such as our starting point right now.

Galatians 5:1 reminds us of our freedom in Christ:
It is for freedom that Christ has set us free. Stand firm, then, and do not let yourselves be burdened again by a yoke of slavery.

Romans 6:18 reminds us we are free for a glorious purpose – righteousness:
You have been set free from sin and have become slaves to righteousness.

Luke 9:23-25 reminds us of the great irony of losing to gain:
[23] Then he said to them all: "Whoever wants to be my disciple must deny themselves and take up their cross daily and follow me. [24] For whoever wants to save their life will lose it, but whoever loses their life for me will save it. [25] What good is it for someone to gain the whole world, and yet lose or forfeit their very self?

And so there it is, in Luke 9:23-24, the great irony of the Gospel. And the extent to which this can be *personally* known rests in the working together of our complete brokenness and compulsory surrender of everything we are, have and hope to be, and His willingness to rein us in by the power of his Holy Spirit living within.

Once He has helped us to measure our life as nothing outside of him, the soil of our soul is readied for the life-changing truths He longs to reveal to us about who we are and how we are to perceive ourselves in light of what scripture teaches.

Only when the Spirit of God is readied and welcomed to do his complete work in us, not only unto salvation, but unto our continual process of becoming perfect *(sanctified)* in Him, can we begin owning the intended newness of life He desires for us in Christ.

Chapter 32

Increasing Deliverance

> *¹ Therefore, since we are surrounded by such a great cloud of witnesses, let us throw off everything that hinders and the sin that so easily entangles. And let us run with perseverance the race marked out for us, ² fixing our eyes on Jesus, **the pioneer and perfector of faith**. For the joy set before him he endured the cross, scorning its shame, and sat down at the right hand of the throne of God. ³ Consider him who endured such opposition from sinners, so that you will not grow weary and lose heart.* – **Hebrews 12:1-3**
> *² looking to Jesus, **the founder and perfector of our faith**, (ESV)*

> *² Looking unto Jesus **the author and finisher of our faith**; (KJV)*

This second verse clearly differentiates between our *initial* surrender *to* Christ and our *ongoing* surrender *in* Christ. Both are equally supernatural affairs. Both are essential as things God desires for us. But sadly, to the detriment of the second, most of our focus as evangelicals begins and ends on the first marker point.

This first marker point is what these verses refer to as our pioneering, foundational or authored time of salvation. This pertains to our initial acceptance of Christ's blood as the atoning sacrifice for our sins. And this initial intervention on God's part is specifically referenced in a way *separate from* the *ongoing* pursuit of our *continuation* in Christ.

The first exchange is merely the foundation or *starting line* for our spiritual journey in surrender to Jesus Christ! Yet we too often live our entire lives as believers *looking backwards* with hearts of gratitude *for that starting line* when we were redeemed. But this tendency does not *advance* us in our Christian experience. I believe this breaks God's heart.

We are not to decrease in dependence upon our supernatural, personal experience with God after that initial exchange! Miraculous it was–but miraculous should our lives be also going forward! We are to *continue onward* into the finishing, the perfecting of our faith.[69]

Hebrews 12:1-3 clearly admonishes us to *finish* and *perfect* the faith which the Spirit began in us. Thankfully, we don't have to work this out alone. To assist us in this lifelong objective, God has given us his Word and the Holy Spirit. He doesn't intend for the continuation and growth of our faith to be something gained through blind trust or reliance upon the disciplines of the flesh. No way! God the Father has given us the Holy Spirit in that first transaction for the purpose of leading us more deeply into himself. And, for me, part of this growth was sparked as I was led into a more thorough understanding of what Christ actually accomplished for me at Calvary.

I pray this will be a flashpoint of growth for you as well as we head into the remaining chapters awaiting our consideration.

But follow me here and think upon this for the time-being; it can only be when we reckon more fully the toll exacted upon our old man that we can live in the gratuitous victory of the new. Until we take in the *fullness* of what transpired when we *died in Christ* and were *raised again with Christ*, we merely live a spiritual life characterized by a grateful heart for the price paid for our sins–that we've been forgiven them (back to the time of his having pioneered our faith). **But, in practice, we walk through the rest of our days dragging along our old man.**

---

[69] I didn't want to pose this question in the context of this paragraph as it would distract from the point being made. However, I do want to pose the following question for your consideration: Why is it that we more so view the foundation of our life in Christ to be one of absolutely unquestioned supernatural intervention while we view the life we live thereafter as one reliant upon the willful disciplines of the natural flesh, merely *assisted by* the Spirit? Now we wouldn't readily admit to this being true in our lives because we scholastically know we cannot please the Lord Jesus in the effort of our fleshly nature. But in actual practice, do we live out our Christian experience as ones *completely* dependent on the supernatural to facilitate within us a life pleasing to God? Think about that. Work it over with God. Is your old man, the one Christ died to rule out, still working to please God in your ongoing Christian walk? This is an important question. We will deal more with this in later sections of this book.

Why is this? It is because in our refusal to recognize our death, we quench the Spirit's communion with us. In such a state (recall chapters 12-17 here), we put a lid on His influence in our lives and will therefore not be able to experientially grasp the extent to which that old trouble-maker has been done away with.

The old man can have no fellowship with the Spirit in this life. They cannot coexist. The Spirit of God could not, in fact, move in until our old man was done away with. This is the story of our salvation. We *had to be* completely absolved of our old life for God to coexist with us!

If the point of 2 Corinthians 6:14 is that light cannot have fellowship with darkness, then we have to ponder what actually happened to us as a prequalification for his very presence to live within us.

In *reality* God has, in Christ, *executed* our old Adam, thus making it *possible* for his Spirit to live within us (Col 1:13, 2:9-12, 2:20, 3:3, Rom 6:3, I Cor 1:30). But we live our *new* lives as though this truth has little practical implication for our ongoing, daily experience! Oh, how this breaks God's heart when we deny in practice what He has *completed* on our behalf in reality!

And so due to the fact that too many of us lifelong Christians have sold ourselves short theologically and have unknowingly quenched the Spirit's movement within, we have relegated ourselves to merely living our lives in a *self*-disciplined, effort-filled, obedience-to-blessing way, but lacking evidence of the victory aiding power of the Holy Spirit in our daily lives.[70]

Now I will admit that as we live our Christian lives in the above mentioned *self*-disciplined, effort-filled, obedience-to-blessing way, cranking it out as an act of our mental and emotional *will*, we *can* and *do* experience *some measure* of physical and psychological satisfaction, contentment, and happiness. But it is short-lived...until we *do* something more to earn such peace of mind again.

Even still, it is quite the hollow experience when compared to the life filled to overflowing with the incomparable presence of the energized Holy Spirit within.

It is when we no longer obstruct His incomparably great power that our life becomes one filled with lasting joy (Neh. 8:10, Ps. 28:7), a life where the darkness retreats from our soul (John 1:4-5, 12:46, Eph. 5:8), a life where deep and personal insight into His Word becomes

---

[70] This would be a good place to read Appendix A, Earning Our Way Throneward

customary (I Cor. 2:9-11, Ps. 119:105)[71], and a life where he continually expands the perception of our *desperate need of* and *increasing deliverance from ourselves in* Him (the Book of Romans).

In summation of these thoughts, our efforts in the merely *birthed* Christian flesh are only a poor reflection of the life-giving discoveries awaiting us once we've *completely given up on* being consoled by, or finding satisfaction in, *anything* this fallen world or our fleshly life has to offer. This is, in my mind, a prerequisite to being fully alive in Christ as he intended for a normal Christian life.

So where would you say *you* live? Are *you* depending on a dead man?

PAUSE to PONDER

- Take five minutes to meditate on the awesome truth that, in Christ, God has executed your old self. Ask the Holy Spirit to reveal the depth of this reality, along with its implications over your life through the following verses: Colossians 1:13, 2:9-12, 2:20, 3:3, Romans 6:3, I Corinthians 1:30.

---

[71] ...beyond the milk Paul talks about–the rudimentary things dealing only with our conversion experience

Chapter 33

Depending On A Dead Man?

It is with great sadness I say, as you know by now, I spent most of my Christian life living only half of what God had intended for me as his adopted child. I was most certainly living a forgiven life in Christ. I was not, however, living experientially in collaborative and reciprocal fellowship with the Holy Spirit.[72]

Many of us know we gained the Holy Spirit at the time of our salvation, but we do not *know* his infilling in *experience*.[73] Rather, we know Him academically. We know of His presence in the, "God said it so I believe it," sort of way.

But how can what we know to be true about our life in Christ become true for us in experience?

While we cannot force the hand of God, you already know how I feel about what I believe to be our ability to resist and quench such experience with the Holy Spirit. If this condition describes you, it is likely you are still trying to live in a dead man. We have already dealt with this in a limited way previously, and we will deal with this in greater detail in the coming chapters.

---

[72] This brings to mind a fantastically challenging series of messages by Hans Peter Royer, Fellowshipping with Jesus; Ref. in Resources at the end of this volume.

[73] I believe there can be many things which can work together to correct this condition—such as an accurate perception of our human condition, our need for brokenness, the critical role of stillness, the release of control over our lives, a subjective knowledge of the death of our old man, and the merciful work of God's Spirit and timing—to name a few. The entirety of this book is purposed to help us correct this condition.

Then, some may not know of his fellowship in experience because they are theologically uninformed about the fact that the Holy Spirit actually came into their life *at the moment of salvation*. In such a case, we should become accurately informed!

We discussed I Corinthians 12:13, Romans 8:9 and Ephesians 1:13-14 earlier under the heading "A Savior Saves; A Lord Owns." Let these be your launching point for further, individual study. But presently, let's take a moment to once again encourage our understanding together in our current context.

Have you repented of your sins and asked Jesus to cover your life with his redeeming sacrifice? Then you have received both remission of those sins *and* the Holy Spirit.

You might say you have only received the first gift, not the second. But, my friend, God offered you two things if you have repented by faith. Why have you only acknowledged or taken in the one? What are you doing about the second? Perhaps the following illustration Watchman Nee conveys could also accompany your quest.

> Suppose I went into a bookshop, selected a two-volume book priced at ten shillings and, having put down a ten-shilling note, walked out of the shop–carelessly leaving one volume on the counter. When I reached home and discovered the oversight, what do you think I should do? I should go straight back to the shop to get the forgotten book. But I should not dream of paying anything for it. I should simply remind the shopkeeper that both volumes were duly paid for, and ask him if he would therefore kindly let me have the second one. And without any further payment, I should march happily out of the shop with my possession under my arm. Would you not do the same under the same circumstances?
>
> But you *are* under the same circumstances! If you have fulfilled the conditions [for your salvation], you are entitled to two gifts, not just one. You have already taken the one, why not just come and take the other now? Say to the Lord, "Lord I have complied with the conditions for receiving remission of sins and the gift of the Holy Spirit, but I have foolishly taken only the former. Now at length, I have come back to thee to take the gift of the Holy Ghost–and to praise thee for it."[74]

If completely honest, I could not say my Christian walk was consciously and perceptively accompanied with a powerful indwelling

---

[74] Nee, The Normal Christian Life; Chapter 7

of the Holy Spirit, leading, impressing things upon me, bringing the Word freshly into my daily experience in newness of insight, and altering the way I deeply desired to live my life. Until recently, I could not fully release my greatest fears unless I yet maintained some measure of control.

Why is this? Why do we find it so difficult to release unto God *completely*, thus enabling his Spirit to move within us unobstructed? I believe it is primarily because we refuse to be moved in directions we cannot control–directions we may feel *could* bring too little surety. Plus, we have several good arguments *for* control!

For example, we as husbands and fathers especially feel our primary call in life is to bring stability, safety, continuity, advancement and instruction to our wives and children. If not, what kind of protector and leader would we be in our own homes? Thus, we must leverage control which enables us to coordinate those things over which we have been given authority.

But we forget we are *first* to recognize our complete allegiance to God–completely and unconditionally. Unconditionally. And we must recognize that our family members do not belong to us. If there is any control we exert over our spouses which is self-serving (to be read manipulative) or which is not preconditioned with the Spirit's tender heart of leadership, then we are leading in a way that needs fulfillment according to self.

But once we have become well-acquainted with our sinful tendency toward control over that which belongs to God, then the groundwork has at least been laid in the direction of releasing these things into the capable hands of the Father.

This is *hard* for innumerable reasons. In the particular case of which I am currently speaking, though our self-serving goes much broader than this, it is the convicting work of the Holy Spirit that helps us differentiate between leadership and manipulation. But unless we recognize the extent to which our old man has been completely killed off, we will likely not be sensitive enough to the inner working of the Spirit in the first place!

Oh, the inter-connectivity of it all!

PAUSE to PONDER

- Honesty with oneself is a first great step to unobstructed surrender to, and freedom of movement for, the Holy Spirit.

- Why might you find it so difficult to release unto God completely?
- Make your own "Top 3 List" of the most challenging things to fully surrender into God's *complete* care–to do with as *He* pleases.

Chapter 34

Don't Make Him Strip You

When I cannot release something, I find it is frequently because I have been too grounded in the soil of this earth rather than the stuff of heaven.

It is important to remember we, like our Old Testament friend Abraham, are pilgrims and strangers in this world. This world is not our home. The Bible tells us this. We're not at home here–at least we're not supposed to be.

Sometimes we get a little too attached to our world and forget this **is not** our home. Our citizenship is in heaven. We are not only to endure this world, but we are to live successfully estranged (not to be read detached) from this earth by living in fellowship with Almighty God as his kingdom citizens first, second and third. We could learn a great deal from Abraham's ability to be released into the hands of God.

Abraham, in his early days, ventured out without knowing where he was going. God was helping Abraham learn dependence. And throughout this early part of his journey with the Lord, it seems as if God was, little by little, one thing at a time, taking *from* Abraham everything that was important to him.

First of all, He told him to leave his country.

And then God told him to leave his father.

And as he went along in his journey, it wasn't long before Abraham separated from his nephew–and he gave the good land to Lot.

And then there came a time when he had the opportunity to become instantly wealthy but walked away from the spoils of war that were in the hands of the kings of Sodom.

And it isn't long before he's being asked to say goodbye to Ishmael, his son by Hagar.

Then, to Hagar.

Little by little, everything that was near and dear to Abraham's heart had been taken away from him. God was working on him. God was preparing him. God was building into him this concept of faith because He was about to test him in order to produce within him something that would change the face of history.

But if Abraham had not had these early experiences, if he had been a stranger to the places of release unto God, he never would have been able to stand for God as he did.

And here's the point: As you see the life of Abraham, you watch God taking away from him everything upon which he was prone to depend. Sometimes I wonder if God isn't doing that to...no, *for* some of us now.

It's easy for us as we grow up in this land of plenty to have everything planned out. We've got everything prepared. We've got our future all laid out–and it's perfect. We know where the portfolios are and our trust in the future is based on what we have accomplished with our lives. And so we refuse to give up our little plans at the great cost of not discovering something that far surpasses *our* plans. God was teaching Abraham to trust in Him, not in the things God had given him.

It is the same with us. We must be stripped of the earth-side things most precious to us. *For God's means of delivering us from ourselves is not by means of making us stronger and stronger...but by making us weaker and weaker.*

That is surely a peculiar way of victory, you say? Perhaps it is...at least in our eyes, yes. Nonetheless, it is the divine way. *God sets us free from the dominion of self not by strengthening our old man, but by crucifying him; not by his helping to do anything, but rather by removing him from the scene of action.*

For years, I have tried to exercise control over myself. But now that I have seen the truth of my condition, I completely recognize that I am, indeed, powerless to do anything. **But in setting me aside altogether, God has done it all.** I praise you, God!

This discovery has brought my human striving, need for control, and self-effort to an end.

And this, now, leads us forward. In order for me to really experience the importance of letting go, I had to have God's help in heightening my spiritual awareness so I could gain access to some things only discernible with his assistance.

PAUSE to PONDER

- Does your theology of God permit you to believe He may choose to give himself glory through multiple reductions in your life?
- Could you ever praise and thank God *for* pain, loss or suffering (I Thessalonians 5:18)?

Chapter 35

Heading Plateward: Rending Our Heart

The direction in which I am now purposed to take this writing could be a dangerous one. It is dangerous in so much that we cannot put a readiness of the Spirit into a script. Remember, we are not really in charge, but He. All we have to offer is a truly repentant heart–a worshipful act of our compliant will, prompted by the Spirit living *dangerously*, but necessarily freed to live authoritatively, inside us.

We have to come to a seeking of the Holy God without any pretense, without any self-saving thought, without any sacrifice of anything we possess or could offer Him of intrinsic, earthly value as if *it* could bring us near to Him. It's as if we must finally approach Him with a completely cogitative AND emotional awareness, brought to bear to such a degree only achievable by the Holy Spirit's convicting hand, that all we can offer of any sufficient value that could ever gain us His face would be unrestricted access to our very hearts, lives, and souls.

We cannot play act this posture. Only God, in his timing, can get us there. You will know when you have been ushered into such a place. It will be unmistakably God's hand.

But open the door he *will* if we but, over time and in due process, come empty-handed! Joel 2:12-13 perfectly illustrates this idea–that only our surrendered hearts, broken by some specific touch of the Spirit of God within, could be a sufficient offering.

> *Therefore also now, saith the Lord, turn ye even to me with all your heart, and with fasting, and with weeping, and with mourning: And rend your heart, and not your garments, and turn unto the Lord your*

> *God: for he is gracious and merciful, slow to anger, and of great kindness, and repenteth him of the evil.* — **Joel 2:12-13** (KJV)

Now stick with me. These verses beg *hard* for a more thorough and contemplative pause. Please come with me. Again, Joel 2:12-13...in **bold** and ***italics***: (parenthesis contain both selected excerpts from John Gill's exposition of the Bible as well as my thoughts for a more contemplative investment into the depths of what this passage is saying)

> ***Therefore also now, saith the Lord*** (Before the terrible and intolerable day of judgment which is near at hand, comes for the objects of God's threatened, wrathful judgment; though just at hand; serious repentance is never too late, now is the accepted time)
>
> ***...turn ye [even] to me with all your*** <u>***heart***</u>; (against whom they had sinned, and who had prepared his army against them, and was at the head of it, just ready to give the orders, and play his artillery upon them; and yet suggests, that even now, if they turned to the Lord by true repentance, not hypocritically, but sincerely, with true hearts, and with their whole hearts),
>
> ***...and with fasting, and with weeping, and with mourning*** (these are external signs of inward grief and sorrow, testifying their hearty return to the Lord; which, though, without the heart, signify nothing but self-deceiving attempts at manipulation of the Holy One)
>
> ***...And*** <u>***rend***</u> ***your*** <u>***heart***</u>***, and*** <u>***not your garments***</u> (The latter of which used to be done in times of distress, either private or public, and could be done as an external token of sorrow and might be done hypocritically. Rather, God was after a truly, sincerely, desperation-like contrition of heart and brokenness of spirit under a sense of sin, which is here requested as evidence of real, godly influenced sorrow and repentance; the acts of which, flowing from faith in Christ are much more acceptable to the Lord than any outward expressions of grief; see Psalms 51:17, Isaiah 57:15, 66:2)
>
> ***...and turn unto the Lord your God*** (consider him not as an absolute God, and as an angry one, wrathful and inexorable; but as your covenant God and Father—as your God in Christ, ready to receive sinners sensible of sin that flee to him for mercy through Christ);

> *...for he [is] gracious and merciful*; (he is the God of all grace, and has laid up a fullness of it in Christ; and he gives it freely to them that ask it of him without upbraiding them with their sins; he delights in showing mercy; and this is no small encouragement to turn to the Lord, and seek mercy of him: and, besides, he is)
>
> *...slow to anger; and of great kindness, and repenteth him of the evil* (NIV; and is abounding in love).

I believe we do this "rending of our hearts" by dying to ourselves and surrendering completely in the knowledge of our having died in Him on the cross, reckoning that we HAVE died and gained that victorious death through the cross. But this is a reckoning only fully reached through the touch of the Spirit. More on this in Part III.

I have begun to wonder if the majority of us lifelong Christians have too little comprehension of what *comprises* the freedom we have been given in Christ. A flyweight knowledge of such a heavyweight topic can leave us with a gratitude that, while it *is* there, is only surface deep...not that we have ever wanted it that way.

A mere acquaintance with the topic, but a lack of a deep understanding of the inner workings which function together to bring us such freedom, renders only shallow, though genuine, gratitude.

We may know the stories, but do we *know* our God? Do we *know* our Savior? Do we have his mind? Has our culture and our own sin nature brought about such self-reliance that we are, as a by-product, unknowingly living lives which repeatedly quench the Holy Spirit?

Do we *know* anything about brokenness? Is pride our unnamed dam, holding back the free-flow of the Spirit in our lives?

While we would say we have surrendered our lives to God, have we merely attained eternal life through Christ's work and are yet to surrender to Him as *Lord*? Have we given over to him that which he rightfully owns?

Remember the illustration of the purchased but *not yet delivered* motorcycle? Are we control freaks? Do we trust the Lord with the most precious people in our lives or are we helicopter spouses and parents?

If you can't tell, I could go on with what the Lord has revealed in my own life as a result of the points of inquisition above. Oh, how I thank God for His patience, grace and mercy. Oh, how I come up so pathetically short apart from the covering of the Blood.

And I am wondering if while living a self-empowered, American "can-do" life, without the intended power of the Spirit alive and well within, ...I am wondering if you, too, may be suffering under a life characterized by a low bar of spiritual expectation.

Like me, could your Christian life be stunted by your own flesh-imposed refusal to surrender to what Jesus always intended for us and what Watchman Nee referred to as, a "normal" Christian life?

Anyway, while the direction in which I am now purposed to take this writing could be a dangerous one – dangerous, as I said, only insomuch that we cannot put a readiness of the Spirit into a script, I nonetheless do want to recount the process through which the Lord has brought me–a process for which I will be grateful beyond words for the rest of my earthly life. And it seems like such holy ground over which the Spirit has traveled with me for the past 18-24 months that I have not, until now, been willing or able (I don't know which) to recount it.

How *did* the Lord move me–rather how did the Lord move us, because it *was* he and I together for sure, *from* a low bar life of spiritual expectancy as an already obedient and faithful Christian? How did the Lord move us to a life afresh in the Spirit, having been crushed with a deep realization of whom and what I am in myself as a self-saver...one trying to be a Christian but without having first, sufficiently become a dead man?

He took us back to the beginning–to the place where it all started.

Now one final strong word of caution as we conclude this chapter and progress to the first of four foundational building blocks; and this is very important.

Each building block is just that–a *building* block. Each of the four bases we're going to touch *build upon* one another. You *could* cerebrally blow through all four bases (in Part III), and close out with the final ongoing challenge in an hour or so. But if this writing is only something to check off your list, please do me, yourself and the Lord a favor and put this book down. You will not be changed by it. Now is not the right time.

It is likely the Spirit will have to reveal some things to you in each of these chapters–whether directly by the content or, more likely, indirectly as he searches your heart.

> *And he who searches our hearts knows the mind of the Spirit, because the Spirit intercedes for God's people in accordance with the will of God.*
> **– Romans 8:27**

A soulish illumination of deep truths from God is not the same as *covering material*—as if only to spill it back out on an exam. Being cognizant of something, and truly *knowing* it deeply and subjectively so as to have it change us *is worlds apart*.

Jesus wants nothing to do with our becoming more acquainted with him academically. To God's great sorrow and angst, this world is *filled* with academic Christians. He himself entered a world filled with the academically religious—and we all know how that went. But he has demanded more of us.

I pray the Holy Spirit would personally instill within you a fear of being one who dares tinker with his Lordship in your life.

My prayer is that with each reading of this book, there would be intermittent, stop-and-go progress as the Spirit desires to use whatever elements of these next four sections to newly arrest your undying allegiance. My desire is that there would be time and space for the Spirit of God to download, install and permanently burn into the hard drive of your heart many of the things which we have known in our heads but haven't let travel deeply enough into our soul so as to meet us with a deep joy only importable by the supernatural Spirit of God who lives dangerously within us.

Paul was passionate enough about this differentiation between *being familiar* with something and *understanding* it that, in Romans, he beseeches God's help to aid him in helping his Roman audience of believers not just *know* the Truth, but *understand* it. You see, Paul understood that our minds are limited—they are fleshly. And because no good thing inhabits the flesh without supernatural intervention through revelation, Paul knew the role the Spirit of God *had to play* in illuminating that which he taught *so that* his audience could *understand* it—**so that it could become their experience**.

And so if you read Romans 1-3, we see this pattern develop: Paul begins the chapter by teaching a truth, but then he *prays* that we'll understand it.

So here's my challenge going forward: **For the remainder of this book, refuse to read or listen past anything until each concept has hit its mark in your soul.** If achievement is your idol, you won't take the time necessary for the Holy Spirit to weave the truths on the following pages into your soul. You will rush to the next sentence so you can finish this book, rather than allowing God to reveal himself to you.

Give the Spirit time to work. He wants to gain in you more than a cerebral comprehension of himself. He wants to remake you through his Truths. What follows is the kind of thing that, while not lengthy in volume, should drive you into deep contemplation and wonder. The best thing I could hear from those reading these next four sections is that it took a month, or the summer, to get through them. There is no rush. Let the Spirit take you to a place where you drink most deeply of Him unto surrender.

It would be appropriate to come to each of the next four sections with a heart conditioned by what this prayer conveys:

> Jesus, I know you intend to be Lord in my life. But I cannot give you all you desire without a deep, personal revelation from the touch of your mighty hand. I beg of you to make my spirit willing. Would you plant in me a greater hunger for your fellowship and lordship than for any pleasure or comfort this world could offer me?
>
> As we move forward into these meditations centered on your Word, I want you to know that I intend to review and reckon upon that which you came to offer me through your Blood and the Cross until it wrecks me. Help me to wait patiently upon you such that I will not push on from one chapter to the next until you have pressed through my intellect and deeply into my soul. Give my soul eyes to see and ears to hear. I give you permission to not only reveal what needs breaking, but to just go ahead and break me each step along the way through a deep repentance and surrender only attainable through an act of your sovereignty in my life.
>
> Without your help, Father, I cannot even discover the things that may be keeping you from freely flowing through the life you have given me. Holy Spirit, I thank you for entering my life the moment you enabled the eyes of my soul to discover that I needed saving. Would you now begin the process of making me wholly yours—through whatever means necessary, that in so doing you would bring yourself glory?
>
> We have come far together, but not far enough. I am no longer satisfied with living in the strength of my fleshly abilities or a strong will. Anything short of your controlling influence over my life is no longer sufficient.
>
> I need you to completely remove me from the scene of my life so that you may use what you own.

Finally, forgive me. Forgive me for not hungering on to more of you as the very central purpose of this life. Thank you for making me new. Please help me know what newness really looks like in *your* eyes.

Amen.

PART III

WHAT IS TRUE OF YOU

CHAPTERS 36-41

FIRST:
THE WORK OF THE BLOOD

For you know that you were redeemed from your empty way of life inherited from the fathers, not with perishable things like silver or gold, but with the precious blood of Christ, like that of a lamb without defect or blemish.
— **1 Peter 1:18-19** (HCSB)

Chapter 36

The Blood of Christ

The first thing that hit absolute pay dirt for me was this whole concept that the Blood and the Cross each play a specific role; the Blood for our salvation and the Cross for our sanctification–the furtherance of our journey Godward.

I don't know that I can effectively communicate the spiritual transformation this understanding has wrought in my life, but one thing is sure; since God has helped me access and come to deeply know *(not just academically but also in a Spirit-revealed way)* this information, I have, much to my spirit's unrestrained joy, discovered anew the greatness of Christ and his finished work on the cross! I am excited to share how this came about with you now.

While it seems I am still an eternity away from what God desires that I grasp in this matter, drinking deeply of this distinction has been another layer-upon-layer building block toward a heady discontent over what the Lord has brought to the fore of my consciousness—about who I am *apart from* His miraculous grace and mercy.

Looking back, I now see the preliminary thing the Holy Spirit wanted to implant within me was an accurate theology of how my new man came to be.

Usually, before something can become our experience it must first be introduced to our conscious mind as an academic or cerebral Truth. It was the Lord Jesus' delight to firstly implant such a cerebral understanding of *how* my life, as a Christian, *became* supernaturally new. More to the point, as a result of a greater perception of the independent roles of the Blood and the Cross, the Holy Spirit catapulted me into a world-view-smashing awareness of how absolutely literal is Paul's declaration in Galatians 2:20; "No longer I, but Christ." This verse is Paul's declaration of our intended condition as normal believers.

About this verse, Watchman Nee says the following:

> He [Paul] is, we believe, presenting God's normal [state] for a Christian, which can be summarized in the words: I live no longer, but Christ lives **his life** in me.[75]

Now we seldom have trouble with the idea that the moment of our salvation was brought about through the spilling of Jesus' blood as our sin sacrifice—though I hope to shed some light upon that occurrence as well. But somehow these two words, His life, seem to make a world of difference to me when speaking of our *continuance in Christ*, our sanctification. It reminds me of what is true; it is not me living my life—Christ merely assisting me, but rather it is actually *He* who is living *his* life…in and through me. And this piece of meat, my body, is now effectively going along for the ride as a surrendered "yes man."

To again reiterate Paul's teaching in Galatians, it is He (Christ) who lives **instead of us**. Thus, we are continually delivered into His hands as *His* vessel. I like Nee's wording when speaking of Jesus' role for us on this point.

> So we can speak of two substitutions—a Substitute on the Cross, who secures our forgiveness, and a Substitute within, who secures our victory.[76]

---

[75] Nee, The Normal Christian Life; Chapter 1

Do you understand what he is saying? Where does this distinction between the blood and the cross find its merit? It finds its merit through the fact that **we**, mankind, **have a dual problem**. And it is for that dual problem that God has provided for us a dual remedy. Our dual problems are: *Sins* and *Sin*. And I've already given away our dual remedy: The Blood and the Cross. But let's begin working this out together, shall we?[77]

As we explore the book of Romans, it is first of all noteworthy that the first eight chapters form somewhat of a self-contained unit. The four and a half chapters from 1:1 to 5:11 form the first half of this unit, and the three and a half chapters from 5:12 to 8:39 the second half. In the argument of the first section, we find the *plural* word "sins" given prominence. In the second section, however, this changes as Paul shifts his focus, using the *singular* word "sin" again and again as this new angle then becomes the subject with which Paul mainly deals.

Why is this? It is quite simple, really. It is the way he addresses our dual problem I mentioned a moment ago. It is that I need forgiveness *for my sins*, but I need also deliverance *from the power of*

---

[76] Nee, The Normal Christian Life; Chapter 1

[77] Now as I lay out the theology of Romans and much of what Paul is teaching us in his NT writings, what will be written upon during this section will be taken extensively from Watchman Nee's book, The Normal Christian Life, because he has an incredibly simple way of explaining its truth in layman's terms. And in my estimation, I could not possibly improve upon it. I will quote from it at length but will not separately notate each idea or quote lest we may have 80% of the next several pages footnoted. Along with other writings, sermons and personal studies of the Scriptures around the same time as my reading the fifth, consolidated printing (2010, November) of Nee's book pertaining to the topic of our "becoming new", his text was especially instructive and assisted the Holy Spirit in bringing my walk with Christ into grateful newness. The Holy Spirit used the truths illustrated therein to begin an awakening of my soul. Because it was through this tool the Lord Jesus impacted me so significantly, I intend to take most of my "aha moments" from his text and will thus be attempting to retrace the things that, for the first time really, gave the Holy Spirit within me the God-ordained pause to exact massive newness in my walk with Him. Therefore, consider what follows in this section to be taken extensively from the pages of Nee's book. I hope to segue them together in such a way that other believers may, too, discover the thrill of a truly new adventure which God intended for all who place their trust in Christ Jesus.

sin. The former touches my conscience, the latter my life. Did you grasp that? Are you with me? Do you see the difference? Don't move on until you follow this difference.

When God's light first shines into my heart, my one cry is for forgiveness, for I realize I have committed sins before Him. But once I have received forgiveness of *sins*, I make a new discovery. Namely, that there is something *wrong within*. While I may have experienced a very real lifting of my sins—a lightening of the burdens I had carried in my separation from God, I find my compulsion *to* sin seems not to have been dealt the same blow. This is when guilt, for the believer, takes hold and we begin working hard to enslave our mind, body, heart and soul to acts of the will—to overcome our tendency toward sin.

In short, we discover that we have the *nature* of a *sinner*. I don't know about you, but while I may have sought and received forgiveness, I want something more than that: I want *deliverance*.

Said another way, as the Lord Jesus draws me individually, I discover a dual need. I need *forgiveness* from what I have *done*, but I also need *deliverance* from what I *am*. Thus, the first eight chapters of Romans where *both* glorious aspects of salvation are presented to us; firstly, the forgiveness of our sins, and secondly, our deliverance from sin. It is a valuable distinction between our two remedies.

The Blood deals with what we have done, whereas the Cross deals with what we are. The Blood disposes of our sins, while the Cross strikes at the root of our capacity for sin. And this second matter is, I believe, the very heart of the Christian's dilemma; we don't really understand the act of redemption God performed through the cross!

The Cross is no mere symbol, the likes of which we use as reflection for gratitude for the forgiveness of our sins. No, for that we should reflect on the crimson drops of blood. Instead, the Cross is our vehicle of victorious self-reduction, brokenness and surrender, carrying in its power our elimination *in favor of* Christ's life becoming our new Life. It is *here* where we realize that old things have passed, and that all things are become new. Oh, the glory of it!

The Cross cannot be a mere emblem which reminds us of the forgiveness of our sins—merely an icon that draws our hearts to gratitude and awe. No. A thousand times, no! We must understand that the purpose of the Cross is more active and lively than simply being a symbol of reflective thankfulness! If it has only become an emblem of reflective thankfulness, has the Cross not merely become an idol? If the cross has only become a visual *representation* of God, which we're commanded not to create, we are misunderstanding the critical role of the Cross over our lives.

Now I don't want to take us down a rabbit trail, as idol worship is a study for another time. But suffice it to say that we must understand the power and ongoing work of the Cross for our lives if we anticipate living victoriously in these bodies of flesh. But more on this shortly. For now, let us touch on the first of God's dual remedy for our deliverance; the half that deals distinctively with the problem of our sins.

We begin, then, with the precious Blood of the Lord Jesus Christ and its value to us in dealing with our sins and justifying us in the sight of God. And this is laid out for us in the following passages:

> *All have sinned.* – **Romans 3:23**

> *But God proves His own love for us in that while we were still sinners, Christ died for us! Much more then, since we have now been declared righteous by His blood, we will be saved through Him from wrath.* – **Romans 5:8-9** (HCSB)

> *They are justified freely by His grace through the redemption that is in Christ Jesus. God presented Him as a propitiation through faith in His blood, to demonstrate His righteousness, because in His restraint God passed over the sins previously committed. God presented Him to demonstrate His righteousness at the present time, so that He would be righteous and declare righteous the one who has faith in Jesus.* – **Romans 3:24-26** (HCSB)

Sin enters as disobedience which first of all creates a separation between God and man, whereby man is put away from God. God cannot have fellowship with him, for there is something now which hinders, and it is that which is known throughout Scripture as "sin."

And our sins must be dealt a death blow in three directions: the directions of sin, since God says we are all under it, of guilt, because our sins give rise within us to a sense of estrangement and wrongdoing before God, and of Satan's charge against us since he, too, knows we have committed sins which disallow relationship with God.

And so to redeem us, and to bring us back to the purposes of God, our sins and their effect on our lives had first to be dealt with by God. And this was achieved by the precious Blood of Christ. It was achieved to overcome all three directions I just mentioned: Godward (because we *have* sinned), manward (because of our guilt), and Satanward (because of our accuser).

Now let's roll on, because this gets **really** good!

Chapter 37

The Role of the Blood

The first stepping stone is to understand that because of our problem of sins, **the Blood**, as the catalyst for our solution, **is primarily for God**. In doing so, it will help us to understand how Jesus' Blood efficiently and completely covered us before God.

Now please note here the tense of this verb above – cover**ed**! It is not **covers** us before God, but **covered** (past tense) us before God–because the act of the shedding of his blood was done in the past, one time–for all time to come. It was, and is...DONE.

This is how the Blood works for God. We need forgiveness for the sins we have committed so that we don't come under judgment; and they are forgiven, not because God overlooks what we have done, but because He sees the Blood. The Blood is therefore not primarily for us, but for God.

Now as we dive in intellectually, understand that what we're doing here is informing, or brushing up on, our theology–in a context that can inform our spirit. You see, as we gain knowledge of Truth, our faith becomes informed as a natural progression of such knowledge.

"But Greg," you say, "faith isn't intellectual–or it's not faith! Faith is more like trust–something you don't have to prove to yourself...or understand cerebrally." Oh yeah!? As you might recall, I used to feel that way too. And although I could again go on for fifteen minutes on this, let's just leave it at this: What do you think Romans 10:17 means if not what it says; faith comes by hearing, and hearing by the Word of God?

When we are informed on a soulish level, the knowledge gained from hearing and digesting the Word can absolutely become our experience. And when we experience Truth–subjectively, deeply, emotionally, we become different, and God's passion is breathed into us. The problem, as John MacArthur says, is that if we just *know* the truths of God's Word, but don't really *understand* them, then we cannot live them. Do you see what we're saying? This idea of our gaining in an intellectual comprehension of good theology as our launch point is such a crucial one—so I want to linger here just a moment longer. Please stick with me.

Think about something I mentioned toward the end of chapter 35, only in our current context: Paul was passionate enough about this differentiation between knowing and understanding so as to effect life change that, in Romans, he beseeches God's help to aid him in helping his Roman audience of believers not just know the Truth, but *understand* it. Remember that?

As I mentioned, if you read Romans 1-3, you see this pattern develop: Paul begins chapter one by describing our position in Christ, and then he prays that we'll understand it. Then again in chapter two, he describes our position in Christ, then he prays we'll understand it. Then, in chapter four, it's as if he says, "Now that you've got it AND understand it, here's how to live it."

You see, Paul understood that our minds are limited—they are fleshly. And because no good thing inhabits the flesh without supernatural intervention through revelation, he knows the role the Spirit of God *has to play* in illuminating that which we know cerebrally so that we can *understand* it—so that it can become our experience.

To paraphrase John MacArthur, the point is this: You **cannot live** what you do not **understand**. And again, as I mentioned before, don't mistake knowing for understanding. You CANNOT live on principles you don't understand. No Christian has ever lived the Christian life who did not know what it was. Gotta have it!

Christians all over the place are frustrated to no end, trying to live a life they don't truly understand—and trying, no less, to do so in their own power. As a man of God, Paul knows that to change a life it cannot just be a matter of *telling* people a new truth, but he has to pray that *God will energize the information*!

That's why, in Acts 6, the Bible tells us that the apostles said, "We give ourselves continually to the ministry of the Word AND PRAYER." Why? Because the ministry of the Word *must be energized by* the Spirit of God. That's why it says in verse 17 of Ephesians 1, that they would receive a spirit of wisdom and revelation in the knowledge of Him, *that the eyes of their understanding would be enlightened* that they would *know* what is the hope of their calling!

It's not enough to just hear sound teaching; it must be prayed in, as it were, by the energy of the Spirit of God released as a response to intercessory and longing prayer.

So while the truths we are about to unpack about the Blood of Christ, and then later, the Cross of Christ, may be old as the hills to you, could it be that, like me–a Christian most all of my life, God's Spirit could illuminate within *you* a spirit of new understanding relative to their value? Could your faith be energized like never before because of a newly appreciated, Spirit-led apprehension of such knowledge?

In part, this is what God has chosen to use in my life to jump start the completion of that which He started so very long ago. And I pray He does so for you as well.

So back to the specific value and purpose of the Blood. If I want to understand the value of the Blood, *I must accept God's valuation of it.*

If I do not know something of the value set upon the Blood by God, I will never know what its value is for me. What must be made known to me is the estimate that *God* puts upon the Blood of Christ. And this can only be done as the Holy Spirit brings us a deep and personal understanding of it. In His doing so, I can *then* come into the good of it myself, and find how precious indeed the Blood is to *me*. But the first aspect of it is Godward.

Throughout the Old and New Testaments the word "blood" is used in connection with the idea of atonement–I think over a hundred times. And throughout, it is something for God.

Let me give us two such examples.

In the Old Testament calendar there is one day that has a great bearing on the matter of our sins, and that day is the Day of Atonement. In Leviticus 16, we find that on the Day of Atonement, the blood was taken from the sin offering and brought into the Most Holy Place, where it was sprinkled before the Lord seven times.

Now follow this very carefully.

On that day, the sin offering *was offered publicly* in the court of the tabernacle. Everything was in full view and could be seen by everyone.

But here now is the differentiation.

The Lord commanded that *no man* should enter the tabernacle itself *except the high priest*. It was he alone who took the blood and, going into the Most Holy Place, sprinkled it there to make atonement before the Lord.

Why?

Because God had commanded that it be done that way. And connected with his going in, there was but one act—the presenting of the blood *to God as something God himself had accepted*, something in which He could find satisfaction. It was a transaction between the high priest and God in the Sanctuary—away from the eyes of the men who were to benefit from its presenting. The Lord required that.

The Blood is therefore, in the first place, not for ourselves, but for God.

And then, even earlier than this, my favorite example. It's my favorite example because of its clarity of the point that the blood is *not* purposed primarily for us, **but for God**.

In Exodus 12:13, we see described how the shedding of the blood of the Passover lamb was instrumental for the saving of life while the Israelites were in Egypt. Remember?

The blood was put on the lintel and on the door-posts, whereas the meat, the flesh of the lamb, was eaten inside the house; and God said: "When I see the blood, I will pass over you."

Here we have another illustration of the fact that the blood was not meant to be presented to man, *but to God*; for the blood was put on the lintel and on the door-posts, where those feasting and then hunkered down inside for the night would not even see it. What is the pronoun in this 13th verse? It is the personal "I." "When I see the blood, I will pass over you." The Lord, Yahweh, was referring to himself. The blood was there for God.

Chapter 38

God Is Satisfied

Understand, then, it is God's holiness, God's righteousness, which demands that a sinless life should be given for man. There is life in the Blood, and that Blood has to be poured out for me, for my sins.

God is the One who requires it to be so. God is the One who demands that the Blood be presented, **in order to satisfy his own righteousness**, and it is He who says: *"When I see the blood,* I will pass over you." The Blood of Christ wholly satisfies God.

Let me say it again. The Blood of Christ was shed *as the Father's requirement for himself*, first and foremost. We the sinners, then, are merely the "by extension" benefactors for whom it was the blood was shed.

So, then, what about *us*? How does this understanding impact us?

As the Lord Jesus reveals more and more Truth to us while growing nearer to Him through the power of the Holy Spirit's conviction onto our lives, there may be times that our increasingly awakened conscience becomes acutely sensitive. This can constitute a real problem for us. The sense of sin and guilt can become so great that it can almost cripple us by causing us to lose sight of the true effectiveness of the Blood. It seems some particular sin may trouble us so many times, that we come to the point where, to us, our sins loom larger than the Blood of Christ.

In such times, the whole trouble with us is that we are trying to sense it; we are trying to feel its value and to estimate subjectively what the Blood is for *us*. **We cannot do it; it does not work that way.**

Remember, the Blood is first for God to see. We, then, must accept God's valuation of it.

If, instead, we try to come to a valuation of the Blood by way of our feelings, we get nothing; we remain in darkness. No, it doesn't work that way. Rather, it is a matter of faith in God's Word. We have to believe that the Blood is precious to God *because He says it is so.*

> For you know that you were redeemed from your empty way of life inherited from the fathers, not with perishable things like silver or gold, but with the precious blood of Christ, like that of a lamb without defect or blemish. – **1 Peter 1:18-19** (HCSB)

If God can accept the Blood as a payment for our sins and as the price of our redemption, then we can rest assured that the debt has been paid. If God is satisfied with the Blood, then the Blood must be acceptable. Our valuation of it is only according to His valuation– neither more, nor less. It cannot, of course, be more; but it *must not* be less.

Let us remember that *He is* holy and *He is* righteous, and that a holy and righteous God has the right to say that the Blood is acceptable in His eyes, and has fully satisfied Him.

And so, can we agree that we have to come to a realization that this whole matter of our having been forgiven our sins *is a matter of historical fact?* I pray it be so! This is the first, foundational *cornerstone* which must be cemented into our understanding in order to, now, have forward progress.

PAUSE to PONDER

- Who demanded the blood sacrifice as the all-sufficient buydown of God's wrath for the sins of mankind?
- As one who has accepted Jesus' blood as sufficient to atone for your life before God, what two illustrations from the Bible can you recall if you ever doubt that God has been satisfied?

Read Exodus 12:1-13 and personally enter into the drama.

Read Leviticus 16:15-17 and note that the blood's work before God was done behind the curtain where no one but the one offering the blood was allowed.

- Never forget that the primary function of the blood was for God...and that He has been satisfied–once for all!

Chapter 39

The Believer's Access to God

So – the Blood has satisfied God; **it must satisfy us also.**

Why do I say we must get to a point where the Blood must satisfy *us* also? It is because we have a conscience. And no amount of trying to *feel* the forgiveness of the Blood will sufficiently aid in clearing our conscience. No, it must come through an intellectual understanding of what it is that allows us unfettered access to God–free from a stricken conscience.

Now we already know how the blood satisfies God, but it also does its work for us–consciously. In Hebrews 10:19-22, we learn that we can draw near to God because our hearts have been sprinkled to cleanse us from a guilty conscience.

> *Therefore, brothers and sisters, since we have confidence to enter the Most Holy Place by the blood of Jesus, by a new and living way opened for us through the curtain, that is, his body, and since we have a great priest [Jesus] over the house of God, let us draw near to God with a sincere heart* **and with the full assurance that faith brings, having our hearts sprinkled to cleanse us from a guilty conscience** *and having our bodies washed with pure water.*
> **– Hebrews 10:19-22**

Isn't that a beautiful and most magnificent word for us from God? Oh, I could just leap for joy when I read these truths from His Word! Having read them only cerebrally and having been thankful for them for some 30 years, I am now moved to my emotional core because these words mean something more to me today than I could ever have imagined–even just 5 years ago.

Coming to a personal, deeply subjective understanding of this myself through the illumination of the Spirit is one of the many deep joys that has become mine.

How about you?

Do you experientially *know* this full assurance of your heart having been sprinkled to cleanse you from a guilty conscience? Oh, that it would become yours as well.

And now when Satan wants to bring me under conviction for a wrong, I have the personal, strong grounds to remind him that it was all covered in one, historic act of crushing victory for us who have entrusted our very lives into the hands of Jesus, the Son of God! And my guilty conscience abates in the light of God's Truth.

But even *that* is only part of the story. Are you ready for this? Because it gets **really** good here!

Our access to God is completely unrestricted because of an even deeper, in this case, surgical procedure. (Let's give ourselves a little preview of things to come in our study together for a moment.)

Let's go to Jeremiah 17, verse 9.

> ⁹ *The heart is deceitful above all things and beyond cure.* Who can understand it? – **Jeremiah 17:9**

So, if our very heart, the core of our fleshly man, is sick and beyond cure, then the *only* solution would be a heart transplant, right? Well Ezekiel, in chapter 36, gives us a preview of a coming attraction! In verses 25-27 he prophecies about God's plans for our heart transplant. Check this out!

> *I will sprinkle clean water on you, and you will be clean; I will cleanse you from all your impurities and from all your idols. I will give you a new heart and put a new spirit in you; I will remove from you your heart of stone and give you a heart of flesh. And I will put my Spirit in you and move you to follow my decrees and be careful to keep my laws.* – **Ezekiel 36:25-27**

And so, what is Ezekiel doing? He's giving them a preview of the New Covenant to come–to be set into motion and fulfilled through Jesus some 600 years later! And so again, what is the only solution to a heart that is incurably sick? A **new** one. Right? That first heart has to be killed off. It must DIE–and be replaced.

Think of it this way. We do not wash and iron clothing we are going to throw away. In the same way, as we will see shortly, the "flesh" is simply too bad to be cleansed; **it must be crucified. The work of God within us must be something *wholly* new.** And thus, Ezekiel says, "a new heart also will I give you, and a new spirit will I put within you" (Ezekiel 36:26).

Yes! Do you see this? Are you following what we're on the cusp of learning here, friend? Let it build within as we continue onward.

Alright then, first, back to where we were before our detour into a preview of coming attractions! The cleansing work of the blood....

The cleansing work of the blood is in relation to the conscience. Remember that portion of Hebrews 10 in verse 22 where Paul writes that our faith in Jesus' shed blood has sprinkled our hearts to **cleanse us from a guilty conscience**? Well this is in recognition of something real–not something about which to turn a blind eye. It means there was, in fact, something negatively intervening between, causing a rift between, myself and God. As a result, I had an evil conscience whenever I sought to approach Him. And that evil conscience was constantly reminding me of the barrier that stood between myself and Him.

But now, through the operation of the precious Blood, something new has been effected before God which has removed that barrier, and God has made that fact known to me in his Word.

When that has been believed in and accepted, my conscience is at once cleared and my sense of guilt removed. I no longer have an evil conscience toward God! It is an absolutely miraculous, beyond explanation, supernatural exchange that takes place.

Just try to tell someone who has experienced this deep forgiveness first hand–this removal of a guilty conscience, that it is nothing more than a psychological crutch! Good luck with that.

And so today, after many years of living in the forgiveness of my Savior, I have found that in order to keep going on with God, I must only reckon upon the up-to-date value of the Blood, and remember it as my sufficiency–my only sufficiency, before Him. God keeps short accounts, and we are made nigh by the Blood every day, every hour, and every minute. It never loses its efficacy as our grounds for access if we will but lay hold upon it.

And as a very important reminder, I once again want to reiterate that it has never been, nor ever will be anything we *do* that can draw us near to God; we only enter into the presence of God by the blood.

Each time we recognize our sins and our tendency toward sin and that we have need of cleansing, we must come to God on the basis of the *finished work* of the Lord Jesus.

As I lie on my back at the onset of most days, I remind myself that I approach God through His merit alone, and never on the basis of my attainment; never, for example, on the grounds that I was extra kind or patient the previous day, or that I have already done something for the Lord that morning. No! I have to come by way of the Blood *every time*.

A clear conscience is never based upon our attainment; it can only be based on the work of the Lord Jesus in the shedding of his Blood. Therefore, our approach to God is always in boldness; and that boldness is ours through the Blood, and never through our personal attainment–at any level.

Think of this. Were you to meet God in person today, on what grounds would you dare approach this most Holy place of God's very presence? Whatever may be your measure of attainment today or yesterday or the day before, as soon as you were to make that move into the presence of God, immediately you would have to take your stand upon the safe and *only* grounds of the shed Blood.

Whether you had a good day or a bad day, whether you have consciously sinned or not, your basis of approach is always the same–the Blood of Christ. God's acceptance of that Blood is the ground upon which you may enter, and there is *no* other.

So, for the present, let us be satisfied with the Blood–that it is there and that it is enough. We may be weak, but looking at our weakness will never make us strong. No trying to feel badly and doing penance will help us to be even a little holier. There is no help there!

So, let us be bold in our approach because of the Blood. Our conscience is cleared because God has said the Blood has done all the work. It is finished!

Perhaps this would be a good point of transition for you before God as it has to do with the Blood's sufficiency for you. Let this be the moment in time for the absolute clearing of your conscience for what you have done, and will yet do into the future that has the potential to threaten the intimacy of your relationship with the Spirit of God within you:

> LORD, I do not know fully what the value of the Blood is, but I know that the Blood has satisfied you; so the Blood is enough for me, and it is my only plea. I see now that whether I have really progressed, whether I have really attained to something or not, is not the point.

Whenever I come before you from this day forward, I thank you that it will always be on the grounds of the precious Blood. Thank you.

And finally, at this point, your conscience is really clear before God. No conscience could ever be clear apart from the Blood. It is the Blood that gives us boldness. "No more conscience of sins"; these are the tremendous words of Hebrews 10:2. We are cleansed from every sin; and we may truly, with Paul, echo the words of David: "Blessed is the man to whom the Lord will not reckon sin." (Romans 4:8)

And so, the first step is one where the blood has the ability to aid us in the clearing of our conscience. But there is also a second step for us to lay hold of—one designed to give us victory over the powerful pull of the accuser of our flesh.

Chapter 40

Overcoming the Accuser

We have an enemy. This enemy is real. He is the accuser of our soul, and accusation becomes one of the greatest and most effective of Satan's weapons. He points to our sins and seeks to charge us with them before God. And if we accept his accusations we go down immediately.

The reason we so readily accept his accusations is that we are frequently caught unaware, and find that we are *still* hoping to have some righteousness of our own. And in doing so, we forget that the grounds for our expectation is wrong.

Satan has succeeded in making us look in the wrong direction. Thereby he wins his point, rendering us ineffective. But if we have learned to put no confidence in the flesh, we won't wonder whether we have sinned, for our understanding and recollection is that the very *nature* of the flesh *is* to sin. Do you understand what I mean?

It is because we have not come to appreciate our true nature and to see how helpless we are that we still have some expectation in ourselves, with the result that, when Satan comes along and accuses us, we go down under it.

You see, God is able to deal with our sins; but He cannot deal with a man under accusation—because such a man is not trusting in the Blood. The Blood speaks in his favor, but instead he is listening to Satan.

Christ is our Advocate, but we, the accused, side with the accuser. We have not recognized that we are unworthy of anything but death; that, as we will see shortly, we are only fit to be crucified anyway. We have not recognized that it is God alone who can answer the accuser and that in the precious Blood, He has already done so.

It reminds me of the life-giving message of one of my absolute favorite songs—it's a Phillips, Craig & Dean song, Let The Blood Speak For Me. If you don't have the song, get it. Let it become a part of your victory:

> Guilty as charged I stand
> Got here by my own hand
> I've no defense, the evidence is clear
> Left to my own design
> I thought the world was mine
> But all I found were chains that bound me here
>
> I can't deny I'm lost in sin
> I could plead my own case but I would not win
> The only hope I see are the stains of Calvary
> So I'll let the blood speak for me
>
> My heart was a prison cell
> My sin I knew all too well
> Condemned to face this empty place inside
> Held captive by selfishness
> No argument I confess
> No pardon due for so much foolish pride
>
> I can't deny I'm lost in sin
> I could plead my own case but I would not win
> The only hope I see are the stains of Calvary
> So I'll let the blood speak for me
>
> The blood says I am whole
> The blood says I am clean
> All is forgiven, I've been set free
> So let the blood
> Let the blood speak for me
>
> The blood says I am whole
> The blood says I am clean
> All is forgiven, I've been set free
> So let the blood
> Let the blood speak for me

Our salvation in this whole matter of Satan's accusatory finger lies in looking away to the Lord Jesus and in seeing that the Blood of the Lamb has met the whole situation created by our sins and has answered it. *That* is the sure foundation on which we stand. *Never* should we try to answer Satan with our good conduct, but always with the Blood.

Yes, we are sinful, but, praise God the Blood cleanses us from *every* sin! God looks upon the Blood whereby His Son has met the charge, and Satan has no more grounds for attack. Our faith in the precious Blood and our refusal to be moved from that position can alone silence his charges and put him to flight.

> *Who will bring any charge against those whom God has chosen? It is God who justifies. Who then is the one who condemns? No one. Christ Jesus who died—more than that, who was raised to life—is at the right hand of God and is also interceding for us.*
> **– Romans 8:33-34**

And similarly, it will be so right on to the end.

> *[10] Then I heard a loud voice in heaven say:*
> *"Now have come the salvation and the power*
>   *and the kingdom of our God,*
>   *and the authority of his Messiah.*
> *For the accuser of our brothers and sisters,*
>   *who accuses them before our God day and night,*
>   *has been hurled down.*
> *[11] They triumphed over him*
>   *by the blood of the Lamb*
>   *and by the word of their testimony;*
> *they did not love their lives so much*
>   *as to shrink from death.* **– Revelation 12:10-11**

Could there ever be a better refrain than this peek we get into our future as ones who have placed our trust in the Lord Jesus? Bless the Lord!

Now before moving on to the role of the *Cross* over how we live our lives here on earth, I also want to bring another very important thought onto the scene as we put the wraps on what it is we are blessed beyond measure to *avoid because of* the Blood shed on our behalf–namely God's terrible and inexhaustible wrath for those who reject His Son.

Chapter 41

The Wrath of God

As we have just discussed, Satan has sufficient grounds to accuse us. In our flesh and apart from the Blood, he knows we are completely sinful and justifiably damned to eternal hell and separation from the goodness of God.

Satan knows well the frightening judgment under which we could never stand were it not for the Blood, and under which he himself will never ultimately stand. He *hates* the Blood. He *hates* our redemption. And so, he works like crazy to accuse our new man—doing everything in his power to resurrect what has been put to death in us.

Our triumph in this life through Christ is Satan's continual reminder of what will be his ultimate undoing and destruction.

But God's judgment and the ultimate destruction of those who have not called upon the name of the Lord is a place we too often refuse to go because it's not a pleasant place. It is much easier to dwell on the love of God than on the wrathful judgment that awaits those who die apart from Christ. By extension, I'm afraid our message to a lost world is becoming one where we are increasingly trying to make God more palatable in the eyes of man—as if God needs our help to effectively market Himself.

We seem ashamed of what the world would perceive as the *less desirable side* of the character of God. As a result, in many of our evangelical churches today we are pedaling a gospel that is offering people the gifts of God rather than God Himself. But God has redeemed us to Himself, *not* his blessings.

> This is why we can't, when we talk about evangelism and the Gospel, tell people that you can believe in Christ and you get forgiveness of your sins, and you get eternal life, and you can get your best life, and you get all of these things.
>
> No. You come to Christ and you get God.
>
> All these things flow from God, but we have taken God himself out of how we preach the Cross and the Gospel, and we offer his gifts instead. He reconciles us to Himself, and *He* is the supreme treasure...not His gifts.[78]

We behave much like the child of an alcoholic father who tries to conceal her dad's bad side, keeping such facts from her friends at school. But when we do this, we are not introducing the world to God, but only to one *part* of God – that being His love and generosity.

I'm afraid we feel it may be easier to emphasize what the world may be willing to hear rather than faithfully discharging the whole Truth of God's nature, the nature of the Great I Am–the One who needs no one to make excuses for or soft-shoe around the entirety of His very nature.

God's character and nature is not like a cafeteria where we can just pick and choose what parts of God we like best! And I'm afraid that when we act like this in the midst of today's create-your-own god culture, we're looking like too many others trying to sell their own version of truth, but not The Truth.

We cannot create our own God. He Is. **And because, as of late, I have come to realize we too often don't go to the *other side* of God's personhood, I want to unapologetically go there now.** For if we diminish God's wrath, we diminish His holiness. And we *must not* diminish His holiness.

It is admittedly a hard thing to grasp the idea of God's wrath being poured out on sinners for all of eternity as an act of His judgment. What's more, if you really want a tough thing to comprehend, try to get your mind around how it is that God will actually be glorified *for* such justice!

How do we mentally deal with how a loving God and the righteous ones of heaven could actually, one day, be worshipped *for* and *during* what will be the torment and judgment of sinners? This is flat out challenging.

---

[78] Taken from Platt's, The Cross of Christ, Secret Church, Part 3

In Revelation 15:2-4, 16:1-7 and 19:1-2 we get a graphic picture of God being worshipped as His justice is being poured out on unbelievers.

> ² And I saw what looked like a sea of glass glowing with fire and, standing beside the sea, those who had been victorious over the beast and its image and over the number of its name. They held harps given them by God ³ and sang the song of God's servant Moses and of the Lamb:
> "Great and marvelous are your deeds,
> > Lord God Almighty.
> Just and true are your ways,
> > King of the nations.
> ⁴ Who will not fear you, Lord,
> > and bring glory to your name?
> For you alone are holy.
> All nations will come
> > and worship before you,
> for your righteous acts have been revealed." **– Revelation 15:2-4**

> Then I heard a loud voice from the temple saying to the seven angels, "Go, pour out the seven bowls of God's wrath on the earth."
> ² The first angel went and poured out his bowl on the land, and ugly, festering sores broke out on the people who had the
> > mark of the beast and worshiped its image.
> ³ The second angel poured out his bowl on the sea, and it turned into blood like that of a dead person, and every living thing in the sea died.
> ⁴ The third angel poured out his bowl on the rivers and springs of water, and they became blood. ⁵ Then I heard the angel in charge of the waters say: "You are just in these judgments, O Holy One, you who are and who were;
> ⁶ for they have shed the blood of your holy people and your prophets, and you have given them blood to drink as they deserve."
> ⁷ And I heard the altar respond:
> > "Yes, Lord God Almighty, true and just are your judgments."
> > **– Revelation 16:1-7**

> After this I heard what sounded like the roar of a great multitude in heaven shouting:
> > "Hallelujah! Salvation and glory and power belong to our God,
> > ²   for true and just are his judgments.
> > He has condemned the great prostitute
> > > who corrupted the earth by her adulteries.

He has avenged on her the blood of his servants." – **Revelation 19:1-2**

When we really contemplate this, when we let these pictures soak in, this is challenging to comprehend. This is the kind of thing around which we can hardly wrap our minds. *We* find it challenging to sometimes even grasp the *love* of God. How *does* He love us in the midst of what we have done to grieve his heart? And that's his *love*! But if that's not hard enough, it is *really* challenging to talk about God's wrath.

And even if we *are* able to get our minds around the necessity of God's wrath, though it breaks us to pieces, what we find in these and other passages in the Bible is above our pay grade. Really? Worshipping God for his wrath as He pours out judgment on sinners? How do we worship God for his wrath? If this isn't challenging for you, then you don't have a heart!

How is it that *as God's wrath* is being poured out in heaven, we see saints in heaven worshipping God? In the grips of this truth, a truth we cannot just whisk away or dismiss with a wrong view of Scripture so that God will somehow fit within what our finite minds can determine to be acceptable behavior for God…it is in a contemplation of these challenging passages that David Platt asks this question:

> What is it about what we will realize on *that* day that maybe we don't fully realize today?[79]

Certainly our inability to figure some things out to our satisfaction points to the fact that we are, in fact, the clay and *not* the Potter. Because certain aspects of the wrath of God are so perplexing, and we so mightily struggle with these things, we may be tempted to make excuses for such difficult Truths, or take them as mere parable or allegory so that we can accept them in another light. But who are *we* to tell God what is right or fair or what is reasonable? These passages are a foretelling of *what will be*. And because of this, we have to accept what Paul wrote to the believers in Corinth:

---

[79] David Platt, Heaven, Hell and the End of the World; Secret Church 13 – March 2013

> *For now we see only a reflection as in a mirror; then we shall see face to face. Now I know in part; then I shall know fully, even as I am fully known.*
> **– I Corinthians 13:12**

> *For we know in part and we prophesy in part, but when completeness comes, what is in part disappears.*
> **– I Corinthians 13:9-10**

And so, again, this picture of the worship of God *as* His wrath is being poured out onto unrepentant, unbelieving sinners is hard for us to process. What is it about what we will realize on *that* day that maybe we don't fully realize today? I think Platt's answer well encompasses what ails us most in this life; we have a perspective problem.

Says Platt,

> Here's what I think it is. On that day, we will finally have a high view of God. We will see God from heaven's perspective. We will see him [and] realize with much greater clarity that He is sovereign over all. That He is glorified above all. That He is Holy in all of his attributes. ...and on that day we will realize that God is righteous in all his ways. We have a tendency in our limited understanding, even our limited misconceptions, to question the rightness of God, the justice of God. But on that day we will conclude, with Deuteronomy 32:4,
>> He is the Rock, his works are perfect, and all his ways are just. A faithful God who does no wrong, upright and just is He.
>
> We will realize God is righteous in all His ways and we will realize that He is loving toward all His creation, that He is merciful and gracious, slow to anger and abounding in steadfast love. And we will have one clear conclusion: This God, our God, is infinitely worthy of eternal worship. ...On the Day of Judgment, we will finally have a high view of God.
>
> At the same time, we will finally have a humble view of man. And we will realize the humbling horror of our sin against God–how we have denounced the sovereignty of God. How we have defamed the glory of God. We will realize that we have dishonored the holiness of God. ...And so we will come to the clear conclusion that God is not only infinitely worthy of eternal worship, but [that]...we are infinitely worthy, in our sin, of God's eternal wrath.

...This is why we have a hard time comprehending the worship of God in His wrath and judgment–because we have things totally backward.

Instead of having a high view of God, we have a low view of God. And instead of a humble view of man, we have a high view of ourselves. ...[on that day], our questions about God's justice will be no more. Our awe at God's mercy will be forevermore. For on that day we will finally understand the depth of hope in the Gospel. How, at the Cross on Good Friday 2000 years ago, God expressed His wrath towards sin, God poured out His righteous judgment towards sin. At the same time, God endured His wrath against sin.

Jesus *drank* the cup of God's wrath in our place–and in this God enabled salvation for sinners. He made Him who had no sin to be made sin for us in order that we might become the righteousness of God.[80] [2 Cor. 5:21]

And so, thanks be to God through Jesus Christ, the triumphant scripture references about which we read above (Romans 8:33-34 and Revelation 12:10-11) pertain both to our present life and our victorious future.

But for us to gloss over the price, and the nature of the penultimate wrath *which had to be appeased* by our Substitute, would be to tragically strike at the very heart of our capacity for gratitude due our Lord Jesus.

Let's not manipulate God only into one *we* craft based on what is most comfortable *for us* to ponder. For to do so becomes the starting line of a dangerous path–one that will lead quickly to today's select, relative and personal truth rather than upon a complete understanding of the God whose we are.

God was, is, and will be frighteningly dangerous beyond comprehension for those not under the covering of His Son's Blood. A one-dimensional knowledge of God may not cause visible trouble on the surface for Christians, but it absolutely damages our knowledge and accurate understanding of who God is and of the great, redemptive price paid on our behalf. And when this happens, we become a Body of Christ identified with what Dietrich Bonhoeffer calls *cheap grace*.

---

[80] Platt, Heaven, Hell and the End of the World; Secret Church 13 – March 2013

> Cheap grace is the grace we bestow on ourselves. Cheap grace is the preaching of forgiveness without requiring repentance, baptism without church discipline, communion without confession...Cheap grace is grace without discipleship, grace without the cross, grace without Jesus Christ, living and incarnate.[81]

In addition, *this kind of a limited view of God is not good for the necessary work of the Spirit in the breaking of our soul.* Focusing wholly, selectively, and exclusively on the warming, radiant acceptance of God is the spiritual equivalent of the warm glow of the Venus Fly Trap. It can become a deadly deception.

What's more, the Blood that has washed us clean in the eyes of God has *also* had to accomplish something to appease the *other side* of God's nature. As a holy and just God, it is the Blood that also satisfies God's **wrath**–a wrath based in justice that, apart from the work of the Blood over our lives, could only condemn us to eternal damnation, torment and separation from anything good.

When we focus only upon the wonderfully redemptive side of the character of God, we completely lose the part of our holy and just God that is brought to us through an understanding of the propitiatory nature of the Blood.

Yes, our God is one who loves endlessly, is faithful and all the rest, but He, just the same, is *also* the God who absolutely had to have His indescribably terrible wrath, pointed directly at us, appeased by its outpouring onto his Son. And without such an appeasement, God's wrath would ravish and overwhelm us forever.

Even in times past, we know that man had an innate sense that even his make-believe gods had to be appeased–bought off, so to speak. And so, what did man do? He would attempt to placate the gods by sacrificing things–including his own children.

And if there were an *especially* great need for things to turn around, they somehow 'knew' that *blood* had to be spilled. Of note, however, it was always *man* who had to sacrifice greatly to win the favor of the gods, regain a good karma...or whatever you want to call it. And, naturally, it was *never* the gods' responsibility to come down and propitiate or buy down their *own* anger and wrath through any number of sacrificial options.

But the God of the Bible is not so selfish. His great love for *us* brought His Son, Jesus, into this world to *be* the sacrifice, to *be* the buy down–on our behalf and unto death. J.I. Packer presents this

---

[81] Dietrich Bonhoeffer, The Cost of Discipleship

piercing reality well from God's perspective when, in chapter 18 of his book, *Knowing God*, he points us to Leviticus 17.

> *For the life of a creature is in the blood. And I have given it to you to make atonement for yourselves on the altar. It is the blood that makes atonement.*
> **– Leviticus 17:11**

Says Packer,

> When Paul tells us that God set forth Jesus to be a propitiation by his blood[82], his point is that what quenched God's wrath, and so redeemed us from death, was not Jesus' life or teaching, not his moral perfection nor his fidelity to the Father as such, but by the shedding of his blood in death.
>
> Along with the other New Testament writers, Paul always points to the death of Jesus as *the* atoning event, and explains the atonement in terms of representative substitution–the innocent taking the place of the guilty in the name and for the sake of the guilty under the acts of God's judicial retribution.[83]

You see, Jesus became a curse *for* us. He hung *in our place* because the Father's wrath *had to be* appeased, bought out, without which the justice of God would be only a ruse. David Platt says this in his book, Radical.

> I wonder sometimes, though, if we intentionally or just unknowingly mask the beauty of God in the Gospel by minimizing his various attributes. Peruse the Christian marketplace and you will find a plethora of books, songs and paintings that depict God as a loving father. And he is that. But he is not just a loving father, and limiting our understanding of God to this picture ultimately distorts the image of God we have in our culture.
>
> Yes, God is a loving father, but he is also a wrathful judge. In His wrath, He *hates* sin.

---

[82] *He is the propitiation for our sins, and not for ours only but also for the sins of the whole world.* - **I John 2:2 (ESV)** ...and *whom God put forward as a propitiation by his blood, to be received by faith. This was to show God's righteousness, because in his divine forbearance he had passed over former sins.* – **Romans 3:25 (ESV)**

[83] Packer, Knowing God

Habakkuk prayed to God, 'Your eyes are too pure to look on evil. You cannot tolerate wrong.' And in some sense, God also hates sinners. You might ask, what happened to God hates the sin and loves the sinner? Well, the Bible happened to it.

One psalmist said to God, 'The arrogant cannot stand in your presence. You hate all who do wrong.' Fourteen times in the first fifty psalms we see similar descriptions of God's hatred towards sinners, his wrath toward liars, and so on.

In the chapter in the Gospel of John where we find one of the most famous verses concerning God's love, we also find one of the most neglected verses concerning God's wrath.

The Gospel reveals eternal realities about God that we would sometimes rather not face. We prefer to sit back, enjoy our clichés and picture God as a father who might help us, all the while ignoring God as a judge who might damn us.[84]

But today we too infrequently go here, choosing to focus nearly completely on the warm, fuzzy, comfortable place of God's acceptance–and thus, a cheapening of God's grace. And this negatively impacts our fellowship with God through His Spirit living within us.

When we focus on a one-dimensional God, we eliminate any identification with what was, in ourselves, to be our inheritance *without* the spilled Blood of our Savior. And our souls cannot therefore identify sufficiently with the utterly soiled nature of our flesh.

The very center of the Gospel is firstly a mental and emotional ingestation of the terrible substitution of Jesus as He took upon Himself the iniquities of us all.

> *⁴Surely he took up our pain and bore our suffering,*
> *yet we considered him punished by God,*
> *stricken by him, and afflicted.*
> *⁵ But he was pierced for **our** transgressions,*
> *he was crushed for **our** iniquities;*
> *the **punishment** that brought us peace was **on him**,*
> *and by **his** wounds **we** are healed.*
> *⁶ We all, like sheep, have gone astray,*

---

[84] Platt, Radical; Chapter 2, Page 30

> *each of us has turned to our own way;*
> *and the Lord has laid on **him***
> *the iniquity of **us** all.* – **Isaiah 53:4-6**

> [24] He himself bore our sins in his body on the cross, so that we might die to sins and live for righteousness; "by his wounds you have been healed." – **I Peter 2:24**

But when you realize that God has taken you from the gutter, so to speak, and made you a son in His own house, you, a miraculously pardoned offender, guilty, ungrateful, defiant, perverse as you were, then your sense of God's love beyond degree, is more than words can express. You will echo Charles Wesley's question,

> Oh how shall I the goodness tell
> Father which thou to me hast showed
> that I a child of wrath and hell
> I should be called a child of God.[85]

But what I have found is that no amount of mental work, memorization of scripture passages or the like is capable of driving our spirits and souls into such an experiential awareness of the extent to which He paid our price. It is not possible. It is not in us to attain such.

It is only in the course of time, and as we learn to surrender everything to the LORD Jesus, making Him truly our Adonai–our Master, that we begin to gain such emotional connectivity to the price paid on our behalf. As mentioned earlier, it is only when the Lord does us this favor that we are finally able to pull our boats to the shore one final time and follow him radically.

May the joy and deep gratitude attainable only through a proper reckoning upon our undeserved sonship and adoption into His family, thanks to the suffrage of Jesus through his shed blood *and appeasement of the Father's wrath*, be an ever-increasing component of our faith!

Oh, what an emancipation it would be if we saw more through the eyes of God as **He** places the value on the precious Blood of His dear Son!

Jesus' blood has obtained our forgiveness, justification, and reconciliation with the Father.

---

[85] Packer, Knowing God

But we must now go a step further in the plan of God to understand how He deals with *the sin principle in us*. **The Blood can wash away my sins, but it cannot wash away my "old man." It needs the Cross to crucify me. The Blood deals with the *sins*, but the Cross must deal with the *sinner*.** Do you see the difference? It is really important that you do.

The purpose of the next section is to help us grasp this difference.

CHAPTERS 42-46

SECOND:
THE WORK OF THE CROSS

Chapter 42

The Cross of Christ

Once I had taken time to bask and glory in a deeper apprehension of the Blood's role for me, having reviewed much of it half a dozen times or more before allowing myself to move on, the Bible a ready companion for exploration on the theme for what seemed like cup after cup of cool water to the soul, I was finally ready (like a rabid dog ready) to break into what I had hoped would be a similarly refreshing and enhanced understanding of the Cross and how it was purposed to remedy my sin *nature*.

In like fashion, I would ask that you not be too quick to merely gather in additional knowledge of the Cross until you have marinated your soul sufficiently, and over a period of days in the least, in the historical and New Covenant purposes of the Blood.[86]

The Blood was purposed for, and deals with what we have *done*; it was needed for forgiveness. But the Cross deals with what we *are*; we need the Cross for deliverance.

So, whereas the majority of the first four chapters of Romans deal with our sin and our justification[87] before God, we now, in the latter portions of chapter 5, begin to turn the corner toward the problem of our conduct.

And in turning this corner, we begin to see the striking difference of theme and subject matter between the two halves of this section of Romans. In both sections, Paul speaks of peace. Romans 5:1 tells us that "being therefore justified by faith, we have peace with God through our Lord Jesus Christ." This means now that I have forgiveness of sins, God will no longer be a cause of dread to me. I who was an enemy to God have been "reconciled...through the death of his Son (5:10)."

However, I very soon find that I am going to be a great cause of trouble to myself.

---

[86] Again, I would ask that you not be too quick to move into this section, merely gathering additional *knowledge of* "the Cross," until you have sufficiently waited on the Lord Jesus to marinate your soul, over a period of days in the least, in the Old and New Covenant purposes of his Blood. It is not a matter of there surely being something new to learn that you've never read before, but it *is* a matter of letting the Holy Spirit pierce your soul with its weight so as to change you. Let its truth wash over you as you *plead with the Spirit* to open the eyes of your spirit to its significance. I dare you to put off your pursuit of this section yet *another* day or two. In its place, spend time waiting on and seeking the Lord Jesus for just one or two more nuggets from his Hand that would help you lay an even deeper hold on the Blood's absolute complete work for the covering of your sins, and in its wake, gaining for you access into the very presence of God, pure and undefiled before Him. Find a couple good articles online pertaining to such. Plead with God for a deeper understanding of its import into your personal life. Pray it in so you may not just know *about* its work, but that you may *know* it intimately, personally. Then review the roles of the OT blood sacrifice again. Let the Spirit teach you about His Blood spilled out for you, and pray it in. This waiting on the Lord is most important. Learning to listen and sup with God through the power of his Spirit living in you is most important. (Psalm 14:2, Hebrews 11:6, Hosea 10:12, Psalm 25:5, 123:2, 130:5, Lam. 3:24-26, I Chr. 16:11, ...)

[87] For a great study in grasping this word and how its understanding should impact our daily Christian walk, listen to John MacArthur's Redemption Through His Blood, Part 1 message listed in the Resources section.

There is peace with God, but there is no peace with myself. There is, in fact, civil war in my own heart.

This condition is depicted in Romans 7 where the flesh and the spirit are seen to be in deadly conflict within us. But from this, in chapter 8 the argument leads to the inward peace of a walk in the Spirit.

Verses 6-7 say, "The mind governed by the flesh is death, but the mind governed by the Spirit is life and peace. The mind governed by the flesh is hostile to God; it does not submit to God's law, nor can it do so."

Therefore, it becomes apparent to us that when we know the precious truth of justification by faith, we still know only half the story. We have still only solved the problem of our standing before God. But as we go on, both in our new life in Christ and in Romans, God has something more to offer us—namely, the solution to the problem of our conduct.

Glory to God, He has not left us alone in the living out of our new life in Christ!

Chapter 43

The Role of the Cross

Recapping then, as we did transitioning into this chapter, we have objectively seen that the Blood deals with our *sins*. The Lord Jesus has borne them on the Cross for us as our Substitute, and has thereby obtained our forgiveness, justification, and reconciliation with him.

But we must now go a step further in the plan of God to understand how he deals with *the sin principle in us*. Again, **the Blood can wash away my sins, but it cannot wash away my "old man." It needs the Cross to crucify me. The Blood deals with the *sins*, but the Cross must deal with the *sinner*.** Do you see the difference? It is really important that you do.

The word "sinner" only begins to come into prominence in chapter 5, and it is important to notice how the sinner is introduced at that point.

In that chapter, a sinner is said to be a sinner because he is *born* a sinner; not because he has committed sins. The distinction is important and there are implications to this difference.

For example, when we use Romans 3:23 to convince someone that he is a sinner, because "all have sinned," we're maybe using that verse the wrong way. *For the teaching of Romans is not that we are sinners because we commit sins, but that we sin because we are sinners.* **We are sinners by *constitution* rather than by *action*.**

As Romans 5:19 expresses it: "Through the one man's disobedience, the many were made (or constituted) sinners."

How were we constituted sinners? By Adam's disobedience.

We do not become sinners by what we have done, but because of what Adam has done and has become.

Think of it this way. When working at Chick-fil-A and spending time with my employees in the kitchen, I spoke Spanish—broken though it was! But in doing so, I am not thereby constituted a Hispanic. I am in fact an American Englishman of Swiss-German descent. I do not become Hispanic because I speak Spanish—by what I do. Neither am I an Englishman of Swiss-German ancestry *because* I speak English. No, I can only be a Hispanic or an Englishman if I am *born* as such.

In like manner, chapter 3 of Romans draws our attention to what we have done—"all have sinned"—**but it is nevertheless not because we have done it that we become sinners!** This is SO important to our going forward that I'm going to camp here for a moment longer.

I recently set Lesli (my wife) up with a question that bordered on the unfair—one that would have elicited the same response from myself were I to have been in her shoes. I asked her, "Who is a sinner?" Her immediate reply was, "One who sins." Yes, one who sins *is* a sinner to be sure, but the fact that he sins is merely the evidence that he is already a sinner; it is not the cause.

One who sins is a sinner, but it is equally true that one who does not sin, if he is of Adam's race, is a sinner too, and in need of redemption. Do you follow me?

There are bad sinners and there are good sinners, there are moral sinners and there are corrupt sinners. Nonetheless, they are all sinners alike. **The trouble lies in what we are.**

One of my early childhood friends was a first-generation American citizen. His parents came from Taiwan. Initially, being so new to America, his parents could scarcely speak a word of English. Now Steve, though clearly Taiwanese, was born in America, and by the time he was learning a language, his parents had begun to speak some English. Therefore, Steve and his sister were unable to speak but the most basic Taiwanese. Nonetheless, he was Taiwanese just the same—because he was born Taiwanese. It is birth that counts.

Similarly, I am a sinner because I am born *in* Adam. **I am not a sinner because I sin, but I sin because I come of the wrong stock.** I sin because I am a sinner.

This realization, though some may say is nothing more than a slightly different slant in perspective, was hitting me like a freight train—and I couldn't wait to draw all the sap out of it.

It was a change in perspective that was going to change everything. It was as if I were, for the first time, intellectually and practically connecting with an accurate diagnosis into the uttermost root cause of my selfish and sinful condition. I had known this to be true of mankind, but it was now becoming *my* story. And my excitement was peaking because I knew the antidote was next—*my* antidote. I knew that what lay ahead was a discovery of how God had intended my normal Christian life to be effected by the Cross. And I couldn't wait!

Reflectively for a moment before moving on, I think the human condition, even for us Christians, is to think that what we have done is very bad, but that we *ourselves* are not so bad. And this is at the center of our transition now between the work of the Blood and the work of the Cross.

We tend to separate what we *do* from who we *are*. If you think about it, you may find this true for yourself as well to some degree.

It's as if we would be ok if only we would do what is right all the time! Then, we'd be good. But, in Romans 5, God is taking pains to show us that we *ourselves* are wrong, fundamentally wrong. The root trouble is the sinner; he must be dealt with.

Throughout most of my Christian walk, I had well come to grips with the idea that it had been my sins keeping me from personal fellowship with God. But at this juncture in what the Lord Jesus was bringing to bear in my heart in a new way, I was becoming much more deeply appreciative for the Blood, and an understanding of its actual role, how it was mostly a sufficiency for God.

The way the Blood works is like this: God, through Jesus' blood, has given us the key to our new car, our new life, and with that we are the owners of this new object—eternal life. It was now ours, and no one could take it from us. The full price had been paid and we now owned the car, our new life in Christ, outright.

But, sadly, that's where so many of us stop!

We own the car of our new life, we know we are redeemed, forgiven, set free from the power of eternal damnation, but we neglect to put the key into the car with an expectation that our conversion was only to be the beginning.

We may familiarize ourselves with the new life, feel its leather-wrapped steering wheel, kick its tires, be appreciative of the trunk space, know the official color of the paint job and the like, but we neglect to grasp that without employing what came to us with the purchase of the car, we cannot actually start up and drive the new car—our new life in Christ!

So, it's like we now have a new car, a new life, but we have neglected to learn about how our new vehicle needs oil, transmission fluid, gasoline and coolant so it doesn't burn up! We've neglected to learn about the source of the life-giving fluids for living this new life—our life as a new creation. Thus, we continue living in our own power, our own strength and effort without the intended fuel!

This is where the Cross comes in. The power of the Cross picks up where the Blood leaves off.

Had you asked me at the point of my conversion, or for that matter just 2-3 years ago, whether there were more trouble on the horizon in my walk with Jesus—as I now attempted to drive my new car, keeping our illustration alive, I'd have said, "Yes, of course! Sure."

This was because I knew I was still living in a body of flesh—sinful flesh. I figured I had been redeemed spiritually for all of eternity, but I was still imprisoned in this body of flesh. As a consequence, what lay ahead was going to continue to be the ongoing, lifelong challenge of bringing my old flesh into alignment with my new life.

But I would have only thought of it as being the ongoing and natural challenge of learning how to follow Jesus into a life of less sin and more victory, because I was going to learn how to control myself in the direction of better behavior—albeit with the help of the Holy Spirit.

I was going to continue putting the water of my own ambition for Christ into my new engine, and change into who Christ wanted me to become...one way or another.

The only problem is that the engine won't run with water in the crankcase—it has to have oil! You see?

You don't put new wine into an old wineskin. Is this bringing new light to the illustration given us in Matthew 9:14-17, Mark 2:21-22 and Luke 5:33-39?

Just as Judaism and its laws couldn't contain or hold the new purposes God had for them in Christ, neither can our old man contain the new purposes the Spirit of God has in store for us when he enters to make us new!

In the same way, I wasn't going to be able to run as a follower of Jesus with *any* amount of tight-fisted, self-controlling effort. But, without getting too far ahead of myself here, the Spirit hadn't yet revealed to me what it meant that I had **died**—*in* Christ. I hadn't seen that yet.

You see, God made it impossible for us to please him with our own ability. What He intends is that we actually understand that when God's Blood was assigned to our case, it put to death that old man. Now how was I going to use those dead faculties to live my new life in Christ? It wasn't going to work.

Just the same, the truth is that *I was working hard to produce* the fruit of the Spirit through a gutty effort, mental discipline—you know, molding myself into becoming a better Christ follower as a result of putting my nose to the grindstone out of a commitment to and great love for God.

I was trying to live in victory in this new life with tools that were already dead and buried! Was I a new creature or not? If so, as Scripture clearly teaches us, then why all this work trying to use the old tools left behind in the old body? Oh, how I pray you understand what I'm trying to say here. It is important that you do.

Dear God, give the reader eyes to see.

You may say, "Greg, what you're saying is merely semantics—merely a looking at our life as Christians through a different *mental* lens." To which I loudly proclaim, "No it is *not!*"

I really don't think I had ever *deeply* connected with the idea that I *myself*, am wrong; that I, *in my very being*, am made of the wrong stock for living rightly with my Savior.

It hadn't come to me that in all of my doing, in all of my working to behave differently, in all of my effort to alter my behavior, in all of my diligent, intellectual reading and wrestling with the words on the paper in the Scriptures, and committing myself to executing it into my life, it hadn't come to me that I was completely incapable of gaining victory over the sinful, prideful, thoroughly selfish body of sin in which I was living—that *I myself* was all wrong from the ground up, and that I had *no chance* of gaining victory through any amount of effort!

I wasn't only separated from God because of my sins, which had previously been my only thought on the matter, but I was also separated from Him because of *what I was*. And I had missed this equally important aspect of the work Jesus had begun that day on that hill.

While I knew my sins had been dealt with by the Blood, without the Spirit's illumination into my soul, I never would have come to the understanding that I *myself* had to be dealt with—and this with the Cross.

I was beginning to learn how deep-seated the trouble was within us as a human race. And it was finally at this point where I was able to come to the Lord and say, "Lord, I see it now! Not only what I have *done* is wrong; *I* am wrong."

And so, the beautiful truth Romans was teaching me was that the Blood procures our pardon from what we have *done*, while it takes the Cross to procure our deliverance from what we *are*!

It was *this* distinction that was gaining both traction and great anticipation within me. For I began thinking that if there were something the Lord Jesus had done in that transaction two-thousand years ago which could deal with *me*, something I had not yet fully understood in my theology, then there was hope to begin living deeper into the One who had taught that I had become a new creation…in itself something I had only partially comprehended.

Was there a key somewhere here that could unlock within me the capacity for a greater love for Jesus?

Merely reckoning upon this idea began to drop my jaw and make me giddy with excitement about what more the Spirit may be preparing to teach me!

I was like a child readying his taste buds for that root beer candy—drooling at the possibilities! I remember to this day how my heart was beating wildly and my mind spinning in anticipation with what I may be getting ready to be taught…and the awaiting newness of victory in Christ that was on my horizon.

And so it was at this time that the conclusion of the first half of Romans 5:19 was beginning to dawn upon me.

At the fall, a fundamental change took place in the character of Adam whereby he, and thus we by extension as his offspring, became a sinner—one constitutionally unable to please God any longer. And it was into this family likeness I was born.

Let me illustrate.

My name is Beaverson. It's not a terribly common name. So how did I come by it? I didn't choose it. I didn't go through the list of possible German/English names and select one. It is not any of my doing at all, and moreover, there's nothing I can do to alter it.

I am a Beaverson because my father is a Beaverson, and my father is a Beaverson because my grandfather was a Beaverson. If I act like a Beaverson, I am a Beaverson. If I act unlike a Beaverson, I am still a Beaverson.

If I become President of the United States, I would remain a Beaverson.

If I become a beggar on the streets of Chicago, I would still be a Beaverson.

Nothing I do or refrain from doing will make me other than a Beaverson.

In the same way, we are sinners not because of ourselves, but because of Adam. It is not because I have individually sinned that I am a sinner, **but because I was in Adam when he sinned.**

That's right. Think about it for a moment here.

Because by birth I come from Adam, I am a part of him. I can do nothing to alter this. And even if I immeasurably improve my behavior, I cannot make myself other than a part of Adam–and so a sinner. Right?

If this is too hard to grasp at first blush, consider this; I could have the following conversation with my son:

"As you know Caleb, Papa Roger's father, Owen Beaverson, was very ill as a young boy. On one such occasion at the absolute worst of his sicknesses, the doctor told your Great-Great Grandma that her son wouldn't make it through the night. It was on that occasion that Owen dreamed about his falling at increasing speed into a dark abyss.

At the moment of what seemed to be complete separation from this life, what felt like arms cushioned him and broke his free-fall from life on earth. The next morning, he awoke to consciousness and began his miraculous and unexplainable return to health–good thing since he hadn't yet come to know Christ.

Now let me ask you a question, Caleb. *What would have happened if your Great Grandpa Owen Beaverson had died that night? Where would you be now?"*

In fact, I just now paused and called Caleb–I just hung up the phone. I asked him this very question. *Caleb, what would have happened if your Great Grandpa Owen Beaverson had died that night? Where would you be now?*

His response? "I wouldn't exist."

"Oh no," I said, "your Great-Grandpa Owen could have died his death and you could have still lived your life!"

"That's incorrect!" Caleb replied. "*I* could not have been born biologically if *he* had died."

Caleb was right!

Do you see the oneness of human life? If your great-grandfather had died at the age of 12, where would *you* be? You would have died *in* him! Your experience is bound up with his.

And in just the same way the experience of every one of us is bound up with that of Adam. And because of this, we are all involved in Adam's sin. And by being born "in Adam," we receive from him all that he became as a result of his sin. We derive our existence from him. And because his became a sinful life, one which paid forward a sinful nature, the nature which we derive from him is also sinful.

So, as we have said, the trouble is in our heredity, not in our behavior!

Unless we can change our parentage, there is no deliverance for us. **Unless we were to die, effectually ending our lives, and then somehow be born again in order to secure anew our parentage in birth through another, there can be no escape for us from our heredity.**

But it is in this very direction that we will find the solution of our problem, for that is exactly how God has dealt with it.

PAUSE to PONDER

- Can you relate to my self-evaluation for most of my Christian life?

  I figured I had been redeemed spiritually for all of eternity, but I was still imprisoned in this body of flesh. As a consequence, what lay ahead was going to continue to be the ongoing, lifelong challenge of bringing my old flesh into alignment with my new life–and I was going to change into who Christ wanted me to become...one way or another!

- If the above picture of self-government epitomizes your walk as a Christian as it did mine, please, for both God's sake and yours, RUN–don't walk–to the next three chapters!

Chapter 44

As In Adam, So In Christ[88]

In Romans 5:12-21 we are not only told something about Adam; we are told also something about the Lord Jesus. "As through the one man's disobedience the many were made sinners, even so through the obedience of the One shall the many be made righteous." In Adam, we receive everything that is of Adam; in Christ we receive everything that is of Christ.

The terms "in Adam" and "in Christ" are too little understood by Christians. But building upon the illustration I posed in the previous chapter pertaining to our heredity as a person, let's look at what Romans is teaching us in this section of verses. Because through it we are presented with a new, hope-filled possibility!

Please follow this prospect, worthy of its own chapter herein. Let it be a pivot-point in your contemplation.

In Adam, as we just agreed, all was lost. Through the disobedience of one man, we were all constituted sinners. By him, sin entered. By him, death also entered–and throughout the human race, sin has reigned unto death from that day on.

But now a ray of light is cast upon the scene. Through the obedience of Another we may be constituted righteous. Where sin abounded, grace did much more abound, and as sin reigned unto

---

[88] I once again take most of these next sections' content from Nee's book, The Normal Christian Life. My objective herein, however, is to write upon only the most key elements which helped me gain a knowledge of what Paul was teaching us in Romans and which began to light up the eyes of my individual soul toward a recognition of my newness in Christ. His word for word exposition I could never improve so I have quoted him at length through much of what follows, beginning on page 20 in said book.

death, even so may grace reign through righteousness unto eternal life by Jesus Christ our Lord (Romans 5:19-21). Our despair is in Adam; **our hope is in Christ!**

Chapter 45

The Divine Way of Deliverance

God clearly intends that our consideration of Romans 5:12-21 should lead to our practical deliverance from sin. Paul makes this quite plain when he opens chapter 6 of his letter. In it, he questions whether we should continue in our sin, and his recoiling response is "God forbid!" He queries rhetorically how a holy God could ever be satisfied to have unholy, sin-fettered children (Romans 6:1-2). So, it is Paul's assumptive conclusion at this point that God has surely therefore made adequate provision that we should be set free from sin's dominion.

But here is our problem. We were born sinners; how then can we cut off our sinful heredity? Seeing that we were born in Adam, how can we get out of Adam?

Let me readily remind us that the Blood cannot take us out of Adam. **There is only one way. Since we came in by birth, we must go out by death.**

To do away with our sinfulness we must do away with our life. Bondage to sin came by birth; deliverance from sin comes by death– and it is just this way of escape that God has provided. Death, then, is the secret of emancipation.

So, read the essence of Romans 6:2 again and rejoice not only in what you have known all your life, but also in that which is hopefully now, through the progressive logic of the scriptures, bringing a new smile to your face!

...How can we who died to sin still live in it? – **Romans 6:2b**

We...YOU(!)...died to sin.

But how can we die? Some of us have tried very hard to get rid of this sinful life, but we have found it most tenacious. What is the way out? It is not by trying to kill ourselves, but by recognizing that God has already *dealt with us in Christ*. This is summed up for us in the apostle's next statement: "All we who were baptized into Christ Jesus were baptized into his death" (Romans 6:3).

But if God has dealt with us "in Christ Jesus," then we have as big a problem as before. How are we to "get into" Christ? Here again God comes to our help.

We have, in fact, no way of getting in; but, what is more important, we need not try to get in, for we *are* in. What we could not do for ourselves, God has done for us. *He has put us into Christ.*

Let me remind you of I Corinthians 1:30.[89] Nee says he thinks it is one of the best verses in the whole of the New Testament: "Ye are in Christ." How? "Of Him (that is, 'of God') are ye in Christ." Praise God!

Do you see it is not left to us either to devise a way of entry, or to work it out? We need not plan how to get in. God has planned it; and he has not only planned it but he has also performed it. "Of *Him* are ye in Christ Jesus." We are in; therefore, we need not try to get in. It is a divine act, and it is accomplished.

Now if this is true, certain things will follow. Just as we agreed our lives are bound up in the ones who came before us, so this is true of our new life being "in Christ." When the Lord Jesus was on the Cross, all of us died—not individually, for we had not yet been born—but, being in him, we died in him. "One died for all, therefore all died" (2 Cor. 5:14). When he was crucified, all of us were crucified there with him.

Let me try to illustrate this remarkable concept that we, being in him, shared in his experience when he died, remembering that God himself has placed us in Christ.

A few years back, I created a training video for new school bus drivers. When someone orders one of my training DVDs on the internet from, say Ft. Collins, Colorado, I fill the order from home by inserting the disk into a large envelope and sealing it. Then, I do something with the envelope. I post mark it and, walking it out to the mailbox in front of my house, mail it to Ft. Collins, Colorado. I do not post mark the disk, but the disk has been put into the envelope.

---

[89] If you do not have your Bible in front of you, opening to every one of these passages, you aren't yet serious. *Get* serious and turn to I Corinthians now and join me!

So then, where is the disk? Can the envelope go to Colorado and the disk remain here in the mailbox in front of my house? No! Where the envelope goes the disk goes. If I were to drop the envelope in the trash, the disk would go there too. And were I to quickly take it out again, I would recover the disk also. Whatever experience the envelope goes through the DVD goes through with it, for it is still there in the envelope.

"Of him are ye in Christ Jesus." The Lord God himself has put us in Christ, and in his dealing with Christ, God has dealt with the whole race. Our destiny is bound up with his. What he has gone through we have gone through, for to be "in Christ" is to have been identified with him in both his death and resurrection.

He was crucified: then what about us?

Must we ask God to crucify us? Never! When Christ was crucified we were crucified; and his crucifixion is past, therefore ours cannot be future.

I challenge you to find one text in the New Testament telling us that our crucifixion is in the future. All references to it are in the Greek *aorist*, which is the "once-for-all" tense, the "eternally past" tense (See Romans 6:6, Galatians 2:20, 5:24, 6:14).

No, God does not require us to crucify ourselves. We were crucified when Christ was crucified, for God put us there in Him. That we have died in Christ is not merely a doctrinal position; it is an eternal and indisputable fact!

PAUSE to PONDER

- As one who has asked Jesus to forgive your sins and come into your life, please take at least one day to dwell upon the following before continuing in this book: I have died in Christ. The *real* me has died in Christ–approximately 2000 years ago. My sin *nature* has been dealt a deadly blow, never to return.
- Sincerely and intellectually take time to think about what this means for your life from this day forward. Then, ask the Holy Spirit to illuminate your conscience mind with its reality.
- Meditate on Romans 6:6, Galatians 2:20, 5:24 & 6:14.

Chapter 46

His Death and Resurrection – Representative and Inclusive

The unique nature of our having died in Christ through the Cross stands in contrast to what we learned earlier about his shed Blood. For unlike the shedding of his Blood as sufficiency for the Father, in his death on the Cross he *included you and me*. The Lord Jesus, when he died on the Cross, shed his Blood, thus giving his sinless life to atone for our sin and to satisfy the righteousness and holiness of God. To do so was the prerogative of the Son of God alone. No man could have a share in that.

The Scripture has never told us that we shed our blood with Christ. In his atoning work before God, he acted alone; no other could have a part. But the Lord Jesus did not die only to shed his Blood; he also died that *we* might die. He died as *our* Representative. In his death he included *you and me*.

Yes, the death of the Lord Jesus is inclusive.

Similarly, the resurrection of the Lord Jesus is, alike, also inclusive. And so there is yet one further, glorious implication of our being included in Christ we must bring to the forefront of our minds and hearts as well.

It is in light of this Truth that the end of I Corinthians speaks both of Christ as "the last Adam" and, too, as "the second man." Follow me here. Scripture does not refer to him as the second Adam, but as "the last Adam"; nor does it refer to him as the last Man, but as "the second man." The distinction is to be noted, for it contains a truth of great value.

As the last Adam, Christ is the sum total of humanity; as the second Man, he is the Head of a new race—one we joined *the moment we placed our trust in him* for our salvation. So we have here not just one, but two unions—the one relating to his death and the other to his resurrection.

In the first place, his union with our unredeemed race as "the last Adam" began historically at Bethlehem and ended at the cross and the tomb. In it he gathered up into himself all that was in Adam and took it to judgment and death.

In the second place, our union with him as "the second man" begins in resurrection and ends in eternity—which is to say, it never ends – for, having done away with the first man in whom God's purpose was frustrated, Jesus rose again as Head of a new race of men, in whom that purpose shall be fully realized!

And, glory upon glory to God the Father, Jesus the Son and the Holy Spirit who all worked together to make our rebirth possible, we have already been born into this new race of men—the *moment* we believed and truly surrendered into Him!

When, therefore, the Lord Jesus was crucified on the cross, he was crucified as the last Adam. All that was in the first Adam was gathered up and done away with in Him. We were included there! It is not our ability to emotionally relate to this fact that makes it so, but merely that it has been done.

As the last Adam, he wiped out the old race; as the second Man, he brings in the new race. What's more, it is in his resurrection that he stands forth as the second Man, and there, too, we are included. "For if we have become united with him by the likeness of his death, we shall be also by the likeness of his resurrection" (Romans 6:5).

Oh, how I pray that the scriptures are coming to life for you! Is God trustworthy? Then what He tells us is true about us is also trustworthy.

As ones who have trusted in Christ for our salvation, we have not only been firstly redeemed unto God through the Blood, but we have secondly *died* to sin through our having been put into Christ, a result of his work on the Cross! This is what gives us free passage into our newness of life, our having become a truly new creation (2 Corinthians 5:17) with a new heart (Ezekiel 36:26-27; 11:19-20) to serve God.

This is an absolutely staggering and life-changing bit of news for us as believers in Jesus—if we but grasp it with the help of the Holy Spirit's work in our life.

To review then, when we trusted in Jesus Christ to forgive our sins, generating within us a newly formed, right standing with God the Father, we, at that moment, were asked to live in a new reality—namely, that of our historic death in Jesus Christ as *the* last Adam, and into the life we now live in him as the second Man. The Cross is thus the mighty act of God which traverses us from Adam to Christ.

So, in light of all of this, take a moment to pause—take a deep breath.

It is at this critical juncture that I need to ask you a very important question.

Have you *truly* surrendered your will to the will of God in your life? If you are not positive, please do so today.

There is no magic formula—only a genuine brokenness and receptivity to the truth of our access to God through his son Jesus Christ. If the weight of these truths we have been discussing has burdened your heart, give Jesus your life. Now.

And if this is the case, it has come only because God, in his sovereign will, has given you the ability to come to him today with all of your baggage. He is ready to lift the weight from your shoulders. He *is* freedom. He *is* life. Give your life to Him—He is able to make something beautiful out of the mess we bring to Him.

Time is marching on, and I believe the return of the Savior and Judge of the world is near. Please do not delay. *Please let go.*

If, right now, you are wondering how to let go of your life, and how to let God put you into his Son for eternal life, let's briefly look at what John says to us in I John 5:12—because John gives us our clear view of how we can know we have the life of God in us!

> ¹² *Whoever has the Son has life; whoever does not have the Son of God does not have life.* – **I John 5:12**

In other words, you can *know* that you have eternal life if you *have* the Son of God.

So the question you need to ask yourself, regardless of whether you have grown up in the church all of your life or have lived a thoroughly sinful, God-rejecting life is this; **how do I *have* the Son of God in order to have a forgiven and eternal life?** John again does us the favor of making this clear in the Gospel of John, Chapter 1 and verse 12.

> ¹² *But to all who did receive him, who believed in his name, he gave the right to become children of God.* – **John 1:12**

Simply put, you must *receive* Jesus Christ to have the Son of God. What does receiving Jesus Christ look like?

It is as simple as asking Jesus to come inside you, to indwell you, to live in you by his Spirit. By childlike faith, you invite him in. Jesus said in John 14:20, that He will be *in* you. Conversely, the apostle Paul writes in Romans 8:9, *"Anyone who does not have the Spirit of Christ does not belong to him."* This is why Paul appealed to the Corinthians to make sure that Jesus was *in them*, according to 2 Corinthians 13:5.

So – have you asked Jesus to be your Savior?

To *have* the Son and gain eternal life, you simply ask Jesus Christ to come *into* you. You do not attain forgiveness of your sins or gain eternal life with God by doing good things, going to church, being on an elder board at your church (Ephesians 2:9), calling yourself a Christian or even by confessing your sin(s) to a priest or pastor. These things would indicate that Jesus didn't need to die on the cross for you, because you are saying that you believe you will gain heaven through some, even part, of what *you* do.

So, again, my question to you is, have you asked Jesus to come *into* you?

If you have not, and if you want to be sure that if you were to die tonight you would wake up in heaven and in Jesus' presence, pray right now and invite Jesus Christ to take up residence in you by his Spirit. But in doing so, please know it is not the exactness of the words that matters, but the condition of your heart before God that matters. So if these words mirror the desire of your heart today, just pray these words to God with me now–life is about to change for you forever!

> Father God, I believe you are there. I believe Jesus Christ is your son. I understand that Jesus Christ died on the cross for my sin. I recognize that when I ask you to forgive me for my sins, based on Christ's sacrificial death for me, when I die my sins will not keep me out of heaven. Though I deserve eternal separation from you, you tell me in your word that by believing in the Son, I will receive eternal life. I receive this gift of grace because Jesus paid the penalty for my wrongdoing. Thank you. Spirit of Christ, come into me and take up residence in me. Live your life in me.

When you sincerely pray like this, not only do you receive eternal life, you receive the Spirit of Christ to live in you. In addition, unique and personal things will start happening as you continue to seek to obey him in your new, reborn life as a child of God.

Now because you are gaining a better, even personal, understanding of the powerful antidotes of the Blood and his Cross over the diseases of our sins and our sinful heredity, the honest truth is that we soon find ourselves longing for these truths to become ours by way of a subjective and personal experience. This, God longs to do in us. But how? How can the intellectual properties of these truths actually become our experience? *This* is what we will endeavor to explore in the *next* section of chapters.

PAUSE to PONDER

- Have you just now asked Jesus to come into your life? If so, I would ask that you act on the next bullets.
- Send me a personal email (greg@twsuproject.org), briefly telling me your story. I would like very much to correspond with you.
- Call (if recipient is 40+ yrs) or text (if recipient is under 40 yrs) a friend or family member you know who has been praying for this day in your life. Tell him or her that you have asked Jesus to be your Savior and to live His life in you.

CHAPTERS 47-54

THIRD: RECKONING INTO CONFIDENT BELIEF

Chapter 47

The Paths of Progress: Knowing and Reckoning

> I do not know how far I may be able to make myself intelligible about it, for there is nothing new or strange or wonderful and yet, all is new! In a word, "whereas once I was blind, now I see".... I am dead and buried with Christ – aye, and risen too and ascended.... God reckons me so, and tells me to reckon myself so. He knows best .... Oh, the joy of seeing this truth–I do pray that the eyes of your understanding may be enlightened, that you may know and enjoy the riches freely given us in Christ.[90] – **Hudson Taylor**

---

[90] These quotations are from Hudson Taylor and the China Inland Mission [1919] by Dr. and Mrs. Howard Taylor; Chapter 12, "The Exchanged Life."

Prior to the spring of 2012, I would *never* have questioned whether my life was truly in God's hands. But I was wrong to believe it was. I think many of us live the Christian life the way I lived my first 35 years in Christ–living palms up but with fingers securing what he'd given me.

My palms up meant that the life He'd given me was merely an open book, showing Him all that I was *doing*, how I was *performing*, as his ambassador–but not his slave. A slave has no will of his own. A slave cannot say, "No" to his master. A slave does not have the liberty to assess whether abandonment to self on a particular matter is going to be the "right" decision.

I was still 'willing my way through life,' first making decisions with a spreadsheet, thinking somehow my say was still important. Meanwhile, I would then ask my Savior (but not yet my Adonai) to give me wisdom and discernment in my (but not our) planning, *rather than* giving Him the spreadsheet of my life with permission to turn it *completely* upside down–because He would find glory in doing so for his name's sake.

As the Lord began teaching me the practical implications of Romans 6, 7 and 8, I began to discover for myself Watchman Nee's observations–that the conditions of living what God intended to be a normal Christian life were fourfold: **knowing** his truth, **reckoning** upon that truth, **presenting** myself to God, and **walking** in the Spirit–set forth in that order. He was now going to be free to write whatever He wanted to write on the tablet of the rest of my life.

I was no longer to be the designer of my future. I was no longer to live safe. I was no longer to be the American Christian, living as if this were my home, thinking first of provision and only distantly of abandonment. And, make no mistake, it has generated some significant challenges.

I feel more an outcast in some ways than one whom others understand. And how to live in love in the face of these issues, I am not yet completely sure. It is difficult.

What I do know is that I have a *long* way to go in this new life of surrender. What I do know is that, be grieved my soul, I will never reach a place where I satisfactorily love my wife and others with whom I do life. I will always, now, have an expectation to love others in a way that is far greater than my earth-side capacities will facilitate. This is surely a difficult dichotomy of living a normal Christian life–while in the body of flesh. Oh, how I, in this regard, long to be free from the remaining elements of this body of sin I insist on bringing back from the grave at the least appropriate of moments.

And yet, of one other thing I am also sure; through this whole process, I have been made new—not just in historic reality, but now in ever-increasing experience.

Chapter 48

The Path of Progress: Knowing

What Jesus surely intends to be our *normal*, post-ascension, Spirit-filled, Christian life began for me as a very definite, cognitive, analytical understanding of theological facts. But it would not be enough to merely know something *about* the truth. A merely scholarly understanding alone of some important doctrine would only make my mind puff with knowledge. No, I needed something more to accompany it, and I knew it.

Words and knowledge are nothing more than evangelical scholarship without a healthy dose of subjective enlightenment into just what this really means for us, for our souls, for our lives in the flesh in the here and now—not just for all eternity to come.

The challenge, as I saw it, was going to be for the Spirit to help me somehow deeply emote over what these truths meant—and moreover, what "dying in Him" on that cross could really mean for us today, as ones born into newness. It had to become a supernatural transaction, one too few of us have taken the time or energy to allow the Spirit of God to sear into our subjective impressions.

Yes, I knew what I was learning would have to become subjectively, individually, experientially *mine*.

It was time to see if God would be willing to turn this whole bit of who I really am in Christ into a difference-making faith walk. And so it was; over a period of a day or two, there came an opening of the eyes of my heart that only the Holy Spirit could exact upon me—to really *see* what we have in Christ.

What began as an academic understanding became a personal *knowing* of the fact that my first Adam had actually been put asunder. I had to come to it internally, deeply, emotionally and spiritually through the eyes of the Spirit within. A merely cerebral learning was about to be a thing of the past. Praise God!

But while it is true that all we need comes to us in Christ, it may seem a bit inadequate in terms of how that alone could so radically recreate our perspective into the Christian life. How does it work its way out to us in this life? How does it become *real in our experience*? These are the questions I was up against.

I want you to follow some thoughts from Romans 6 with me now. And in doing so, ask the Spirit of God to bring it to light within you. But first a thought from Romans 5.

Chapter 5, verse 8 says that Christ died for us. Do you believe that to be true? Do you this day question whether He died? Do you this day question whether your sins were forgiven on that historic day, nearly 2,000 years ago?

When you saw all your sins taken away on the Cross, what did you do?

Did you say, "Lord Jesus, please come and die for my sins?"

No, you did not pray in the form of request at all; you only thanked the Lord. You didn't plead with Him to come and die for you, for you realized that He had already done so! Right? Do you follow me?

Well what is true of your forgiveness is also true of your deliverance from yourself—your old Adam. The work is done. There is no need to pray for our death, but only to praise. In his death we all died says Romans 6:1-11. And none of us can really progress spiritually without seeing this—not academically, but in absolute belief and self-awareness.

Again I ask you, do you believe in the death of Christ? Of course you do.

But the same Scripture that says He died *for* us, says also that we died *with* Him. Look at it again: "Christ died for us" (Romans 5:8). That is the first statement, and that is clear enough, yes? But, then, is this any less clear? "Our old man was crucified with Him" (Romans 6:6). "We died with Christ" (Romans 6:8). Read it in *your* Bible!

When are we crucified with Him?

What is the date of our old man's crucifixion and death?

Is it tomorrow? Yesterday? Today?

If Christ was crucified and we were crucified with Him, then how can our death be historically any *less* real than our Savior's?

This truth must indwell us as a prerequisite to our gaining any further traction in our walk with Jesus. *Stick with me here.*

Why do you believe the Lord Jesus died? What are the grounds for that belief? Is it that you *feel* he has died? No, you have never felt it. Anyway, emotions can be unreliable at best. You believe it because the Word of God tells you so.

When the Lord was crucified, two thieves were crucified at the same time. You do not doubt that they were crucified with him either, because the Scripture says so quite plainly.

So, you believe in the death of Jesus and you also believe in the death of the thieves with him. Now what about your own death? Your crucifixion is actually more intimate than was theirs! They were merely crucified at the same time as the Lord–and on different crosses. But you were crucified on the same cross as He, for remember, you were in Him when He died!

How can you know? You can know for the one very sufficient reason that God has said so. It does not depend on your feelings.

If you *feel* Christ has died, *He has died*; and if you *do not* feel that He has died, *He has died*. If you feel that you have died, you have died; and if you do not feel that you have died, you have nevertheless just as surely died.

These are divine facts. We must get used to living in the light of the divine as being every bit as real and true for us as the chair on which you are sitting or the road over which you are driving as you listen to these words.

Get this!

That Christ has died is a fact. That the two thieves have died is a fact. That you have died also **is a fact**.

Let me tell you, *you have died*! You are done with! You are ruled out! The self you loathe was on the Cross in Christ. And "he that is dead is freed from sin" (Romans 6:7). This is the Gospel for Christians! Oh, rejoice in this my friend!

And think about this as well. God's way of deliverance is altogether different from man's way. Man's way is to try to suppress sin by seeking to overcome it; God's way is to remove the sinner.

But we too infrequently realize this was God's intention. Rather, many Christians mourn over their weakness, thinking that if only they were stronger, all would be well.[91]

The idea that *"because failure to lead a holy life is due to our impotence, and that something more is therefore demanded of us,"*

---

[91] I vetted this out more extensively in a separate writing, but elected not to include it here. You can find it in Appendix A.

leads naturally to this false conception of the way of deliverance.

If we are preoccupied with the power of sin and with our inability to meet it, then we naturally conclude that to gain the victory over sin we must have more power. "If only I were stronger," we say, "I could overcome my violent outbursts of temper," and so we plead with the Lord to strengthen us that we may exercise more self-control.

But this is altogether a fallacy; this is not Christianity!

God's means of delivering us from sin is not by making us stronger and stronger, but by making us weaker and weaker.

That sure is a rather peculiar way of victory, you say; but it is the divine way. God sets us free from the dominion of sin, not by strengthening our old man, but by crucifying him; not by helping him to do anything but by removing him from the scene of action.

Says Tozer,

> Jesus came to bring an end to self; not educate it or polish it, but put an end to it. Not cultivate it, give it a love for Bach, Plato and Da Vinci, but to bring an end to self. This position pronounces a death sentence on everything related to self or the ego. The Apostle Paul set the standard when he said, "not I, but Christ," Galatians chapter 2 verse 20. The "I" must be eliminated in its entirety for Christ to hold his rightful position in our lives.[92]

For years maybe, you have tried fruitlessly to exercise control over yourself. Perhaps this is still your experience; but when once you see the truth Paul is teaching us in Romans 6, you will recognize that you are indeed powerless to do anything–but that in setting *you* aside altogether, *God* has done it all. Such a discovery brings human striving and self-effort to an end.

I will never forget when the concept of the previous several paragraphs really hit the depths of my soul–so that I unconditionally *knew* the extent of our being historically and factually removed from the scene. These are truths with which I would have shaken my head in agreement for most of the years of my walk with Jesus, but I didn't really *understand* them. I had never really had a personal revelation from the Spirit to *know* of how God's way of deliverance could and should practically play out in my life.

But when he helped me get ahold of these truths and drove them into my spirit, it provided the way to be free from a life of striving. And its impact is still changing me today. It was a truth as

---

[92] Tozer, The Crucified Life; Part 4, Chapter 13

practically real as the truth I'd been more acquainted with—that my sins had been forgiven. And this is a perfect segue to what came next. Let's walk through it together now.

Regarding this truth I had more easily come to grasp in my own life, that my sins were and are forgiven through His work on the Cross, let me ask *you* this question.

How do *you know* your sins are forgiven?

You do know this, don't you—to such an extent that you'd be willing to *die* for this knowledge? Is it because your pastor told you so? No, you just *know* it.

If I ask you how you know, you simply answer, "I know it!" Such knowledge comes by divine illumination. It comes from the Lord himself.

Of course, the fact of forgiveness of sins is in the Bible, but for the written Word of God to become a living Word from God to you, he had to give you "a spirit of wisdom and revelation in the knowledge of him" (Eph. 1:17).

In order for you to entrust your life into His care, what you needed was to know Christ in that way…in a subjective, personal, revealed only from God, kind of way.

And just as your salvation from sin unto life in Christ was revealed to you, it is always a similar process which would seem to move us into any new apprehension of Christ…when you know it in your own heart—when you "see" it in your spirit. It happens when a light has shined into your inner being, and you are wholly persuaded of some fact.

And so, I have come to believe that what is true of the forgiveness **of** our sins is no less true of our deliverance **from** sin. This is why Paul can say that we have been *set free from sin* and have become slaves to righteousness (Romans 6:18). Do you see it?

And in this passage from Romans, Paul makes everything depend upon such a discovery.

> *Knowing this, that our old man was crucified with him, that the body of sin might be done away, that so we should no longer be in bondage to sin.* - **Romans 6:6**

For me, there was an absolute point in time when what Paul is trying to teach us in Romans finally hit its mark in my mind *and* heart. It was a 30-45 minute window, actually—as if the Lord were turning on a light with a dimmer switch, kept low initially, but then slowly turning it up until it had a brilliance sufficient for its full weight to detonate into the plane of my awareness–my emotional, experiential, *knowing* world.

It just so happened to begin as I was looking out a hotel window in Pennsylvania–at a row of pines, the hotel's attempt at buffering our view of the nearby highway, and its illumination continued as I listened over and over to the Spirit's replay of what I'd been learning. And it continued while walking a distance of about one mile–to a Walmart where I purchased a light blue, long sleeve, half-zipper, pullover sweatshirt.

As I looked at the underpass I was again about to walk beneath on my return to the hotel, I remember tearing up with an experiential *sense* that I really *had* died that day on the cross…and *was* made new. I don't know that I will *ever* forget that moment…that afternoon. Those are not things we can manufacture, but are purely merciful acts of God's grace.

And for me, it began with an accurate understanding of what the Blood and the Cross mean for our lives as ones forgiven and remedied unto God.

When once the light of God dawns this distinction and its real, historic and yet very personal meaning upon your heart, as with any new Truth from his Word, you *see* yourself **in** the story. **In** the Truth. **In** Christ. And suddenly you find yourself swept away with a completely new sense of its reality to you. Personally. Actually. Experientially. And it changes you. You cannot be the same.

It is not now because someone has told you, and not merely because Romans 6 says so. It is something more even than that. You know it because God has revealed it to you by his Spirit. You may not feel it; you may not understand it; but you *know* it, for you have seen it. Once you have seen yourself in Christ on that day at Calvary, nothing can shake your assurance of that blessed fact.

This is *not* the case with merely an academic knowledge of something. **It** doesn't change you. It merely becomes part of your knowledge bank. And I am convinced–utterly convinced, that we can be some measure of a Christ follower with a cerebral acquisition of information *about* him while not experiencing what God intended us to possess by way of power and authority of the Spirit's life within. I think many of us are living, satisfied and pacified, with well less than what God really intended for us as ones born anew **into** his Son.

What I've found is that as we discover Spirit-revealed Truths, acknowledging them as facts from God of our condition, position or place as his children, our *reckoning of these Truths begins* the marvelous, Spirit-infused process of these Truths actually becoming our *experience*—not merely our academic understanding.

But we must not be misled by any other source of today's relative and substitutional truth through this process. Truth is not for us to create as we see fit, or to strive for as merely "an experience." This would be a dangerous mistake—were we to try to create such an encounter. There can be no newness of life found any other way than through the One who *is* the Truth.

Dietrich Bonhoeffer reminds us of this in a single sentence within the pages of his book, The Cost of Discipleship. He says,

> He himself [Jesus] *is* the way—the narrow way, and the straight gate.

He then goes on to say,

> He and He alone is our journey's end. When we know that, we are able to proceed along the narrow way through the straight gate of the cross and on to eternal life. And the very narrowness of the road will increase our certainty. The way which the Son of God trod on earth, and the way which we too must tread as citizens of two worlds on the razor edge between this world and the kingdom of heaven, could hardly be a broad way. The narrow way is bound to be right.[93]

If you ask a number of believers who have entered upon the normal Christian life how they came by their experience, some will say "in this way" and some will say "in that." But while the specific experiences that result from our becoming aware of the power of such illumination in each of our individual lives, we must remember that any true experience of value in the sight of God must have its origin in the person and work of the Lord Jesus. That is a crucial test, and a safe one.

Let us, therefore, not seek out experience for the sake of experience alone. For in doing so, we are picking up our old man, and have not let God be God. He knows what we need. Ours is the responsibility of surrender—true, broken, daily, moment-by-moment release of ourselves, our lives, through the grace of God.

Continuing on this very important theme of our receiving a new understanding from the Lord Jesus Christ about the nature of his finished work on the cross being a game changer for us in living lives pleasing to and in communion with Him, it matters less how, exactly,

---

[93] Dietrich Bonhoeffer, The Cost of Discipleship; Page 191

we come to such an awareness, than the fact that its full impact become impressed upon us.

For example, and to clarify what I mean, consider the following.

When Hudson Taylor, the founder of the China Inland Mission, entered into what we're calling the normal Christian life, it was in the following way that he did so.

If you've read any of the accounts of his spiritual life, you remember how he tells of his long-standing problem of how to live "in Christ"– how to draw the sap out of the Vine into himself. He knew that he must have the life of Christ flowing out through him, and yet felt that he had not gotten it, though he saw clearly enough that his need was to be found *in* Christ.

"I knew," he said, writing to his sister from Chinkiang in 1869, "that if only I could abide in Christ, all would be well, but I *could not.*"

The more he tried to get in, the more he found himself slipping out, so to speak, until one day light dawned, revelation came, and he saw.

> Here, I feel, is the secret: not asking how I am to get sap out of the Vine into myself, but remembering that Jesus is the Vine–the root, stem, branches, twigs, leaves, flowers, fruit, all indeed.

Then, quoting a friend's words that had helped him, he continues:

> I have not got to *make* myself a branch. The Lord Jesus tells me I *am* a branch. I am *part of him*–and I have just to believe it and act upon it. I have seen it long enough in the Bible, but I believe it now as a living reality.

It was as though something which had indeed been true all the time had now suddenly become true in a new way to him personally, and he writes to his sister again:

> I do not know how far I may be able to make myself intelligible about it, for there is nothing new or strange or wonderful–and yet, all is new! In a word, "whereas once I was blind, now I see" . . . . I am dead and buried with Christ – aye, and risen too and ascended . . . . God reckons me so, and tells me to reckon myself so. He knows best . . . . Oh, the joy of seeing this truth–I do pray that the eyes of your understanding may be enlightened, that you may know and enjoy the riches freely given us in Christ.[94]

Oh, it is a great thing to see that we are in Christ! Think of the bewilderment, illustrates Nee, of trying to get into a room in which you already are! Think of the absurdity of asking to be put in! If we recognize the fact that we *are* in, we make no effort to enter. If we have more revelation, we should have fewer prayers and more praises. Much of our praying for ourselves is just because we are blind to what God has done.

Nee remembers one day in Shanghai, talking with a brother who was very exercised concerning his spiritual state. He said, "So many are living beautiful, saintly lives. I am ashamed of myself. I call myself a Christian and yet when I compare myself with others, I feel I am not one at all. I want to know this crucified life, this resurrection life, but I do not know it and see no way of getting there."

Another brother was with them, and the two of them had been talking for about two hours, trying to get the man to see that he could not have anything apart from Christ, but without success.

> The man said, "The best thing a man can do is to pray."
>
> Nee and his friend then asked this brother, "But if God has already given you everything, what do you need to pray for?"
>
> "He hasn't," the man replied, "for I am still losing my temper, still failing constantly; so I must pray more."
>
> "Well," Nee and his friend said, "do you get what you pray for?"
>
> "I am sorry to say that I do not get anything," the man replied.

They tried to point out to the man that, just as he had done nothing for his justification [forgiveness for sins and a right standing before God], so he need do nothing for his sanctification [purification and freedom from sin].

> Just then, tells Nee, a third brother, much used of the Lord, came in and joined in on the conversation. There was a thermos flask on the table, and this brother picked it up and said, "What is this?"

---

[94] These quotations are from Hudson Taylor and the China Inland Mission [1919] by Dr. and Mrs. Howard Taylor; Chapter 12, "The Exchanged Life."

"A thermos flask."

"Well, you just imagine for a moment that this thermos flask can pray, and that it starts praying something like this: 'Lord, I want very much to be a thermos flask. Wilt thou make me to be a thermos flask? Lord, give me grace to become a thermos flask. Do please make me one!' What will you say?"

"I do not think that even a thermos flask would be so silly," their friend replied. "It would be nonsense to pray like that; it *is* a thermos flask!"

Then this brother said, "You are doing the same thing. God in times past has already included you in Christ. When he died, you died; when he lived, you lived. Now today you cannot say, 'I want to die; I want to be crucified; I want to have resurrection life.' The Lord simply looks at you and says, 'You *are* dead! You *have* new life!' All your praying is just as absurd as that of the thermos flask. You do not need to pray to the Lord for anything; you merely need your eyes opened to see that he has done it all."

That is the point, writes Nee in light of the book of Romans,

"We need not work to die, we need not wait to die; we *are* dead. We only need to recognize what the Lord has already done and praise him for it." Light dawned for that man. With tears in his eyes he said, "Lord, I praise thee that thou hast already included me in Christ. All that is his, is mine!" Revelation had come, **and faith had something to lay hold of**!

And this is precisely the point I am trying to make. We can work hard, study, memorize, serve as members on elder boards, and do good things while producing truths from our very lips, but if we have not had the Spirit's illuminating light gain in us an understanding of some truth regarding a matter of God's choosing, then we will have a hard time living in its light!

And in so many words, this is what I had been doing for so many years. I was doing all the work but seldom gaining experiential confidence in my faith because it had little to lay hold of subjectively–only intellectually. And when we live in such a low bar of expectation for the Holy Spirit, we are not living supernaturally, but only clinically, cerebrally.

Oh, how God must ache for us when we pull up so short of the normal Christian life He intended. Oh, how his heart must be saddened by our perpetual struggles in this life when there lies supernatural power, authority, insight and victory just beyond *ourselves*. Oh, how it must displease God when his bought children are satisfied with so little to sustain us spiritually.

We are content with living a Christian life in the knowledge of the trinity, but without implementing the gift of the Spirit's power provided us at Pentecost.

Again, it's like C.S. Lewis' quote I mentioned at some point previously:

> "It would seem that Our Lord finds our desires not too strong, but too weak. We are half-hearted creatures, fooling about with drink and sex and ambition when infinite joy is offered us, like an ignorant child who wants to go on making mud pies in a slum because he cannot imagine what is meant by the offer of a holiday at the sea. We are far too easily pleased."[95]

It is as if we stop short of fully realizing the power and authority living within us as ones possessing the Spirit of the Living God.

But the Cross has gone to the root of our problem. And here I will begin pointing you to, rather than quoting at length from the source of much of this deliberation, Nee's book. Without his book, I would anticipate that much of what comes hereafter will be lost on you.

In your copy of The Normal Christian Life, read the single page beneath his final header in Chapter 3, The Cross Goes to the Root of Our Problem. It is his illustration of what it is like for God to have fundamentally taken care of the *root* problem of our sin nature. It is critically helpful.

As Nee says, "the finished work of Christ really *has* gone to the root of our problem and dealt with it. He has made full provision for sin's rule to be utterly broken."[96]

"Knowing this," says Paul, "that our old man was crucified with him, that the body of sin might be done away, that so we should no longer be in bondage to sin" (Romans 6:6). *"Knowing this!"* Yes, but *do* you know it? "Or are ye ignorant?" (Romans 6:3, ASV).

Oh, may the Lord graciously open our eyes.

---

[95] C.S. Lewis, The Weight of Glory
[96] Nee, The Normal Christian Life; Chapter 3, Page 35

Chapter 49

The Path of Progress: Reckoning

At this point, I was big time ready to move on in what the Lord Jesus was teaching me. I was so gripped with the **knowing**, there was little chance of diverting my attention from **reckoning**, the second of Nee's four steps of analysis *from Romans*.

In order to get to the **presenting** of myself unto God and then **walking** in the Spirit as God had intended, I wanted first to see what Paul had to teach me about how he desired that we reckon ourselves before God in the light of what I now knew.

But, in all honesty, I couldn't help but wonder how or for what purpose a mere repetition of "reckoning" was going to be important. I was soon to find out that it was important for the sufficient reason that God asked us to do it–and He has purpose in everything he requires of us!

Enter chapter 4, The Path of Progress: Reckoning, in your newly purchased book, The Normal Christian Life,[97] where Nee quickly clears up some of what were my mistaken assumptions about the role such reckoning is to play in our Christian life.

---

[97] For the audio book, go to Audible.com. For the hard cover book, go anywhere–just get it. For my preferred version, go either here: https://tinyurl.com/y8egoe8j or here: https://tinyurl.com/y83gb6n4, Then, continue with this reading. If you do not own a Bible, the most important and absolutely critical book, inspired by God to bring you Truth which can transform unlike *any* other because it is a living, supernatural text, what are you waiting for? Beg, borrow or….well, don't steal one. Just get one and always line up what man teaches with God's transformative Word.

> *Reader Note:*
>
> **At this point, I wish to pick up the pace so that the remainder of this book will look more like a tutorial study guide.** I intend this for two reasons: **The first reason** is to drive you personally into both Nee's book and the book of Romans. I badly want you to pan for your own gold. **The second reason** is to keep this book, containing recollections of my personal path of progress, moving in the direction of highlights which I pray will not only remind me of God's faithful and new in-breaking, but may also thoughtfully give a more loosely tethered framework to you, the reader, around which you may ponder such poignant truths as the Spirit leads *you* onward as well. Have your Bible and Nee's short book handy going forward.

God's Word makes it clear that the *knowing* of our personal history in Christ is a crucial first step, *and that it is to precede reckoning*. God is also then equally clear in telling us to *reckon* upon such truth–that there is a very important role for this practice as well which helps to clear the way for our ongoing progress.

Note that Romans 6:6: *"Knowing this, that our old man was crucified with him"* comes first in Paul's delivery of this chapter. Only thereafter does he, in Romans 6:11, give us our next command: *"Even so, reckon ye also yourselves to be dead unto sin."* That is the order.

Again, God's Word makes it clear that 'knowing' is to precede 'reckoning.' "Knowing this...reckon." The sequence is most important. Our reckoning, as Nee here reminds us by looking directly into this 6th chapter of Romans, must be based firstly on [our] knowledge of divinely revealed fact. If the Spirit has not branded our personal experience with our *knowing* what He says to be true about us, then our faith has no foundation on which to rest. However, if we *know*, then we *reckon* spontaneously.

But in discussing this matter, we should not over-emphasize reckoning.

Says Nee,

> People are always trying to reckon without knowing. They have not first had a Spirit-given revelation of the fact; yet they try to reckon, and soon they get into all sorts of difficulties. When temptation comes, they begin to reckon furiously: "I am dead; I am dead; I am dead!" but in the very act of reckoning, they lose their temper. Then they say, "It doesn't work. Romans 6:11 is no good." And we have to admit that verse 11 is no good without verse 6.
>
> So it comes to this; that unless we know for a fact that we are dead with Christ, the more we reckon, the more intense will the struggle become, and the issue [result] will be sure defeat.[98]

The secret of there being true value in reckoning, as Paul commands us to do, is first a *new understanding* from the Spirit into the depths of our souls of what is true about us. It is the kind of revelation God desires to do in us—as Paul so clearly prays for on behalf of the believers in Ephesus.

> *I keep asking that the God of our Lord Jesus Christ, the glorious Father, may give you the Spirit of wisdom and revelation, so that you may know him better. I pray also that the eyes of your heart may be enlightened in order that you may know the hope to which he has called you, the riches of his glorious inheritance in the saints.* – **Ephesians 1:17-18**

As the Spirit within us gives "the eyes of [our] hearts," as Paul says, a deeply personal understanding of the truth that we have been most completely dealt with through the death of our old nature in Christ, then our reckoning of such a fact will never again be a halfway, indefinite or vague thing.

It is God who must do this work in and for us. He will do this through his Word and the power of his indwelling Spirit as he opens our eyes to the fact of our union with Christ. *Thereafter*, we can reckon valuably and to great benefit for our ongoing, victorious and theologically accurate walk with the Spirit of God in Truth. **Most simply said, it is not a reckoning *toward* death, but *from* death.**

So what, then, does reckoning mean?

---

[98] Nee, The Normal Christian Life; Chapter 4, Page 38

> **Reader Note:**
>
> In Chapter 4 of your copy of **The Normal Christian Life**, read the page and a half under the header **The Second Step: Even So Reckon...**

In short, and from the Greek, reckoning means doing accounts.

Reckoning is not a matter of wishing something to be so. It is not a form of make believe, but rather an accounting of *what is*. It is taking an inventory of facts for the purpose of recollection.

Reckoning can never make what is untrue, true...in this case that our old man is dismissed from the scene. God tells us to reckon ourselves dead, not that by the process of reckoning we may become dead, but because *we are dead*. He never told us to reckon what was not *a fact*.

So let's put the wraps on this idea in order to move on to our next weighty and very intellectually honest assessment.

While the Spirit's revelation of some truth should lead us to reckoning spontaneously upon that truth he has awakened within us, it is not something God has left to chance, for we must not lose sight of the fact that we are presented with a *command*: "Reckon ye...."

There is a definite attitude to be taken. God asks us to do the account; to put down "I have died," and then to abide by it. Why? Because it is a fact.

When the Lord Jesus was on the cross, I was there in him. Therefore, I reckon it to be true. I reckon and declare that I have died in him. Paul said, *"Reckon ye also yourselves to be dead unto sin, but alive unto God."* How is this possible? "In Christ Jesus." Never forget that it is always and only true *in Christ*.

If you look at *yourself*, you will think death is not there. But it is not a question of a faith in yourself. Rather, it is a recounting of your faith, belief and confidence in *him*–as a matter of historic fact. You therefore look to the Lord and know what he has done. "Lord, I believe *in you*. I reckon upon the fact *in you*."

Stand there all day!

Chapter 50

Temptation and Failure – the Challenge to Faith

This heading, as well as others previous to this, is again from The Normal Christian Life text. But as the Lord was walking me through these truths from the writings of Paul's epistle to the Romans, I remember thinking, "Ok, so what then about the fact that I am *still* tempted by sin in this life? How can my old Adam be dead and yet still seem to haunt me?"

As odd as it may seem, at this point in my learning I remember this sub-title being tremendously reassuring. Was there going to be an answer to the practical, intellectually honest struggle of how my historic death could possibly still *not* have vanquished my struggle with selfishness and pride and any other number of things that presented themselves to my old, dead man?

"Perhaps," I thought, "just as You [Spirit] have now revealed to the eyes of my heart so subjectively and experientially for the first time–that I am dead, you will *now* bring a *similar understanding* to *this* very challenging and real matter of concern as well!"

I clearly recall there was an incredible expectancy growing within me–an increasing confidence in God's provision for our lives as his newly born children...that He was going to have an answer.

I remember thinking, in so many words, "Well what about *this*, Lord? How is it, if my old Adam is dead, that I am *still* undeniably met with periodic failure in the face of the illness that used to plague my old man?"

But I now knew He was going to meet my charge. I just needed to learn of it. And I couldn't read God's words through Paul, and how Nee may help shed light on such truth, fast enough.

In trying to convey how much I was anticipating God's revelation of what was surely to come, I can only come up with this very poor, earth-side comparison...and, unfortunately, an illustration understandable by depreciatingly few people.

On my wedding day, I couldn't shake the thought that what I had imagined, anticipated, and waited and preserved my physical, virgin body for my whole life, was going to present itself in all its experiential beauty and reality before *that very* day came to an end...unless, God forbid, I were to have a heart attack and die–or be killed in some freak car accident that day! I liked my odds.

I was, for the first time, about to experience God's gift of sexual experimentation with the woman of my prayers and dreams–without reservation...and at the request of, and in obedience to, my God!

It was going to be something incomprehensibly new, something so completely fulfilling and life-giving that it was destined to change me forever.

And so it was that the anticipation welling deep inside my soul for the Truths I was surely about to discover was not dislike the heart-pounding, emotionally charged, palm-sweating moment when, on that wedding night, all the bags were set aside and our eyes and hearts pondered the opportunity of the *single* bed which would change our outlook on life for the rest of our lives together on earth.

Maybe a few of you can relate! My anticipation of what God was surely about to reveal to me was not unlike this kind of anticipation. How is yours?

Ok, back to our present reality.... Here was my personal, current "state of the union."

I had, thus far, become deeply appreciative of the two greatest facts in history: that all our sins are dealt with by the Blood, and that we ourselves are dealt with by the Cross.

But what now of this matter of temptation? This is a most key and crucial matter to understand, both theologically and practically.

Building now upon that which we have learned thus far, and now know, Romans has some practical implications for us going forward.

> **Reader Note:**
>
> In Chapter 4 of your copy of **The Normal Christian Life**, beginning directly under the header **Temptation and Failure, the Challenge to Faith**, read a couple pages through the short paragraph which begins, "So it is a question of our choice…." Read and rejoice in the practical implications of the Cross in disposing of ourselves in the face of temptation and sin!

My Cliffs Notes version, which will never do without contemplating and mentally walking through what I just recommended you read in Nee's book as he walks you in and out of passages from Romans, is that our victory over our *appetite for* sinful thoughts and behaviors is what God has met in us.

We learn from Paul that our old self was crucified and "done away with" (Romans 6:6). This "doing away with" of our old body of sin is not one that is teaching us about its annihilation, but rather that it has been "put out of operation," "rendered powerless," or "made ineffective."

In so doing, God has not removed the sin, but has rather removed the sinner. The Cross has disposed of our old man, and so when faced with temptation, we are no longer "employed" to that temptation, but set free from it. Romans 6:7 and 11 imply *deliverance from* a power that is still very present and very real—not from something that no longer exists.

Essentially, while sin is very much out and about, our victory as believers comes in knowing *that the slave who served the old master is now out of reach!*

Thus, we can say that "deliverance from sin" is a more scripturally accurate picture for us than "victory over the presentation of sin," as if to say that somehow sin is completely out of the picture or no longer exists.

And so in our reckoning upon our death as fact, we can rejoice in God's having positioned us no longer as slaves to sin, but as "instruments of righteousness unto God" (Romans 6:13).

Yes, sin is still there, but we are knowing deliverance from its power in increasing measure day by day! The eyes see, but do not lust. The heart observes, but does not covet. In time, we are made free in Christ—we no longer live, but He does the living through us. Oh, the joy of our living in this knowledge!

To some degree, then, it is a matter of where *we* will *choose* to live. I suggest you read that prior sentence again. And again. And again.

Will we live in a lie of Satan—that the power of the Cross was insufficient to gain us victory in this life? Or will we reckon upon, call upon the Truth of, and live in the light of what has become a fact for us—that we are new and no longer slaves to sin?

Will we live in what our physical life sees as the tangible facts of daily experience or will we build our life on the mightier fact that we are now "in Christ?" It is this very building of a new life, born into us by The Truth, that must change *everything* for us. Has it completely changed you yet, dear Christian? If not, cry out to God for it – for this is yours in Christ! Raise the bar of your expectation of the God of the universe, dear friend!

As Nee points out, "the power of his resurrection is on our side, and the whole might of God is at work in our salvation (Romans 1:16), but the matter still rests upon our making real in history what is true in divine fact."[99]

Nee then goes on to do more of what he typically does. Rather than neglecting that which begs to be answered in us, he takes the questions that naturally cry out for an honest and needful answer *and deals with them* head on!

His analysis of how we actually *become in practice that which we know we are* in our new creation, is absolutely brilliant. In doing so, he draws a powerful line between our increasing deliverance from sin, and how it is that this deliverance can come to be real in our lives.

He takes Hebrews 11:1, that "faith is [the] substantiating of things hoped for, [the] conviction of things not seen,"[100] and connects such *substantiation* to *evidence* of our newness in Christ! **It is a terrific hinge point and an eye-opening look at how our increasingly victorious walk with Christ becomes our own proof of the Life within.** Glory to God!

And so because Galatians 4:19 tells us that God's desire is that Christ be formed in us, don't miss studying this below-mentioned section from chapter 4 of Nee's book. At stake is this intellectually honest question—one which *must* be answered in our own minds before we can honestly journey on from this point.

How *do* we *substantiate* something?

---

[99] Nee, The Normal Christian Life; Chapter 4, Page 44
[100] Hebrews 11:1; Darby Translation

The fact is, God has given us the ability to do so every day. We could not, in fact, live in the world *without* doing so.

> *Reader Note:*
>
> In Chapter 4 of your copy of **The Normal Christian Life**, and under the header **Temptation and Failure, the Challenge to Faith**, read from about 2 pages into this section where the paragraph begins with the question: How do we "substantiate" something? Pour over Nee's ruminations thoughtfully through the end of this section. ***Don't miss this!***

PAUSE to PONDER

- If you have made it this far in this book, it is because God has chosen to bring you here–*but you must now do your part*. Now is not the time to be intellectually lazy or let Satan deal the blow of 'task completion' to this experience. FIGHT IT! If, anywhere along the way, your personal experience has not come along for the ride, I plead with you to turn back. Return to where the eyes of your heart blinked shut and things fell dark. Tell the Holy Spirit that you *refuse* to be deterred in your all-out quest for all He has for you–if only He would bring his illumination into your awareness.

- Honestly reflect right now; if anywhere along the way you thought, "I am not gaining a personal enlightenment beyond the words on the page–I must be too dull to get this..." **Please go back**! You are not dull. God is a rewarder of those who seek Him with all their heart. The revival of our nation and the bride of Christ, the Church, rides on an inbreaking of the Holy Spirit. What God wants to deliver into your soulish experience is worth it. Stand on, and read out loud to God, Matthew 7:7-11. If necessary, invest a month in what precedes this page. God is faithful to finish what He has begun in you– Philippians 1:6!

Chapter 51

Abiding in Him

Oh, that God would be made much of as his Spirit helps us internalize what we have just learned.

It is a *huge* thing to be able to regularly reckon upon how Jesus' life is now being lived *in our place*–substitutionally. Once the Spirit of God helps us personally substantiate what it is we believe, it exponentially increases our faith and lifts our confidence in the truth that God is personal, intimate and now *is* our life.

Is there something new coming alive within you based on what the previous paragraph, as well as what the previous fifteen chapters, have been saying? Be honest. We can fool others, but we cannot fool ourselves–nor our God.

If not, I plead with you to STOP now. Go no further. Put this book down.

Rather than plowing onward to 'finish what you started' in this reading, STOP. For if you have merely picked up this book as a task to be completed, or if it has become that for you, its entire writing has been for naught. You have, in fact, completely wasted your time up to this point. The point of God's words and the truths He desires to have remake us into different people are meant to change us.

If your life is too busy right now to wait on God, then it is better to let dust gather on this volume. In fact, if I may be so bold, it is better to also let dust gather on your Bible–than to live a pretending life. If this describes you presently, admit it. God will respond better to your honesty than your self-reliance, self-absorption and shallow living.

Today, God needs men and women who are finished playing games. He *hates* our religious overtones. He hates gaining only a token of our time.

Oh, how I pray we understand the depths of what God is telling us today through Amos 5, verses 21-23. It should make us quake in fear and evaluate ourselves, our motives, our hearts. How God hates the sacrifice of a partially surrendered heart.

> *"I hate, I despise your feasts,*
>   *and I take no delight in your solemn assemblies.*
> *Even though you offer me your burnt offerings and grain offerings,*
>   *I will not accept them;*
> *and the peace offerings of your fattened animals,*
>   *I will not look upon them.*
> *Take away from me the noise of your songs;*
>   *to the melody of your harps I will not listen."*
> **– Amos 5:21-23** (ESV)

Your alternative is to return to the previous chapters, pull out your Bible, get on your knees, and *refuse to go any further* in your walk with Jesus, let alone in this book, until God has met this charge in you through the illuminating power of the Holy Spirit living inside you.

Tell God you refuse to venture any further in the Christian life until He has truly stirred your soul with a newness of understanding of the things covered to this point.

Our God rewards those who seek him with such stubborn hearts. As I wrote at the conclusion of the last chapter, I now say again; Matthew 7:7-11 will gain in you this confidence to wait expectantly on his Spirit–to make, experientially in you, what you may have only known intellectually to this point in your walk with Jesus.[101]

Yes, when God surrenders our heart, mind and soul to the point where we have truly delivered the vehicle of our life into his hands, our experience becomes the substantiation we need to remind us of who we are *in* Christ Jesus.

But if God's Spirit reveals to us our death, resurrection and newness in Jesus as a fact of history, and begins to substantiate this in our life, what then?

---

[101] I have just recently come across a song called Clear the Stage, by Jimmy Needham. He encapsulates what I pray to be the desperation of your heart at this point. Give it a listen.

"What then....," becomes the source of deliverance for our *next* step–into which the rest of our lives may be lived!

Satan knows, as children of the King, we have been eternally stolen from his snarling clutches. But certain as the sun rises from the east and sets toward the west, Satan will, time and time again, work to return our eyes to the body of flesh which houses our *now* new, patterned after the risen Jesus himself, Second[102] Man. And in doing so, his desire will be to choke out our effectiveness as empowered and adopted children of the King, and to minimize the glory God himself will receive throughout our remaining days on this earth.

In other words, Satan's strategy will change. Be ready.

Practically speaking, while we reckon upon the fact that our old Adam *has* died *in Christ* and is now unemployed, Satan will take the *mere presentation of* our old slave, the sinful nature, and work to convince us that we have not *really* been made new at all.

"Why the familiar temptation?" he would like us to wonder. "What about it?" he will say. "There's something moving inside. I thought your old man was dead."

What we need to *know* in these moments is that while the things our fleshly eyes see, and the covetous tendencies to which our heart used to be enslaved *will* revisit us, we *have* just as surely been given over to new ownership–and are *no longer owned by or enslaved to* these old companions.

Instead, we are being continually, moment-by-moment, delivered from them as slaves to righteousness in Christ Jesus our LORD (Romans 6:14, 6:6)!

> *Reader Note:*
>
> For a fun "lighten things up" interlude, give a listen to two older, yet still favorite songs of mine which speak to our newness no longer being enslaved to what will still, nonetheless, present itself to us during our remaining days on earth: **Just A Few of My Old Friends**, by Morgan Cryar, and **Old Man Down**, by the Allies.[103]

---

[102] Though not yet fully redeemed–that final victory will be met when we join Jesus in heaven.

[103] You can find both of these on YouTube. Source: Cryar's album Keep No Secrets, '84 & the Allies' album Long Way From Paradise, '89

How is it, then, that we can be delivered daily unto righteousness and live to gain God the glory and honor due Him? There is only one way. It is by the mighty power made available to us *as we abide in Him*. Apart from Him we can do nothing (John 15:5), but through Him who gives us strength we can do all things (Philippians 4:13).

And how do we gain access to this abiding authority in Him? It is surely now, and will for all our remaining days be, by His accomplished, all-inclusive death and resurrection *apart from us* (Romans 6:6; Ephesians 2:5-6; Colossians 2:10). And we, mind-blowingly, get to participate in the full benefits of the historic work which He, alone, executed–on our behalf and for our deliverance.

Too often, we forget to live in what *is*–rather than what we *feel* is. We make paramount the emotion of our momentary experience and neglect to take the mental walk, if you will, back into what we *know* about whose we are *and in whose power we now gain the victory!*

But if we reckon upon the fact that our old Adam *has been* put asunder, along with the times past, impotent efforts put forth by that *dead* man, we will eventually cease in our efforts to reemploy the tactics *of* that old man to effect deliverance from our sinful nature. For we now know there is no help there.

But if we *take that walk* into our history and *recount, or reckon upon, that from which Christ has set us free*, we will be happy as a clam at high tide to release what we may have once again begun to resurrect from the grave. And in doing so, we will subjectively remember how that old man struggled and struggled and could never meet the adversary's charge.

Then, in joy...in JOY we will turn to the Victor of our soul...and find deliverance. Yes, the Lord Jesus asks us to abide in Him (John 15:4) not because doing so may somehow give us the edge, but because it is the *only* way to effect ongoing deliverance.

We must trade our striving for abiding. Read John 15, verses 1-9 right now.

This abiding is no mere psychological self-talk or deep breathing technique. This abiding is not a deluxe edition of some yoga-like, transcendental meditation. This abiding is not the Christian's version of Buddhism or Hinduism. For if so, then we are merely putting our trust in the vane religion of the world, not a life in Christ Jesus.

No, we must begin to differentiate between living in the attempts of the flesh and living in the Spirit.

To live in the flesh is to do something out from myself. To live in the flesh is to derive strength from the old, natural source of life–the life we inherited from Adam.

But once we are in Christ, in order to enjoy in experience what is true of me as one in Christ, I must learn what it is to walk in the Spirit. This is where the rubber meets the road of our new life as Spirit-filled, Spirit-led followers of Jesus.

It is a historic fact that in Christ my old man was crucified, and it is a present fact that I am blessed with every spiritual blessing in the heavenly places in Christ (Ephesians 1:3). But if I do not live in the Spirit, then my life may be quite a contradiction of the fact that I am in Christ. For what is true of me in Him will not be expressed in me.

May I say it with force here; **it is the very ministry of the Spirit that He may make real in us all that is ours through the finished work of Christ.**

Only as we first give up utilizing the powers of the old man can we exhibit and subjectively know the ongoing deliverance and authority of the Spirit in our daily lives. The cross has been given to *procure salvation for us*; the Spirit has been given to *produce salvation in us*. The difference between our trying and trusting is worlds apart. In Watchman Nee's words, it is the difference between heaven and hell.

This trusting into the Holy Spirit's rule and authority over our lives is not something just to be talked over as a satisfying thought. It is a must-have in stark reality!

"Lord, I cannot do it, therefore I will no longer try to do it."

And this is the point at which most of us fall short. So, let us become accustomed to living in actual practice in this way; "Lord, I cannot. Therefore, I will take my hands off. From now on, I trust thee for that."

We refuse to act. We depend on Him to do so...and then we enter fully and joyfully into the action He initiates.

This abiding in Christ and releasing and refusing to move onward in our own initiative must not be mistaken for passivity. This refusal to act out of our old man does not mean living a do-nothing life. Rather, it is a most active life, trusting the Lord like this–drawing life from Him, taking Him to be our very life, and letting Him live his life in us as we go forward in his name!

Think of it. Our responsibility is to listen and then act. Once we become better practiced in this order of things, we can move with greater confidence and authority than ever before.

Now in this whole matter of reckoning upon our increasing deliverance through the Spirit, I want to make this very important note. Do not confuse this kind of life with a refusal to ever move with practical intention in a direction you already know to be wise.

We are accountable before the Lord Jesus to live not as unwise, but as wise people (Ephesians 5:15). Being ones delivered into the hands of the Holy Spirit, trusting in His provision and not in our own strength, we must not forget that God has also given us the responsibility to work toward obedience as an act of our will.

It is a wonderful thing, this working together with the Lord.

We cannot look at some weakness in our life and say, "Lord, I have released myself into your power to gain deliverance from this, but it continues to dog me. Every time I go home, I drive right past that club–and half the time, I stop in and fall back into that old pattern of sin."

At this point, we have to look ourselves in the mirror and ask a question. "Am I doing all I can to walk in practical obedience, yes, gaining strength from the Spirit, *but also not merely acting like a victim of my circumstances?*"

In such cases, I have a recommendation; go home a different way! Take another exit! Drive an extra five minutes if you must, **but do not label the Spirit impotent while you go on making poor choices.**

Listen to me. We are called to be holy. We do not need to seek God on this matter–ever. And like most things in our lives as followers of Jesus, this is a *choice* we make every day. You will find great help in this direction by reading a book I have included in the Resources Appendix–Jerry Bridges' book, Pursuit of Holiness. I want to emphasize it as a must read.

And so in conclusion of this matter, I want to wrap up this essential teaching of our LORD Jesus with Watchman Nee's thoughts, constructed from John 15.

> "Abide in me, and I in you." This is a double sentence: a command coupled with a promise. That is to say, there is an objective and a subjective side of God's working, and the subjective side depends upon the objective; the "I in you" is the outcome of our abiding in him. We need to guard against being over-anxious about the subjective side of things, and so becoming turned in upon ourselves. We need to dwell upon the objective–"abide in me"–and let God take care of the subjective. And this he has undertaken to do.

...So in our walk with the Lord, our attention must be fixed on Christ. "Abide in me, and I in you" is the divine order. Faith in the objective facts make those facts true subjectively. ...The same principle holds good in the matter of fruitfulness of life: "He that abideth in me, and I in him, the same beareth much fruit" (John 15:5). We do not try to produce fruit or concentrate upon the fruit produced. Our business is to look away to him. As we do so, he undertakes to fulfill his Word in us.

How do we abide? "Of God are ye in Christ Jesus." It was the work of God to put you there, and he has done it. Now *stay* there! Do not be moved back onto your own ground. Never look at yourself as though you were not in Christ. Look at Christ and see yourself in him. *Abide in him.* Rest in the fact that God has put you in his Son, and live in the expectation that he will complete his work in you. It is for him to make good the glorious promise that "sin shall not have dominion over you" (Romans 6:14).[104]

---

[104] Nee, The Normal Christian Life; Chapter 4, Page 51

Chapter 52

Nothing of the Old Can Inherit the New

At this point, it would be good to briefly reckon upon whose you are. In whose kingdom are you citizen? Is yours a dual citizenship? Should it be? These are not intended to be trick questions.

> *Jesus said, "**My kingdom is not of this world**. If it were, my servants would fight to prevent my arrest by the Jewish leaders. But now **my kingdom is from another place**." –* **John 18:36**

> *I will not say much more to you, for **the prince of this world is coming**. He has no hold over me... –* **John 14:30**

> *As for you, you were dead in your transgressions and sins, in which you used to live when you followed the ways of this world **and of the ruler of the kingdom of the air**, the spirit who is now at work in those who are disobedient. –* **Eph. 2:1-2**

> *But seek first **his kingdom** and his righteousness... –* **Matthew 6:33**

> *If you belonged to the world, it would love you as its own. As it is, **you do not belong to the world, but I have chosen you out of the world**. That is why the world hates you. –* **John 15:19**

> *But **our citizenship is in heaven**. And we eagerly await a Savior from there, the Lord Jesus Christ. –* **Philippians 3:20**

These and other references throughout the Bible teach us two things: There are two kingdoms up and running, and there are two citizenships to which we may belong. When we choose to place our trust in Jesus, our life, and thus our citizenship, is transferred over from the world (John 15:19) to a kingdom of another place (John 18:36). As we have already discussed, the act of Christ's death on the cross was the marker point of history which gave us access to a new sphere of promise, and made possible our entry into an eternal kingdom of abundant and everlasting life in the presence of God.

This occurrence brought man access to two, coexisting kingdoms, both running parallel in time. The only matter at stake today is to which kingdom we profess our allegiance.

Here, now, I will doff my cap to Mr. Nee once again as I could never bring the current matter to bear any better. And, once again, we will point you to his work in The Normal Christian Life to have him bring the Word to practical application.

On these two kingdoms, Nee says this:

> The kingdom of this world is not the kingdom of God. God had in his heart a world system–a universe of his creating–which should be headed up in Christ his Son (Colossians 1:16-17). But Satan, working through man's flesh, has set up instead a rival system known in Scripture as "this world"–a system in which we are involved, and which he himself dominates. He has in fact become "the prince of this world" (John 12:31).
>
> Thus, in Satan's hand, the first creation has become the old creation, and God's primary concern is now no longer with that, but with a second and new creation. ...nothing of the old creation...can be transferred to the new. It is a question now of these two rival realms, and of which realm we belong to.
>
> ...God, in redemption, delivered us out of the power of darkness, and translated us into the kingdom of the Son of his love (Colossians 1:12-13). Our citizenship henceforth is *there*.
>
> But in order to bring us into his new kingdom, God must do something new in us. ...Unless we are created anew we can never fit into the new realm. "That which is born of the flesh is flesh"; and "flesh and blood cannot inherit the kingdom of God; neither doth corruption inherit incorruption" (John 3:16; I Corinthians 15:50). ...Our fitness for the new kingdom is determined by the creation to which we belong. Do we belong to the old creation or the new? Are we born of the flesh or of the Spirit? *Our ultimate suitability for the new realm hinges on the question of origin.*[105]

---

[105] Emphasis mine

> ...God wanted to have us for himself, but he could not bring us as we were into that which he had purposed; so he first did away with us by the Cross of Christ, and then by resurrection provided a new life for us. "If any man is in Christ, he is a new creature; the old things are passed away; behold, they are become new" (2 Corinthians 5:17).
>
> ...The greatest negative in the universe is the Cross, for with it God wiped out everything that was not of himself: the greatest positive in the universe is the resurrection, for through it God brought into being all he will have in the new sphere.[106]

And so thanks to Nee's concise evaluation of the Scripture's teaching of these two worlds before us, the old and the new, we now find ourselves "set up" for the playing out of a greater understanding of how our new life in Christ can become the dominant lens into which we live out the rest of our days in this body of flesh.

And the sooner we see that the old cannot inherit the new, thereby denouncing the alternative of a life depicted by the inner turmoil of civil war, the more speedy will be our walk into a life characterized less by self-striving, self-confidence (okay, just less of self-everything), and more by a patient surrender and a daily being made new in the Spirit of God who will be at work within us.

At the same time, greater will become the ache within us to live in light of, and in congruence with, what we now grasp to be true about ourselves; also recognizing what is no longer true about us—about what we have left behind, but yet tend to struggle with—but what has, in fact, been put to *death*!

PAUSE to PONDER
- If you have placed your faith in Jesus, your earth side citizenship is trumped by your Kingdom citizenship. Celebrate the messages of John 15:19 and Philippians 3:20—that God himself has hand-picked you out of this world to inherit the new citizenship of his Kingdom!
- When temptation rears its head, it is opportunity to rehearse your new citizenship and the power of God at work within you!

---

[106] Nee, The Normal Christian Life; Chapter 5, Pages 53, 54, 55

Chapter 53

Remembering Burial Means an End

How many ways can we remind ourselves of our death?

I suppose we can do so in at least as many ways as God gives us to ponder upon its practical living out. For it is God's desire that we have absolutely no remaining doubts about the fact that our old Adam is dead—gone—his end has come as a matter of the past, once for all.

And it is God's desire that we *never* revisit or live in that old man's powerlessness again! How could we? He *is* dead (Romans 6:6-7).

It was about now, in studying and being exposed to still *other* ways the Bible talks to us about our death, that I was beginning to grasp the seemingly continual undercurrent of the value of our meditation upon the fact that our old, first creation man *has died*!

Passages about baptism, for example Romans 6:3-4[107], point to the fact that *we **were** buried*. I suppose you could say that this ongoing theme was starting to give me hope. If it was needful for Paul, I thought, to reckon upon and rehearse this truth in a plethora of variant ways, then my struggle to practically do this new life *without* picking up the tools of *my* deceased, old man was not something so completely unique.

---

[107] *Or don't you know that all of us who were baptized into Christ Jesus were baptized into his death? We were therefore buried with him through baptism into death in order that, just as Christ was raised from the dead through the glory of the Father, we too may live a new life.* – **Romans 6:3-4**

And if both the writer of Proverbs and Peter understood this tendency of the old, rebellious man to, like a dog returning to its vomit[108], pull out the old tricks to remedy the insurmountable dilemma of escaping our old sin nature, then my Lord Jesus could understand my plight!

Moreover, He was giving me ample and repetitive illustrations purposed to help me grasp the finality of what He had done on the Cross! Oh, the measure of grace this realization gave me was eclipsed only by my hunger to grow more into the release and surrender of all I have and am into His infinitely more capable hands.

For example, what is my answer to God's pronouncement of my old creation? Romans 6:4 explains that baptism means burial: *"We were therefore buried with him through baptism into death..."* Therefore, my answer is to ask for baptism. Baptism is, then, the representation that *I have died*!

I have no interest here in arguing the specifics of *how* one is baptized—that is not the point I desire to make here. The point to be made is that we are given baptism as an illustration of what *actually* happened to us when we became surrendered unto the Cross of Christ—it illustrates *burial*. And whom do we bury but one who has died?

"The reason we step down into the water," says Nee, "is that we have recognized that in God's sight, we have already died. ...God's question is clear and simple. Christ has died, and I have included you there."[109]

Now bear with me as I pass along one more short illustration to which we can surely relate. Nee says this about the nature of our burial:

> In China we have two emergency services, a "Red Cross" and a "Blue Cross."
>
> The first deals with those who are wounded in battle but are still alive, to bring them succor and healing; the second deals with those who are already dead in famine, flood, or war, to give them burial.
>
> God's dealings with us in the Cross of Christ are more drastic than those of the "Red Cross." He does not set out to patch up the old

---

[108] *As a dog returns to its vomit, so fools repeat their folly.* – **Proverbs 26:11**; *Of them the proverbs are true: "A dog returns to its vomit," and, "A sow that is washed returns to her wallowing in the mud."* – **2 Peter 2:22**

[109] Nee, The Normal Christian Life, Chapter 5, Page 57

creation. ...God has done the work of crucifixion so that now we are counted among the dead; but we must accept this and submit to the work of the "Blue Cross," by sealing that death with "burial."

Isn't that an outstanding illustration? What I feel we want to do is patch up our old man, make him better—when all the while God has made us a new creation, completely *new*!

Through the death and burial of our old Adam, God has seen to the exit of that man we continually try to improve. For God has not planned that we make amends with our old Adam! May we rather walk in what he *has* done in removing our citizenship from this old world while promoting us into the new world of his Son's victory!

As we said earlier, there are two kingdoms up and running. There is the old world and then there is the new world. Between the two there is a tomb—**a tomb**.

This is the meaning of Romans 6:2 where Paul tells us that: *"We are those who have died to sin; how can we live in it any longer?"*

Oh, dear brother and dear sister, please **stop** trying to prop up your old creation, the one worthy only of eternal destruction. *Why* live subject *to* him any longer? Remember the tomb, wherein which the Scriptures clearly tell us we were adjoined in Christ Jesus, means we, who are given over to Christ for the redemption only He can bring, *have died, been buried*, and *have been raised to newness of life* as new creations!

Chapter 54

Being Joined in Christ Means Resurrection

Here I simply want to point you to the last header in Chapter 5 of The Normal Christian Life text, **Resurrection unto Newness of Life**, which again so eloquently pictures our new health through the resurrection by way of the concept of grafting.

While the absolute completion of our newness will only be accomplished in its full measure when we are ushered into God's presence in the heavenly realms, we are, nonetheless, partakers in the second man of God's creation here and now.

This newness of life is our next step of focus. It is one of great importance since it is where our entire life is now already being lived going forward into eternity.

Romans 6:5 says, *"If we have become united with him by the likeness of his death, we shall be also by the likeness of his resurrection."* Jesus has been brought to Life that we may share in the fullness of that resurrection.

Remember we were conditioned by God to stand in his presence through the Blood. Furthermore, remember we are also made capable of walking delivered from the talons of the old Adam through the work of the Cross. And because these two things are true, the death we long for in order to get to the other side in shared victory with our Lord and Savior is already a thing of the past. We *have* that victory. We *are* more than conquerors (Romans 8:37).

We *must* live as though our death *is* past and we have been resurrected in newness *already*...precisely because we have! He is our deliverance. He is our victory. It is **He** who now lives in us.

> *I have been crucified with Christ **and I no longer live, but Christ lives in me**. The life I now live in the body, I live by faith in the Son of God, who loved me and gave himself for me.* – **Galatians 2:20**

And so if all this be true, how is it that we still struggle to live empowered lives? How is it that we continue to resource ourselves so frequently with the arsenal of our old Adam, working to pull ourselves up with all of the self-hyphens we recounted earlier? How is it that our lives appear to be less empowered by the Spirit and more so empowered by the impotence of what is supposed to have died?

I firmly believe it goes back to a delivery problem—never fully delivering ourselves into His hands. While He has purchased our motorcycle (recall here chapter 27) and has legal right to its use, we still have it in our garage...or maybe sitting just by the curb, by the mailbox, so to speak, waiting for pickup. But remember, too, that God will not take that which desires not to be given over.

And so when all is said, it is *here* we must become dead honest with ourselves.

It is *here* we must consider whether we are breaking God's heart as we quench the Spirit's work within us.

It is *here* we *must* consider whether we have completely presented ourselves to God for his purposes–for *his* Glory alone.

And it is here we will now focus our attention in the next section.

CHAPTERS 55-59

ROUNDING THIRD AND HEADING FOR HOME

Chapter 55

Presenting Ourselves to God

Ok, so I'm not doing such a grand job generating a mere tutorial guide, am I? Some things just *cannot* be given the pink slip. And this introspective consideration of whether we have completely presented ourselves to God for his purposes is one of them.

This introspective contemplation into the extent to which I'd presented myself to God was one of the final nails in my coffin to being willing and able to relinquish everything I thought **I** possessed to a point of *actual* surrender.

In this matter, and in a way only Tozer can communicate, he says this:

> The old self must go, regardless of the cost. In the old self life there is nothing redeemable. No matter how much the old self is cleaned up, it still contains an irredeemable core of corruption. The new man is in Christ, and from now on we must recognize ourselves to

be dead to sin—but alive to God in Jesus Christ. The question that presents itself is, how do we deal with the old self?[110]

In short, we must remember that the old self has already been dealt with and the matter is settled. Once this has become a settled thing in our heart, we are free to present our new man to God to do with us as He pleases.

But how *do* we present ourselves to God? We do so by *letting go* of the knot at the end of our proverbial rope—the one we have been taught to cling to with everlasting endurance. We do so by recognizing we are owned by, enslaved to, a fully worthy God in whom we have an *unreserved* trust. We do so when we can come to Jesus as more than just Savior, but also as Lord, without agenda or veto power.

The only way Romans 6:12-13 makes sense is if we come to Him without the encumbrances of the old man, and with the Spirit-revealed understanding that we have been crucified, buried and raised anew—with newness of faculties to walk with God.

> *Therefore, do not let sin reign in your mortal body so that you obey its evil desires. Do not offer any part of yourself to sin as an instrument of wickedness, but rather offer yourselves to God as those who have been brought from death to life; and offer every part of yourself to him as an instrument of righteousness.*
> **– Romans 6:12-13**

So what do we offer? Our new creation—it is all we *have* to offer if the old is passed away, right? But we make this *so* difficult.

What we do, in practice, is continually offer our old faculties to the Lord Jesus and ask Him to strengthen them, make them new, and regenerate them.

In doing so, we are asking Him to do something that will never solve our problem. In doing so, we are asking Him to do something He committed his life unto death to resolve in *another* way!

Why, when our Savior has done the work of rendering that old man useless, would we ever ask Him to resurrect that old bag of death?

Let me say it again—and shout it from the mountain top; when we behave in this way, **we are asking Him to do something He has already resolved another way!**

---

[110] A.W. Tozer, The Crucified Life; Part 4, Chapter 13

Remember the thermos flask? Why ask for something we already are? If we've said it once, we've said it ten times—that is all wrong! God must look at us in pity and think:

> "Why doesn't he *get* it? I cannot strengthen what I have destroyed—nor do I desire to do so because there neither was, nor ever would have been, any solution there.
>
> What he's still trying to present to me cannot be regenerated. His physical, tangible world is still eclipsing the realities of the spiritual world which I have already birthed into his life—and at *his* very request.
>
> What he asked for I have given.
>
> Instead of making something incapable of victory stronger, I have made him altogether *new* and completely capable of living *in* me.
>
> Does he not understand I have given him a new heart? Why would I want to regenerate or strengthen that which never had any ability to generate life?
>
> Oh, give him eyes to see, Spirit. Open his eyes!"

And so Paul is pressing us, in verse 13, to present ourselves unto God, as alive from the dead. What is referred to here is not the consecration of anything belonging to the old creation, but only of that which has passed through death to resurrection.

Thus, the presenting or offering spoken of is the outcome of my knowing my old man to be crucified.

Without this knowledge having entered into our consciousness as belief—leading to a confidence in its truth, we will not be able to present unto God anything with which he can work.

If this truth has not yet traveled from your mind to your heart, I beg of you to retrace your steps before pushing forward. Merely getting through material in a cerebral way will *never* gain spiritual sight. Knowing, reckoning, *then* presenting to God; *that* is the divine order.

Says Nee about this prerequisite before our being able to present ourselves unto God:

> When I really know I am crucified with him, then spontaneously I reckon myself dead (verses 6 and 11); and when I know that I am

raised with him from the dead, then likewise I reckon myself "alive unto God in Christ Jesus" (verses 9 and 11), for both the death and the resurrection side of the Cross are to be accepted by faith.

When this point is reached (emphasis mine), giving myself to him follows.

In resurrection he is the source of my life—indeed he *is* my life; so I cannot but present everything to him, for all is his, not mine. ...he has condemned all that is of the old creation to the Cross. Death has cut off all that cannot be consecrated to him, and resurrection alone has made consecration possible. Presenting myself to God means that henceforth I consider my whole life as belonging to him.[111]

---

[111] Nee, The Normal Christian Life; Chapter 6, Page 64

Chapter 56

"Presenting Yourselves..."[112]

It was a great thing when I discovered I am no longer my own, but His. It was a great thing when I discovered that it was *His* life in me now and not my own.

For the first time, really, I felt the pressure to perform was off.

These days, I wonder how many of us really *know* that because Christ is risen, we are alive unto God and *not* unto ourselves. As I look around, I cannot help but think the number is few–very few. For, though painful, we must look at the evidence.

Reckoning upon the fact daily that I am alive unto God and not unto myself has brought regular, *informed* surrender to my life. Somehow, growing in the knowledge and understanding of the roles of the Blood and the Cross over the life I have been given to live has opened the door to the Spirit's activity within. And this not of myself, it has been a gift of God. I pray He may find such an inroad into your spirit as well.

As the days progress, I challenge you to make it a habit to consciously live in light of what is true about you as one born anew. It must change everything. Make Romans 6:19 a definite act. "Present yourselves unto God."

There must come a day in our lives when we pass out of our own hands into His, and from that day forward we belong to Him and no

---

[112] Again, as noted in footnote 69, we are continuing in the thought process laid out by Nee in his book, The Normal Christian Life. While some sentences are nearly direct quotes, others sections are a melding together of his thoughts.

longer to ourselves. This means we are given over to the will of God to be and do whatever He requires.

At this stage of presenting ourselves, it is our *will* that is in question. That strong, self-assertive will of ours must go to the Cross, and we must give ourselves over wholly to the Lord.

What the Lord asks of us should make perfect sense. Could you rightly expect a tailor to make you a coat if you don't give him any cloth? Would you ask a builder to build you a house if you didn't follow up that request by providing him with building materials?

In the same way, you cannot expect the Lord to live out His life in you if you do not *give* Him your life *in* which to live! **Without reservation, without controversy, we must give ourselves to Him to do as He pleases with us. This is not Paul's recommendation or plea. It is God's command to us.**

Romans 6:13 is a directive. "Present yourselves unto God." **It is a matter of obedience.**

Chapter 57

Recognizing God's Ownership – The End of the Beginning

Now comes the test...the test of our trust, the tell-tale gauge of whether we have been broken off from our old man. For once this truly takes place in our spirit through the illumination of the Holy Spirit, we have been *made capable* of presenting ourselves effectively before the Lord Jesus.

Once the Spirit of God has weaned us from ourselves and our conviction of this matter has become personally and subjectively real, we are *joyfully* compelled to give Him what He already owns. And at this point, we are being readied to move *from* merely being a servant *to* becoming a slave of our Vine, our glorious heavenly Father and King Jesus!

What is the difference between a servant and slave? I'm glad you asked. It is an excellent question, and our relatively concise treatment of the answer will now have us rounding third and heading for home in our objective for this project.

For after God has sufficiently broken and mercifully brought us to a point of *actual* (not play-acted or merely desired) surrender, *and* we are consistently practicing the presentation of our newly redeemed faculties to Him *without controversy, and* the agenda we used to have for our life has been given over to the One who no longer has to arrest it from us, *then* **He** is fully sufficient to take it from there. And that, as they say, is the understatement of the century—and certainly of this book!

John MacArthur wrote a book he simply titled, **Slave**, The Hidden Truth About Your Identity in Christ.[113] In the book, he, every which way to Sunday, explains the implications and inferences of the original Greek word "doulos," translated best into English as slave. I wouldn't dare take you there in this writing, but only point you to it as a thorough treatment of what this one aspect of our walk with Jesus, as Lord, must look like if we are to fully live as He intends.

Instead, thanks to Watchman Nee's ability to help us practically comprehend things spiritual, I'm going to gift you the next chapter, taken directly from his treatment of this topic in The Normal Christian Life. May these words challenge our present standing as we examine the extent of our current enslavement to the One we call Lord.

---

[113] See Appendix B at the end of this book. It is the bulk of an interview done by Lillian Kwon, a Christian Post reporter, pertaining to MacArthur's book, Slave. I include this here as a concession. You likely wouldn't get through the whole book as it is a bit redundant (like parts of this book, right?). The transcript of the interview is a touch difficult to read in a few places, but it does get at the main purpose for my including it here at this point in this writing. We are to be ones given over completely to God, having given up our previous "freedoms" as ones now enslaved to God for *his* purposes in and through us. But oh, the irony of it all! Never before and in no other context again will there be any way to gain so much freedom as when one becomes a slave (Greek rendering: *doulos*) of the Lord Jesus. This, too, of interest: http://www.biblestudytools.com/lexicons/greek/nas/doulos.html. Slave (doulos) is used 120 times in the NT alone.

Chapter 58

Servant or Slave?[114]

If we give ourselves unreservedly to God, many adjustments may have to be made: in family, or business, or church relationships, or in the matter of our personal views.

God will not let anything of ourselves remain. His finger will touch, point by point, everything that is not of him, and he will say: "This must go."

Are you willing?

It is foolish to resist God, and always wise to submit to him.

We admit that many of us still have controversies with the Lord. He wants something, while we want something else. Many things we dare not look into, dare not pray about, dare not even think about, lest we lose our peace.

We can evade the issue in that way, but to do so will bring us out of the will of God. It is always an easy matter to get out of his will, but it is a blessed thing just to hand ourselves over to him and let him have his way with us.

How good it is to have the consciousness that we belong to the Lord and are not our own! There is nothing more precious in the

---

[114] Nee, The Normal Christian Life; Chapter 6, Pages 67-68. This section, unless noted, is directly from these pages. Any emphases are mine.

world. It is *that* which brings the awareness of his continual presence, and the reason is obvious. I must first have the sense of God's possession of me, before I can have the sense of his presence with me.

When once his ownership is established, then I dare do nothing in my own interests, for I am his exclusive property. "Know ye not, that to whom ye present yourselves as servants unto obedience, his servants ye are whom ye obey?" (Romans 6:16)

The word here rendered "servant" really signifies a bond-servant, a slave. This word is used several times in the second half of Romans 6.

What is the difference between a servant and a slave?

A servant may serve another, but the *ownership* does not pass to that other. If he likes his master, he can serve him, but if he does not like him, he can give in his notice and seek another master.

Not so is it with the slave. He is not only the servant of another but he is the *possession* of another.

How did I become the slave of the Lord?

On his part he bought me, and on my part I presented myself to him. By right of redemption I am God's property, but if I would be his slave I must willingly give myself to him, for he will never compel me to do so.[115]

The trouble with many Christians today is that they have an insufficient idea of what God is asking of them. How glibly they say: "Lord, I am willing for anything." Do you know that God is asking of you your very life? There are cherished ideals, strong wills, precious relationships, much-loved work, that will have to go; so do not give yourself to God unless you mean it. God will take you seriously, even if you did not mean it seriously.

---

[115] This is a mystery–the working together of our will and his acceptance of us. Let it be yet another opportunity for us to rejoice in God's willingness to credit us with what *he* compelled us to accept!

When the Galilean boy brought his bread to the Lord, what did the Lord do with it? He broke it. God will always break what is offered to him. He breaks what he takes, but after breaking it he blesses and uses it to meet the needs of others.

After you give yourself to the Lord, he begins to break what was offered to him. Everything seems to go wrong, and you protest and find fault with the ways of God. But to stay there is to be no more than just a broken vessel—no good for the world because you have gone too far for the world to use you, and no good for God either because you have not gone far enough for him to use you. You are out of gear with the world, and you have a controversy with God. This is the tragedy of many a Christian.

My giving of myself to the Lord must be an initial, fundamental act. Then day by day I must go on giving to him, not finding fault with his use of me, but accepting with praise even what the flesh finds hard. Therein lies true enrichment.

I am the Lord's and now no longer reckon myself to be my own, but acknowledge in everything his ownership and authority. That is the attitude God delights in, and to maintain it is true consecration.

I do not consecrate myself to be a missionary or a preacher; I consecrate myself to God to do his will where I am, be it in school, office, or kitchen, *wherever he may, in his wisdom, send me*. Whatever he ordains for me is sure to be the very best, for nothing but good can come to those who are wholly his.

May we always be possessed by the consciousness that we *are not* our own.

Chapter 59

Sliding Home – Face First

Would you pause right now?

If the Lord has used any of the words on these pages to hit their mark, please take a moment to pause. It is never words on paper doing the work, but the Spirit himself interceding for us with groanings too deep for words (Romans 8:26). There may be something holy, eternal, outside yourself that God is wanting to do in you. Please listen. Let Him finish what He has started.

In light of what we have learned, our posture now before the King can no longer be so self-hyphenated.

Daily we must view our sin and the disposition of the flesh through a consistently God-centered view more so than one that is self-centered. Instead of being more concerned about our own victory over sin in this life, we must continually grow in our understanding about how our sin and the wayward condition of our heart apart from Christ grieves the heart of God.

The whole idea here has been to point us to the fact that it is God's work and not ours that has achieved, and continues to achieve for us, the ultimate victory. Both in this life and for all eternity to come.

It will, for all our earthbound days *and* on the day of the final judgment, be only the Blood of Jesus that bids us to confidently approach Him. And it will, for all our days, be only the Cross of Christ which gains for us a life that can daily be lived in a way that brings Him glory.

And once we have, by His grace and mercy alone, attained to some new measure of fellowship with Him, may the heartbreak of dispossessing that deep fellowship keep us attuned to His Word, living in His presence, and obediently following hard after Him.

It is at *this* place of presenting yourself, completely surrendered, that I desire to release you into the hands of the One who, I pray, is being given access to live within you unquenched, awakened.

It is here, at the door step of the irony of freeing enslavement, where I pray your chin is being lovingly raised in the tender hands of the One who has purchased you from death to life.

It is here, eyes fixed on the Author and Perfector of your faith, longing to find the life He has in store for you, that I desire to set you down and walk away.

But you're in good hands...the best, actually.

I place you here into the hands of God, having pleaded, and still pleading with Him on my knees, for all who have read to this point. I now present you to The Lord as an act of trust–that you would fall face first into the dangerous yet safe, fearsome yet calming, unpredictable yet reliable, inconceivable yet trustworthy hands of The Almighty God.

When the Lord determines our steps (Proverbs 16:9[116]) and we confidently walk in them with predetermined obedience, we no longer fear what man would deem unconventional, unwise or imprudent. This is so because we dwell with Him as foreigners, strangers, as all our ancestors were (Psalm 39:12b).

More importantly, *we* no longer trust our horizontal, earth-side judgment, but live *His* life and accept his path for us in the light of eternity.

It is here, as we practically present ourselves unto God, that we can embrace the challenge of walking in the trustworthy Light instead of the darkness of our own council (I Cor 13:12[117]).

---

[116] *In their hearts humans plan their course, but the Lord establishes their steps.* – **Proverbs 16:9**

[117] *For now we see only a reflection as in a mirror; then we shall see face to face. Now I know in part; then I shall know fully, even as I am fully known.* – **I Corinthians 13:12**

It is here where we are becoming, *in practice*, **His** (I Cor 6:19-20[118]; 7:23[119]).

So, as we began this writing, midway through our Introduction, we now return.

When we receive a Truth from the hand of God so weighty we don't know what to do with it apart from falling on our knees in jaw-dropping, revelatory awareness, we are on the playing field–the domain, of the Holy Spirit.

With Spirit revealed Truth comes understanding. With such understanding comes knowledge. With such knowledge comes belief. With belief comes release. With release comes humility. With humility comes *brokenness*. With *brokenness* comes repentance. With repentance comes surrender. With surrender comes purpose. With purpose comes calling. With calling comes dependence. With dependence comes a hunger for Truth. And once God has us here, we're cooked and hooked because the cycle, glory be to God alone, starts all over again–in a deep hunger for Truth!

If any of these individual characteristics is not true of you, look at what precedes that stage and you will know where to begin. Begin there–on your penitent knees.

But do not begin by asking the Lord to make you stronger or to help you work harder in that area. No, there is no help there. Rather, ask Him to make you weaker–weak enough, in fact, to become useful in making much of Him and abiding wholly in Him, the Vine of our sustenance.

Remember, the Lord's way is to remind us of our utter insufficiency apart from Him–while pointing us to the Cross where the work was already done.

Oh, that God would be willing to reveal His Truths to us. Oh, that what we teach would be guided by the Spirit of God, actively living in those whom God has gifted with the responsibility to lead. Oh, that Truth would take its *full course* in all our lives that what God desires to tell us today would make straight the path to His being willing to set us, as it were, on fire.

---

[118] *Or know ye not that your body is a temple of the Holy Spirit which is in you, which ye have from God? And ye are not your own; for ye were bought with a price: glorify God therefore in your body.* **– I Corinthians 6:19-20** (ASV)

[119] *You were bought at a price, so do not become slaves of other human beings.* **– I Corinthians 7:23** (CJB)

I pray that we will be a people who refuse to gorge our spiritual stomachs on the entertaining pleasures of this world. Rather, may we choose to find our satisfaction in the eternal treasure of His Word.

I pray that God will awaken in your heart and mine a deeper and abiding passion for the Gospel as the grand revelation of God, and that it would affect great change in whom it is we are becoming.

Come in supremacy, Lord Jesus, through the One you left for our edification, instruction and, yes, empowerment.

After **revealing** your truth to us, **breaking** us—as you are in the habit of doing with those you love and call, **accepting our repentance** in your great mercy, **enabling** us to **surrender** every hindrance before your throne, then, give us a willing spirit. Make us bold. Make us courageous. Make us a surrendered, holy sacrifice, deeply secured in the palm of your hand where we shall fear neither death nor life, neither angels nor demons, neither the present nor the future, nor any powers, neither height nor depth, nor anything else in all creation, because nothing will be able to separate us from your all-consuming love and security for all time to come.

And, finally, *be* Lord of our lives.

CHAPTER 60

Walking in Obedience[120]

This is a purposely unwritten chapter. Its pages will be written upon differently, perhaps, than were they being lived previously. They are yours to fill.

Use them as your own resource pages, including things you have read or heard that have become part of your journey into surrender. Use them to reflect upon what the Spirit has and is doing in you. Use them as the beginning of a journal, chronicling what God is teaching you. Use them to record Aha! Moments that take your breath away as your fellowship with the Holy Spirit brings newness of vision. Use them in whatever way you desire...they are yours to fill.

---

[120] Initially this chapter was titled Walking in the Victory. I have changed it to ...Obedience. Word choice is not merely window dressing, but a window into the soul of intention. This may seem to be merely splitting hairs over semantics, but there is, as Jerry Bridges writes in Chapter 1 of The Pursuit of Holiness, "a subtle self-centered attitude at the center of many of our difficulties..." Pride is self-confidence. The moment we begin to live usward instead of Godward, we are on a very dangerous precipice. When we begin to perceive such things, we are gaining ground in the direction of a healthy fear of self and sin. And so in this case, God wants us to walk in obedience, not victory. Obedience is oriented toward God. Victory is oriented toward self. Again, as Bridges points out in the same chapter referenced above, "Until we face this attitude and deal with it, we will not consistently walk in holiness. This is not to say that God does not want us to walk in victory, but rather to emphasize that victory is a byproduct of obedience."

I remember hearing that the teacher can only teach a student to read, or encourage her with recommendations of what to read. But after that, the student is on her own. I do not consider myself to be a teacher; I do, however, consider myself a forgiven and redeemed sinner, boldly asking my Lord to duplicate in others what he has exacted upon my life.

But beyond the words on these pages, we cannot take the walk to such a destination together. It must be traveled alone. It is always traveled alone. A.W. Tozer says,

> To penetrate into the very presence of God is a very lonely journey. Although there may be companions along the way as we live the crucified life, nobody can experience our experiences for us. Moreover, we cannot experience anybody else's experiences. It boils down to simply this: God and us. And when we come into his presence, we come by ourselves.[121]

You have to find God as the deer longs for streams of water.[122] You have to seek God alone.

I pray God has used something from the words on these pages to help you, and through the scriptures to which they point. I have done my level best to help you. But when He meets you, it will be by yourself. You cannot take the authority of someone else with skin on. You cannot delegate your walk with God to a pastor, a mentor or anyone else. God has given you direct access to himself through Jesus. But you must stand in His presence alone. God must deal with you alone.

Some of the resources included at the end of this writing will teach you more about the Person of the Holy Spirit who can live actively within those who profess Jesus *both* as Savior *and* Lord. Chapters 7-10 in The Normal Christian Life is a great place to strengthen your knowledge and understanding of our Helper. But again, its value is best realized so far as it points you

---

[121] A.W. Tozer, The Crucified Life; Chapter 4
[122] Psalm 42:1 (HCSB)

back to God's Word—and then on to the One who is our end game—to God himself.

Let the header of this chapter remind you of your responsibility now as one who has given up ownership—to walk in the truth of the victory Christ Jesus has won *on your behalf* for all time to come. Instead of just *walking*, walk now in newness. You must do this in the power of the Holy Spirit. There is *no* other way.

Instead of just putting in the work for the rest of your days, ask, seek and knock[123] until your time can be filled with a Holy Discontent[124] of God's own choosing. Don't be afraid—he knows you and will unite your giftedness and talents with something that breaks both of your hearts, into which He may ask that you pour the rest of your life. Are you willing?

There is yet much to discover and much through which to struggle if you desire to walk in the victory of your newness in Christ. *Refuse* to let an over busy life of good works distract you from fellowshipping with Jesus.[125] He wants your *life*, not sacrifice.[126]

The quest in the Lord is lifelong! The resources included at the end of this writing are intended to be part of your quest.

Read the Bible every day.

---

[123] *Ask and it will be given to you; seek and you will find; knock and the door will be opened to you. For everyone who asks receives; the one who seeks finds; and to the one who knocks, the door will be opened.* – **Matthew 7:7-8**

[124] Bill Hybels, Holy Discontent. Did I say to read this book? A thousand times, yes. ATTENTION: Here is a Goldmine for you. If you are like me, you need to have emotion and relatability lead your interest. Take about forty-five minutes and watch the very presentation that drove me to actually purchase a book—this book. Granted it was 4-5 years before I read it, but this message was the seedbed for the Holy Spirit. Though it's a third-party video as a whole, you can watch the message Bill delivered at the '05 Leadership Summit HERE: http://vimeo.com/23836269

[125] See the audio message by Hans Peter Royer in Resources by this same name.

[126] Keith Green, To Obey Is Better Than Sacrifice. Get this song and be challenged.

[This page intentionally left blank]

[This page intentionally left blank]

[This page intentionally left blank]

[This page intentionally left blank]

APPENDIX A: Originally written in my blog on July 20, 2012

Earning Our Way Throneward?
TWSU

Friday, July 13, 2012 – Thursday, October 17, 2013

This idea has been rattling around in my mind for some time – many months in the least. I haven't quite been able to nail it down yet. And I doubt this paper will do so. Nonetheless, we may make some headway.

As Christians, we fundamentally and intellectually know that nothing we can **do** could **ever earn** us a spot in heaven. We get that. We know the theology. But I do believe we somehow think that **after** conversion, what **we do will earn us** greater proximity to an incalculably holy and incorruptible God. And in doing so, my question is, "What ARE we thinking?"

We know we can't **earn** a right standing with God for salvation, but I think we believe that a rigorous study of the scriptures and our consciously working or willing our way into becoming more Christ-like through our mental toughness and all-around effort is somehow earning us a kind of special proximity to God. And I **do believe** we see this as the path we must travel in "taking our minds captive, and enslaving our bodies to the Lord," if you will.

Our angle on it is more like what sociologist Christian Smith once called "moralistic therapeutic deism," or the idea that Christianity can be summed up as "God wants you to try a little harder to do a little better…." And then there's what Phil Vischer, creator of "VeggieTales," has been learning. In the words of BreakPoint's John Stonestreet, Vischer's more biblically accurate puppet series, "What's in the Bible?" with Buck Denver, captures an entirely different message than did his "VeggieTales." Vischer—himself the voice of Bob the Tomato—admits the message taught in many "VeggieTales" wasn't fully ripe Christianity. In his own words, "You can say 'hey kids, be more forgiving because the Bible says so.' But that isn't Christianity." His new work helps children learn about the unity of Scripture, how each piece fits together to form the great story about Jesus Christ, **who came to save us from trying to please God ourselves**.

I urge you to honestly evaluate yourself over the course of this next week or two, Greg...in light of this tremendously important nuance – namely, how you **really** approach your growth as a Christian. Coming to a right conclusion of what you believe you and God each brings to the table in your relationship is vital to living victoriously in your journey with Jesus – so stick with this.

Again, it's like we believe our evolution into becoming more effective and faithful ambassadors of the living God (call it...cough, cough...sanctification) is a product of **our** mental discipline and **our** ability to gain control of the tendencies of our wayward Adam. But in doing so, we are denying the primary and purposed power of our new supernatural strength through the indwelling of the Holy Spirit. I think without really thinking about it, we primarily and repeatedly pick up our old Adam and work diligently to reform him into becoming something better, something valuable – and we ask God to help us do so. **We try SO HARD!** But, in doing so, we have it all wrong. Our old man doesn't need to become better. He needs to be replaced. And so I think in trying to make ourselves better, we're working it backwards. Victory will never come that way, but only repeated disappointment and disillusionment regarding the power we're supposed to now house within. In doing so, our theology is all wrong! I like the new Amy Grant song, "Don't Try So Hard." Taken in this context, it says, in song, what I feel we need to hear as do-it-yourself Christians. The next entry, inserted April 28, 2013 after her song came out, is that song. Listen to it.

I think something like this was going on in Galatian thinking in the churches in Galatia – and Paul addressed it. As Galatians chapter 3 indicates, they were diminishing the place of the Holy Spirit's work and responsibility in their lives in lieu of human work/effort. It says,

"You foolish Galatians! Who has bewitched you? Before your very eyes Jesus Christ was clearly portrayed as crucified. I would like to learn just one thing from you: Did you receive the Spirit by the works of the law, or by believing what you heard? Are you so foolish? After beginning by means of the Spirit, are you now trying to finish by means of the flesh?"

The Galatians, like all other believers, began their Christian lives in the power of the Spirit. But they were coming under the influence of Judaizing teachers who were touting imperative alignment with their laws of the past – the necessity of circumcision, literal physical circumcision, and obedience to the Mosaic Law as a necessity for salvation. They were essentially asking people to be saved by the Lord Jesus Christ, and then to follow hard after imposing ceremonies, circumcision, and the Mosaic Law. But the problem in doing this was that the gospel of grace Paul was so desperately trying to teach them was in danger of disappearing – and in its place was rooting a system of human effort.

I wonder how often we subconsciously do this in our own way.

Paul called this, *being bewitched*. The Greek word he used means to fascinate...to charm in a misleading way. Who has charmed you away from reality? Who has charmed you away from the truth? They had become willing victims, succumbing to a flesh-pleasing kind of spirituality. They received the Holy Spirit by faith. They began the Christian life by faith. Is it going to be perfected by a work of or through effort in the flesh? Is it going to be perfected by fleshly methods, ritual...by circumcision and the keeping of the Law and ceremonies...in their case?

Paul's point is pretty simple. If a person receives eternal salvation through trust in Christ, and believes that he has received the fullness of the indwelling Holy Spirit who takes up residence in all believers at the point of salvation, the power of God therefore being placed at his disposal, **why would he turn to human effort to achieve spiritual goals?**

The Holy Spirit is the Christian's source of life and power. As I heard John MacArthur say, the Holy Spirit is to the Christian what the Creator is to the creation. Without God the Creator, the world does not come into existence. Without God as the sustainer, it does not continue in existence. It is God who created it and God who sustains it.

And so it is with the Holy Spirit and the Christian. Without the Holy Spirit, we wouldn't be the new creation. Without the Holy Spirit we wouldn't be regenerated. And without the Holy Spirit we would not continue to be sanctified. It is His divine power that must do all the work; it does not happen in or through our effort. Apart from such power through Him, we would immediately fall back into the spiritual deadness from which we came. Again, the creation cannot survive without the upholding power of God the Creator. Neither can a Christian sustain Christian life by works nor by ceremony nor by religious ritual; it can only be sustained by the Holy Spirit.

The provision of the indwelling Holy Spirit is given us to put an end to this matter of our fleshly efforts to earn God's favor or live according to His demands of us. He is sent in order to take care of the inward side of these things for us. And He is certainly able to do so—as we are told when we "*walk* after the Spirit" (Galatians 5:16). And to our point here, it is helpful to note the wording of this verse. **First**, ours *is not a working* after or with the Spirit, but a *walk* after the Spirit. Simply put, in Christ our life is not a work; it is a walk. As Watchman Nee says, "Praise God, the burdensome and fruitless effort I involved myself in when I sought in the flesh to please God, gives way to a quiet and restful dependence on His working which worketh in me mightily" (Colossians 1:29). **Second**, to walk *after* implies subjection. When we walk *after the flesh*, as Romans 8:5-8 discloses, there is no question where that leads us. Doing so only brings us into conflict with God. But to walk *after the Spirit* is to be subject *to* the Spirit. There is one thing the man who walks after the Spirit cannot do—and that is be independent of Him. I must be subject to the Holy Spirit. The initiative of my life must be with Him. Again, as Nee says, "Only as I yield myself to obey him will I find within me the Spirit in full operation, and all that I have been doing to please God being fulfilled–no longer *by* me, but *in* me! As many as are led by the Spirit of God, these are the sons of God (Romans 8:14).

Where we are not sustained by the Holy Spirit, we drop right back into spiritual deadness. And in so doing, we begin to own that low bar of expectation that so grieves the Spirit and terribly stunts our growth. No, we live in the Spirit. We are being kept by the Spirit. He is the source of our life. He is the sphere of our spiritual existence. No one is saved without the Spirit; neither can one be sanctified without the Spirit.

So why, back to Paul's challenge to the Galatians, would you begin understanding the power of the Spirit that saved you, and then turn from the work of the Spirit by grace in your heart backwards to those things which you left, those outward, external, fleshly, shadowy, symbolic elements? Why begin in the power of the Spirit and try to perfect what was begun in the flesh?

Taking a slightly different tack at the matter, Timothy Keller, in his wonderful book, King's Cross, used a phrase in Chapter 4 that caught my attention and, once again, brought me back here to the idea of my "Earning Our Way Throneward" phrase.

Under his header, Religion versus the Gospel, he talks about how we may actually believe we can "reach God by working [our] way through certain 'transformations of consciousness.'" The phrase **transformations of consciousness** hit me. Now we know we cannot **earn** our way **to** God through diligent, conscious efforts at goodness, but I'm not so convinced most of us don't somehow feel we can work to **relate** better **to** God through **our** own "transformations of consciousness."

Why do we have this continual need to prove our value? Why do we believe that our conscious efforts to do good will, over time, transform us into ones worthy of God's approval? Well, why do we see an evangelical pastor with a doctorate more valuable to the Kingdom of God than an eight year old boy who has just given his heart to Jesus in Sunday school? Now, you may say, give it a few years, and depending on what this little boy learns, what he does, whom he impacts – maybe he will, in fact, be of greater value to God! But that means his value is based on what he DOES.

Why DO we feel this way? It's because we are preconditioned to believe that productivity according to the world's measuring system brings value and usefulness to that individual. Every culture points to certain things and says, "If you gain those, if you acquire or achieve those, then you'll have a 'self' – you'll know you're valuable. More traditional cultures would say that you're nobody unless you gain the respectability and legacy of family and children. But in individualistic cultures like ours, what brings value or worth is different. Our culture says you're nobody unless you gain a fulfilling career that brings money, reputation and status.

Regardless of such differences though, every culture says identity is performance-based…achievement-based. And Jesus says, that will never work. If you gain the whole world, he says, it won't be big enough or bright enough to cover up the stain of inconsequentiality. No matter how many of these things you gain, it's never enough to make you sure of who you are – that the value of what you bring is good enough. We're simply a product of our society's inability to assign value to anything that isn't somehow earned.

And so because of this, we naturally bring this tendency right into our worlds of religion. Religion is, as we know, man's attempt to earn his way to God. It's filled with a consuming need to do good in order to be accepted – as a move toward attaining a right standing with the greater being. There's a code of conduct, and if you follow it to some degree or another God will somehow look upon you with more favor. This is religion.

I strongly believe we too often look at the scriptures as "religion" rather than the gospel. **Religion is, fundamentally, advice. But the Gospel of Jesus Christ begins and ends with "news".**

There's a HUGE difference between the two, and moreover, as Keller also points out, they are two completely different things. Most people in the world believe that, if there is a God, you relate to Him by being good. Most religions are based on that principle – though there are many different variations on it. Some religions are nationalistic. In other words, you connect to God by coming into a certain people group, and taking on the markers of society membership. Other religions are spiritualistic. You reach God by working through certain transformations of consciousness. Yet still other religions are legalistic. There's a code of conduct, and if you follow it, God will look upon you with favor.

But they all have the same logic. If I perform, if I obey, I am accepted. And I'm afraid that, in our human DNA, we are terribly embedded with our need to **earn** favor – and this doesn't go away just because we have become Christians. That's why all religion is somehow imbued with this quality. This need to earn favor is one with which we seem to be born. And it is deeply subconscious. We don't realize it is there – yet subconsciously for most all of us at some level, it **is** there, driving our attempts to relate to God. And I believe it is so deep-seated, only the Holy Spirit can reveal it to us as it lives its way out through various facets of our life.

The Gospel of Jesus is not only different from that, but diametrically opposed to it. Again, religion says that if I obey, I am accepted. But the Gospel says that I am fully accepted in Jesus Christ – **and therefore**, I obey.

Advice calls for us to **do something** proactive, something effort-filled...religion. Advice comes with it an assumption that if we walk according to it, then our condition or circumstance may improve; if we get the **right** advice, and we enact it, then we'll find that things work out okay.

The gospel, however, as "news", is just that – news. News is something you simply receive. The good news of the gospel isn't calling us, inherently, to **do** anything that could gain us a more proximate position before God. No, it is information...news. We either accept or reject it. News is factually based information we cannot manipulate or "work on" to have it become more real or valuable to us. And as such, the Gospel of Jesus Christ is not an if/then proposition to God's favor, leaving **us** as some kind of agent for bringing the good to pass. No, the Gospel is news to which we cannot ad any amount of effort or action in order for its application to come about in our lives. All we need to do is accept the news – the truth of the Gospel into our lives. There is precisely nothing we can DO to add to it in order for it to have its truth invade us. We must simply accept it for what it is. And so, once again, when it comes to our initial acceptance of the Good News for salvation, we get all of this.

But once we're "in", I'm thinking we have a natural human tendency to want to continue to "earn" an increased "in-ness" unlike we needed to earn our "acceptance" in the first place. **So in so much as the header of this paper would lead one to believe, I'm not really wondering herein if we believe we can earn our way into a relationship with Jesus – I/we know better. Rather, it's more of a ponderance over why we tend to work, intellectually, so hard at applying and bringing to recollection that which we study so diligently in his Word when it's not a text book like that. Rather, it's a supernatural empowerment mechanism to help us relieve ourselves of religious necessity!**

Certainly, we think, we couldn't earn a right standing before God. But now that we know him as our Savior, it's a different story. Now, we think, we have to grow our walk with Him by working hard to follow the advice written in the many pages of His Word. Why all the self-effort all of the sudden? Just because we are now in relationship with God because of the forgiveness of our sins, do we now carry around a burden of proof to which we must attain? No. Rather, our actions of obedience and compliance should only be as a natural outgrowth of our overwhelming gratitude for the good news we received without merit. **And the only good we can do that has any merit at all will only and always be because enough of our "self" has been slain and surrendered so as to be in alignment with the Spirit living within us.**

How do I, now that I'm in Christ, approach God? Is there ever a time where I feel better or worse about approaching him? If so, it may be time for a perspective check. It's natural to feel embarrassed or ashamed when approaching God when in the throes of disobedience – the proverbial dog with his tail between his legs. Similarly, it's natural to feel more confident and self-satisfied when approaching God after doing something especially kind or helping the poor. But in doing so, we are telling ourselves there *is* a connection between my doing and God's reception of me. Still, we should know that regardless of our recent "performance on the job," we are in our human "goodness" never nearer or further from God since we are but refuse in both cases – *unless* coming solely on the grounds of his blood *every* time! **He** knows we are only able to be in communion with him based on his blood...but do WE? Do we *really*?

On a foundational level, am I feeling like I can approach him with a greater expectancy of reception when I have recently done something good or have been on a seeking and obedience hot streak? My approach to my Lord must always and continually be under cover of the finished work of the Son, Jesus. **I must consciously approach God through his merit alone, and never on any basis of my attainment – never on the ground, for example, that I have been extra kind or patient today, or that I have done something for the Lord this morning.** No, I have to come by way of the blood *every* time.

I guess the temptation for so many of us is that because God has been dealing with us, because he has been taking steps to bring us into something more of himself, and has been teaching us deeper lessons, he has, therefore, set before us new standards. And that only by attaining to *these* can we have a clear conscience before him. No. A clear conscience is never based on our attainment. It can only be based on the work of the Lord Jesus and the shedding of his blood.

What, after all, is our basis of approach to God? Do we come to him on the uncertain ground of our feeling, the feeling that we may have achieved something for God today? Or is our approach based on something far more secure; namely, the fact that the blood has been shed, and that God looks on that blood and is satisfied? For sure, our boldness before God is ours through the blood, and never through our personal attainment.

Initially, our standing with God was secured by the blood of Christ as Ephesians 2:13 says – that we are "made nigh in the blood of Christ." But thereafter our grounds for continual access to God is still by the blood and nothing less – as Hebrews 10:19 & 22 says – "Having therefore...boldness to enter into the holy place by the blood of Jesus...let us draw near." To begin with, I was made nigh by the blood, and to continue in that relationship, I must come solely and completely through the same avenue – and that not of ourselves, but through his redemptive blood.

Now one last thought before moving back to where I was before starting this slight but very important detour of thought. All of this is not to say that we should live careless lives. We know the Word very clearly demonstrates to us (see the book of James among other NT passages) that our lives after redemption through Christ are to reflect the fruits of our newness. Just because we are accepted before God because of his blood and not our works, this is not to somehow communicate that our need to carry out the rest of the teachings of scripture which tell us how a life surrendered to Christ should be lived out, is nothing more than extra credit. For the evidence of our progress will always be reflected through the song of our lives.

Anyway, back to the Word, how I approach it and my vs. the Spirit's role in administering it into me, I now look at my contemplation of the Word of God less like a behavioral task list or a piece of advice, and more as a praise list. It is news! And I accept it as such. And **it is now the Holy Spirit's responsibility to change and mold me as a result of its ingestation into my life.** The more I contemplate and reckon my right standing with God through his Son, the more I understand whom it is I have become – a new creation...Christ IN me...due to no effort of my own. And the more the Holy Spirit brings TO ME the desire and power to "become," the more I realize I could never conjure up this desire and power myself, no matter how hard I work at it. No, I now know that my spiritual progress will never be a result of my effort to "get there" (wherever I may think 'there' may be), but rather on **his ability to supernaturally help me lose more and more of me in the process** – allowing for a more discerning heart to where it is He is leading me in this amazing journey.

I'm afraid that if there's too much of **us** via our **effort** in pouring over the Word to academically perceive of it, <u>and too little of Him via the insight that comes through a spirit released to hear the utterances of His voice within</u>, then our human tendency to continually strive toward "becoming" is through our cranial capacity alone...and we dry up, dead, listless, passionless. If we study or behave in any way such that we are hoping it will gain us favor from God in a direction toward anything this world has to offer, then we are simply using God as a means to an end...our end...an end that is bent on self-service.

But Jesus won't be a means to an end; he will not be used. In short, it is **HE** who must be our goal, not a life lived a certain way. For if He **is** our goal, then our life will follow – and one filled to the brim with purposes beyond what we could create through a logical progression of our own making.

I don't want my life to be lived out of duty. I don't want to look at what I do and say, "Yes, I have reason to have a little warmer feeling before you today, Father." No, my confident approach before God will always be because of what He ALONE has done. I continually want to understand that I bring nothing but open palms and a ready life. There is nothing I can perform that can **earn** my Father's full acceptance, love and relationship. It has always been and will always be His free gift to me through the price paid when he took me with him onto that cross and, as a result, made me into a new creation.

But *still*, we try to remake ourselves with our own effort. We DO THINGS that help us identify differently – working to live or be different without the power of God to make the changes...to make us NEW. It's like when I substitute on an Eli Lilly corporate shuttle bus route. There are two halves to the route – one on the corporate side and then for the 2nd half hour, each hour, it becomes a parking lot shuttle. So twice an hour as I filled in last week, I got out to change the identifying magnet on the side of the bus. And each time I got out of the driver seat, I told the passengers I was remaking myself. And then once when I got back into the driver's seat, I said, "There, now I'm new!" But our Christian walk is not supposed to, and cannot, work that way. We don't make ourselves new in any way. We are merely the recipients of what Jesus has already done. We are recipients of the work through the indwelling of the Holy Spirit who seals the deal in us.

Now the natural rebuttal to all of this may be that I might say that God certainly responds with favor to a life lived in obedience to Him. Yes, this is true. The Old Testament is replete with such examples. Based on how the Israelites behaved, He would bless or curse them. But the blessing resulted from their obedience as a result of reverent fear of who He was in their presence in most every case. It wasn't because they planned to carry out the law and then did so because they could. No, it was only through continual prodding and poking, literal *life and death reminders*, that they could do anything right it seems. And we're no different. Only if He is willing to continually poke, prod, surgically remove our selfish pride (which comes in more forms that we can imagine until we're really sensitized to it by His Spirit) and do all the work can we live rightly motivated. There's just too much flesh in the way otherwise.

I have not, in the past, thought certain motives were selfish – until the Lord showed me more what selfishness looked like – what it was beyond my ability to understand and self-diagnose it. Our mind cannot accurately process selfishness. It's too much a part of our DNA. There's too much darkness there for us to be able to evaluate it fully. Only through the Light do we finally realize how utterly dark, sinful and prideful our every motive is that has as its aim anything but that which is centered on and delivered from Him. My good works are lower than a smashed M&M beneath the foot of an elephant. They are inconsequential before the Holy God as it would go toward earning his favor (Isaiah 64:6). Anything I think is good is only so in light of my having been made new in Christ. And only then can it be purified as lovely before a throne of infinite purity and holiness. It is all about Him. All goodness is His. Any goodness I have is on loan from God – so we don't even own that. It is not our goodness, but His.

Oh glory to God! **When we really and truly realize that we have *nothing to give* but "up", we can finally begin a life which brings a smile to the face of Jesus.** I cannot "do good" and then feel good about my ability to transact that thing. Again, I say "no." I can only feel infinitely grateful that He has been willing to deliver into my body the strength to have done something that shadows His goodness. **And because the Spirit of God holds the key to all understanding – all goodness, my striving has ceased.** It is now His responsibility to do the work in me. I cannot do it – hard as I try. It is at this point, I can finally watch God's power manifest itself. It is a tremendously humbling place to be.

So the sum total of my current, very insufficient and almost seemingly futile attempt to put to words that which He is allowing me to discover in myself, is that there is nothing good in me but that which He has placed there. I can, therefore, point at precisely *nothing* and say to God, "See, here's proof that I'm gaining ground." No, in such a case, it is only He who is gaining ground – in me.

APPENDIX B:

Interview: John MacArthur on Being a 'Slave' for Christ

BY LILLIAN KWON, CHRISTIAN POST REPORTER
February 21, 2011/6:44 am

Renowned evangelical preacher John MacArthur has been studying Scripture for more than 50 years. Yet in his new book, *Slave: The Hidden Truth About Your Identity in Christ*, he reveals that only recently he discovered a centuries-long "cover-up" by New Testament translators.

"Slave" is the word that almost every English translation of Scripture has avoided using, in favor of the term "servant." But MacArthur insists that the image of a slave is absolutely critical for understanding what it means to follow Jesus.

MacArthur, pastor of Grace Community Church in Sun Valley, Calif., and author of more than 150 books, recently spoke to The Christian Post about his new book, the anti-government protests in North Africa and the Middle East, and his 50 years in ministry.

CP: You were a Christian your whole life and you've been studying Scripture for most of your life, and you're saying that only recently you discovered what you call a "cover-up" of the term slave? Can you tell me when and how that happened?

MacArthur: It was probably four years ago or so that I was flying over to London. I had been given a copy of a book called *Slaves of Christ* by Murray Harris and I started to read this book and began to dig into this issue. By the time I got over there and had followed the path of the book – the book deals with the word doulos which is the word in Greek for slave; every Greek dictionary will tell you it means slave, it doesn't mean servant, it doesn't describe a function; it always and only means slave. And yet it just wasn't translated that way in any English version (of the Bible) so Harris was dealing with that issue.

I followed that up by trying to find some other studies on that, other information and I wound up looking at a journal article by a scholar from back in the 1960s in which he pointed out why the translators back in the 16th century didn't translate the word slave. And he pointed out the fact that even back then there was so much stigma around slavery that they didn't want to use that word. And so they started a trend and every other English translation up until today followed that trend. They will use the word slave if it refers to a physical slave, an actual slave or an inanimate slave like slave of sin or slave of righteousness. But whenever it refers to a believer, they wouldn't translate it slave. So this just kept going and going.

Order Online: <u>Slave: The Hidden Truth about Your Identity in Christ</u>

Once I began to realize this I thought how have I missed this for so long? I guess it's just that I never was prodded into it and once I did it just became apparent that because we don't have the word slave, we therefore really don't understand the paradigm that defines us as Christian.

CP: So what did this discovery do to your own personal faith?

MacArthur: It's just so profoundly enriching. It didn't add any new theology. It didn't add any new understanding of the gospel and the realities of my relation to the Lord. It just put it in its proper paradigm. It elevated my understanding of what it means to say Jesus is Lord and it lowered my understanding of what it means to say I'm his slave. It's just a very defining concept, a paradigm that's unmistakable.

When you think that the word "Lord" is used 747 times in the New Testament we all understand that all Christians say Jesus is Lord. That's our common confession. But I don't think people get it. That's topside of the word doulos. If he's Lord, I'm his slave. And all of a sudden, all the sayings of Jesus – "deny yourself," "take up your cross," "follow me," "why do you call me Lord and not do what I say" – all these things took on new meaning because that sets the paradigm so clearly.

CP: So how different do you think Christianity would look today if they did translate that word to say slave?

MacArthur: I think it would change everything. Even true Christians, the people who truly believe and are genuinely converted and understand the gospel, now if they understand the concept of slave, have a much richer, a much more defining way to understand what the Lord has done for me, the benevolent grace which he dispenses to me – I'm a slave but I've become a friend and a son and a citizen and a joint heir and I reign with him – this is a new way to understand slavery, not in terms of American abusive African slave trade but in terms of I am owned by a master who loves me and wants to provide everything in his limitless resources out of that love to make my life eternally joyful. That is a concept of slavery that's easily embraceable.

I think also because there's a misunderstanding of this ... this is an interesting thing, just to illustrate it, I read the other day the No. 1 group in the world in drawing audiences is YouTube; No. 2 is Joel Osteen. How in the world did that happen? But what's his message? This message is whatever *you* want, whatever *you* desire, whatever *you* dream, whatever *your* heart longs for, Jesus wants to come along and give it to you. So now you have an inverted Christianity in which you are Lord and he's your slave. That doesn't exist if you understand what it means to confess Jesus is Lord and you're his slave. That has been allowed to flourish to such a massive degree along with the health, wealth prosperity message which basically says the same thing – you're in charge and Jesus will give you what you want. This whole inversion is because of a skewed understanding of doulos.

CP: You've long expressed your frustrations with contemporary Christianity. Do you think what you've discovered pretty much gets at the root of what the problem is in the churches?

MacArthur: I really do. That's such a good perception on your part because I think this is it. Until you understand what it means that he is Lord and I'm his slave, you're going to get all kinds of things wrong. It's what I've been saying for years. I wrote books – *The Gospel According to Jesus*, *The Gospel According to the Apostles*, and *Hard to Believe* and *Reckless Faith* – all these books attempting to get at the issue. But the issue really comes down to this idea that we understand what it means that he is Lord and I'm his slave. That is the most clarifying, far reaching paradigm because everything fits into that.

CP: Lately, many pastors have been expressing similar frustrations with how many Christians are essentially just minimalist or comfortable believers or are identifying with the faith only nominally. So let's say churches all had a copy of your book and all began teaching that to be a Christian is to really be a slave. Would this cause a major exodus or a revival?

MacArthur: I think the first thing it would do is it would define who the true believers are. It's a big problem. We've got churches still with non-believers; many of whom know they're non-believers and many of whom don't. They're going to say "Lord, we did this, we did that" and he's going to say "I never knew you." The first thing it would do, it would provide a plum line, it would provide a reality against which people can measure the legitimacy of their profession. So I think one of the things that would happen is people would say "I don't want that" like the rich young ruler. He runs to Jesus and he says "what do I do to inherit eternal life?" and if Jesus says to him "believe in me," he's going to say "okay, I'll believe in you" and if Jesus says "pray this prayer," he would have prayed the prayer. But instead Jesus went after the issue of who's Lord. OK, let's find out who's in charge of your life. "Sell everything you have, give your money to the poor." And he spun on his heels and left. He wasn't about to let somebody else tell him what to do with his money. That's a lordship issue. That's what Jesus is saying – you're going to acknowledge me as Lord and are you going to deny yourself and give your life to me? It's basically like the First Commandment – have no other gods, Deuteronomy 6, love the Lord with all your heart, all your soul, all your might, all your strength, no room for any other gods. That's why Jude 4 says that Jesus Christ is our *only* master and Lord. So I think that message of the true essence of the lordship of Christ would be a plum line in which people can measure the legitimacy of their profession.

APPENDIX C:

RESOURCES

Before I just list a bunch of resources God has chosen to powerfully use to begin awakening *my* soul to its depth of depravity, surrender, and education toward becoming subjectively new, I have to offer one final caveat.

As I have been careful to point out previously, there is no sure way to place your life onto a collision course for spiritual illumination, around which the God of the universe should ever be obligated to bring you individual awakening. The only thing you *can* do is lose the fear of what God may do if you earnestly and utterly give him permission to take you to a place of personal brokenness, leading to abandonment of yourself. All you can offer is all of you—without reservation, without controversy. You see, broken abandonment is the prerequisite course Jesus intended when He asked that you not only be willing to, but actually take up your cross and follow Him into what He intended to be your normal Christian life. It is undoubtedly the divine way.

If you fear being broken and torn asunder to some degree or another according to *His* operative knife, welcome to the club. But if you cannot yet move past that fear, trust leading the way, do not venture into the life of being a practicing Christian. If what is comfortable, or there even be one claim to veto power of what He can touch in your life, is your priority, you had better not begin such an adventure. Make no mistake, God knows each and every one of your finger holds. And if you give Him free reign, He will not stop until He has pried your willful fingers from each one. And if you don't think this will take a trust *in Him* beyond what you can conjure up in your own strength and willpower, you have another thing coming.

Let's be honest—it is a frightening place to stand, this "whatever you will" place. Frightening indeed. I have come to see this emotion possesses us because we have not had sufficient experiences to know that only in personal abandonment is our footing most sure. And it is terrifying to stand at the disposal of a fearsome, all powerful God with a dead honest release of yourself. Your eyes will open wide. Your pulse will quicken. Your sense of losing control will peak your attentiveness. In short, it is not a place for the faint of heart. And it is a place only attainable once you can honestly say that you trust wholly in His goodness, and that He has the best at heart for your life...regardless of how it appears to you from an earth side perspective. To *know* this should be your ground for submission is one thing, but to actually *go there* with the knowledge that God may *seemingly* wreck your life and/or the life of your family, surely taking you to a place of absolute trust in Him–this is another thing altogether. And don't think He won't. For it is the only way to a surrendered, wholly God-glorifying life.

Now don't worry, I will get to that list of resources. But if we don't really come to acknowledge that any framework is just that–a scaffolding of context intended to heighten our desire for, and understanding of, what is true about who God is and who we are, we will place too great an expectancy on the formula.

We have a natural tendency to control things. Brilliant deduction, yes? But seriously, think about the implications of the reality that our flesh cries out for control–even as we approach the resources I recommend below. Our old man, the one we say has died, is needy. He has need of veto power. Everything in us tenaciously hangs on to the reins of oversight, lest we live irrationally, imprudently. We tend to believe we know what is best for us, our spouse, our children, our friends, and our coworkers–even for complete strangers. We often say things like, "What she should do is _____ (fill in the blank)." Or, "Why doesn't he _____ (again, fill in the blank)."

So here's the rub. When we must govern the circumstances in our life, we are doing life horizontally, leaning on our own understanding. But Proverbs 3:5 entreats us to lean *not* on our own understanding. What do you suppose this means? If *we* could understand what is best for our life in Christ, God would not have commanded us to *stop* living on our own understanding! But our understanding is what we know best. And so we live estranged from living radically, dangerously, counter-culturally, counter-intuitively. It takes a lot of breaking for the Lord to show us that we do not and cannot possess the ability to live wholly surrendered to Christ unless we let loose of our cognitive demand for control.

So all that to say that the resources I list below, while not able to deliver your soul into a subjective, effectual and personal surrender into the God who calls you unto such abandonment, are, in my estimation, an excellent place to begin such exploration.

Please take your time to work through these resources. There is no reward for getting through the material in the next 4-6 months. Maybe let them wash over you through the course of the next year or so. For me, they made their way into my heart and mind through many hours of audio uptake—many between the silent hours of midnight and 5am on trips to and from the east coast while driving a motor coach. If the resource is in book form, as opposed to a sermon/message, I usually purchased the hard copy only after being changed by its audio message. Take each of these supplemental resources (outside of the Bible as your main and uniquely life-giving text) for what they are—nuggets of supplemental, insightful council which should lead us deeper into our walks with Jesus Christ. Test them all against the Scriptures continually. Live in God's Word.

The Bible, *by God*
There are no words to uplift or explain the benefits of this "resource." It is God's access to our spirit and soul. You must deliver it into your spirit daily. There is absolutely NO substitute. If you forgo this resource in lieu of anything else on this list, you are crazy. No other academic or spiritual resource on this planet is alive. This is the resource that gains the Holy Spirit access to your heart, soul and mind. The Bible points us to God supernaturally.

Holy Discontent, *by Bill Hybels*
The message behind this book is what, to the best of my ability to recall, initiated within me a hunger for more. This is the reason I have it listed here. There was something in its message God used which made my heart yearn for more. It was the '05 Leadership Summit where I had heard this message, and during those thirty-three minutes, the Holy Spirit had begun planting the seeds God would generously fertilize some six years later. Though it's a third party video as a whole, you can watch the message Bill delivered at the '05 Leadership Summit HERE: http://vimeo.com/23836269. Then, purchase the book.

The Normal Christian Life, *by Watchman Nee*
This, as you know by now, is the backbone of the constructs of chapters 4-7 of this book. I unapologetically quoted at great length much of what Nee communicates so effectively in the first few chapters of his book since I could neither be more concise nor more illustrative of the truths we find in the book of Romans. It has been used powerfully to affect change in the spiritual lives of huge numbers of Christians. Much of its message in this collected form had its origin as separately spoken messages. It is therefore not wholly systematic. None of the subjects he covers should be regarded as exhaustive, but should be approached prayerfully–not as a treatise, but as a message to the heart. After working very contemplatively through this work, I began to understand how it was that the Holy Spirit used Nee's ministry to bear remarkable fruit in individuals and in many groups of spiritually virile Christians.

The book of Romans, in The Bible *by co-authors God and Paul*
This is God's holy, inspired Word.

The Crucified Life, *by A.W. Tozer*
I used to think Tozer was a really tough read. In working through some of his devotional resources in times past, his writings seemed so deep and intellectually taxing that I could barely concentrate long enough to comprehend what he was trying to communicate. In the interest of full disclosure, however, you should probably also know I was on Methylphenidate as a child–okay, most of us called it Ritalin. Note that some believe I still should be taking it regularly. *Look, a squirrel!* Now where was I? Oh yes, I used to think Tozer was a tough read, but this book has changed this. The message and his style in writing it is stellar. It will add a glorious dimension to the intended pursuits of this book I have so poorly written by comparison. Chapters 7, 8, 9, 10 and following had me shaking my head ferociously as I listened while riding my bicycle and driving the motor coach, thinking about how wonderfully he was communicating so much of what I was trying to say in several sections of this book. Please do yourself a favor and download this audio book if you have time and space for undistracted listening, ...then get the book. It will minister deeply to your soul and make inquiries of your life

which will challenge you. I don't think Tozer would be heart-broken were you to start in Chapter 7. I'm just sayin'.

A Gospel Primer *for Christians* – Learning to See the Glories of God's Love, *by Milton Vincent*

Many Christians think the gospel is only for unbelievers. Milton Vincent has learned that we Christians need the gospel every day to keep us from falling into a performance relationship with God. In this little book (the kind I most like), you will find as practical a way I have found to do our reckoning–the importance of which we discussed in the sixth section of this book (chapters 47-54). This book is a rare jewel of thoroughly biblical, modern authorship. The Gospel is of first importance for us as believers. Regarding this thought, C.J. Mahaney says this in The Cross Centered Life; *"If there's anything in life that we should be passionate about, it's the gospel. And I don't mean passionate only about sharing it with others. I mean passionate about thinking about it, dwelling on it, rejoicing in it, allowing it to color the way we look at the world. Only one thing can be of first importance to each of us. And only the gospel ought to be."* This is a book you will read for 60 seconds – then have a day's worth of reckoning to do. I have a special friend to thank for my introduction to this treasure–thank you Jeff Leffew.

Redemption Through His Blood, Parts 1 and 2, *a sermon message by John MacArthur from his radio broadcast, Grace To You*

This should be the first MacArthur message to which you should listen, *but only after working through Nee's book*. This can be found for free in the radio/podcast archives at www.gty.org, MacArthur's site. This is an indispensable supplement to what we learn in Nee's book about the Blood, its purpose, its power and what it means to us as believers. This is a multiple times listening requirement and one for frequent re-visitation.

Divine Promises Guaranteed, Parts 1 and 2, *a sermon message by John MacArthur from his radio broadcast, Grace To You*

This should be the second MacArthur message to which you should listen–after Redemption Through His Blood. This message, like all of the MacArthur messages to follow, builds upon the previous one. This lays out the extent of what it means that we be in Christ, what belongs to us as believers, and how this should help us live in awe of our adoption as Sons of the Living God! John's so easy to listen to and always has a passionate, driven and purposeful delivery. These two podcasts from his radio broadcast, Grace To You, are no exception.

Our Resources in Christ, Parts 1 & 2, *a sermon message by John MacArthur from his radio broadcast, Grace To You*
Again, this multi-part podcast I heard on Moody Radio's airing of Grace To You, is one which very effectively builds upon his Divine Promises Guaranteed message. This, however, was aired and is archived as three separate podcasts, the first part being more lengthy and, therefore, being broadcast over two days. What does it really mean to inherit what is ours as believers in Christ? Oh the beauty of it! May it change you all the days of your life as a continuing part of your journey into newness in Christ.

The Essential Ministry of the Holy Spirit, Parts 1, 2 and 3, *a sermon message by John MacArthur from his radio broadcast, Grace To You*
Having heard and digested well his previous three podcast messages, downloading them into my iTunes, I was pumped to hear this series of messages on my local moody radio station's broadcast of Grace To You. What a treasure to be able to listen to such incredible, scripturally accurate teaching from God's Word while driving in the car, riding your bicycle, or while doing the dishes at home! As the Spirit draws you into deeper fellowship with himself and as he moves you through the many phases of personal breaking and surrender, your spirit will be peaked when you hear or read others who are also living through an apprehension of such life-changing truths. You will realize you are not alone! You will realize that the Holy Spirit is yet doing a work in His Church amidst the changing landscape of so many who are losing touch with the head of Christ. These six podcasts are rich, rich, rich.

Why We Believe the Bible is True, Parts 1 and 2, *a sermon message by John MacArthur from his radio broadcast, Grace To You*
Much like Tony Evans' Heaven's New Community message, this and its counterpart message, Why We Believe While Others

Reject, help to round out our understanding of, and cause us to sit back in awe of, God's plan. Listening to these messages should drive you to a great sense of humility. It deals with one of the long time questions of the Church. John, like always, walks through this topic scripturally and once again drives us into a quest for a deeper walk with the God of the universe—a God who specifically chose you from the foundations of the earth, to know him. What amazing grace. It is sometimes good for us to not completely understand God and his ways. This is, in part, what reminds us that he is God and we are not.

Why We Believe While Others Reject, Part 1, *a sermon message by John MacArthur from his radio broadcast, Grace To You*
And, as mentioned above, this is the other side of the coin of God's providential authority. This message, and reckoning upon its truth, has given me a more active prayer life on behalf of, and heart for, the lost. Rather than my coming away with the idea that "the lost are the lost," I think about how Hans Peter Royer talks about Fellowshipping with Christ in one of the sessions I am also strongly recommending you digest a multitude of times. He talks about how our walks with the Spirit of Jesus can literally become so continual that seeing a person becomes the same as praying/interceding for that person. The power of our intercession on others' behalf will, I believe, only be brought to light once we reach eternity in heaven. But John helps us contemplate the terrible fate of those chosen to be objects of God's wrath, so to speak. Oh may our hearts be heavy for those estranged from Christ.

Fellowshipping with Jesus, Parts 1a-1c, 2a-2e and 3a-3d, *a series of short messages by Hans Peter Royer from his being asked to speak at a pastor's conference here in America*
This, I doubt you will find anywhere. But if you're looking for one of the more powerful teachings I have ever heard on how we can grow in our fellowship with Jesus Christ, making your walk with Him new, powerful, meaningful and real, this is an absolute must have part of your growth arsenal. Contact me at lilbeav2@gmail.com and we'll try to get you hooked up with this series of three messages, totaling about an hour and a half. There are several things I heard from this message many years ago to which I have referred in the quiet of my heart and mind

many a time, though I could never pinpoint where I had heard them. Recently, when I found this treasure again in an old box of cassette tapes, I realized these truths had come from this man's honest, very practical message to a group of pastors where he spoke during what appears to be their morning breakfast sessions. This is so good my sons and I made it the subject of one of our 20 mile stints on *two* separate occasions during the 2014 Brickyard to Bridge Bicycle Ride. If you're a bicyclist, please join us in July of any year, God-willing, until Jesus returns. As of this writing, we have two years in the books.
http://brickyard2bridge.tumblr.com/

And, if you would like to contribute to our cycling/fundraising efforts for this ongoing, annual effort, know your funds would be used wisely: www.yfci.org/B2B.

Don't Waste Your Life, *by John Piper*
Again, my ability to experience lengthier books has been due to audible.com! There are sections of this book that will make you want to be very reckless with the life God has given you to live on this planet. This is a good thing. If you complete this book with some added conviction and determination to follow Jesus at any cost, keep the pedal down by heading directly into Platt's book, Radical. Then, Not A Fan, by Kyle Idleman.

Radical, *by David Platt*
Just get started with this book – that's all you'll need. If you get the audio, David reads it himself. My prayer is that you will not only reward your spirit with this book, but that you will also find your way into what David calls his Secret Church messages. You will learn a bit of how these marathon teaching sessions came to be in reading this book. If you want a doctorate in Bible, you can find them here: http://www.radical.net/

Pursuit of Holiness, *by Jerry Bridges*
As mentioned numerous times already, I first gain familiarity with books through my earplugs. Often, as I have long drives through the middle of the night, I find the Lord pursuing me—as I pursue him through the conscious choices I make in deciding what to do with that time. I also use my time running and bicycling to work through hours and hours of life-impacting writings from godly

servants. It is during these times that the Spirit does much of his pruning. While people learn in different ways, I would again ask that you consider downloading many of these books in the form of an audio book. Use them while you're working out, taking a long walk (by the way if you're not in the habit of taking walks with Jesus, start) or drive...you get the point. This additional avenue of putting the thoughts of God-fearing disciples of Jesus into your heart and mind gives you opportunity for much more exposure to things the Lord may like to deliver apart from sitting down quietly, specifically, to read...or if you're like me, fall asleep to, a book. Thus, I ingest most of my learning while moving anywhere between 7 and 70 mph. This personal little discourse here should not take away from what I have to say about this bombshell of a book. In short, **this is a book you DO NOT want to miss**. Jerry puts many key things into this powerful package, Pursuit of Holiness. It is an excellent complement to portions of The Normal Christian Life where some may get derailed, thinking Nee is reducing the extent of our personal responsibility in our pursuance of living in increasing deliverance from our old man. Don't let the fact that this book recommendation is last on this initial list communicate it is less than highly recommended. It could even be that I saved the best *for* last. But one warning here as well. Don't read/listen to this one time only. It will be the second and third times through that will give you pause and drive its thought-provoking, scripture-rich message into your ongoing, reckoning consideration.

Jesus, Continued..., Why the Spirit Inside You is Better than Jesus Beside
   You, *by J.D. Greear*

Why does God often feel more like a doctrine we know *about* than a Person we *know*? It is because our on ramp to living a life of deep fellowship with the Holy Spirit is cluttered with debris, among other things. Greear is spot on with his honest, easy to read conveyance of what the filling of the Spirit *is* and is *not*, and how we can position ourselves for the Spirit's in-breaking. This truly excellent and extremely relatable book will teach you not only of the prerequisites to living in communion with the Spirit of God within you, but will also overwhelm you with whom it is we have living within us. Maurice England does an excellent job with the audio version if you prefer that...as do I for a first run-through of a book. The illustration of a bicycle with one wheel is good in itself, and the sub-title is indicative of its content. *Please read this simple, easy to follow book.*

FURTHER RECOMMENDED READING/LISTENING:

Forgotten God, *by Francis Chan*
Life-changing, theological truths don't have to be complicated or 'hard reads.' While there is a place for us to learn about the person of the Holy Spirit through relatively complex and academic works like The Holy Spirit, by John Owen, there are also great treasures to be found for the common man in less daunting reads. Francis Chan, as always, presents simple truths about the person of the Holy Spirit in this truly wonderful, life-giving book that will make you think practically about your Helper. Remember to consider audio books from audible.com as a great way to consume great stuff. Chan narrates this book himself – a good thing given his passion for this tragically misunderstood, vastly ignored and absolutely critical member of the Godhead. Learn more about the One living in you and be changed.

Not A Fan, *by Kyle Idleman*

Knowing God, *by J.I. Packer*
Take this in small chunks, but even if it takes you a year to work through this in audio format alone, it's worth it. Sometimes it's worth it to chew steak rather than merely drinking milk all the time!

Bonhoeffer, *by Eric Metaxas*
Can you say "audio version?" Much less daunting.

Adonai–The Owner of All, *a sermon message by Tony Evans from his radio broadcast, The Alternative (Aired on or around April 15, 2013)*
You could have a tough time finding this message, but it's worth it. It put more pieces together in my journey. Tony explains how it is that we have too frequently have become Christians who want God to get us to heaven, but who do not want him to own us on earth. This, in only the way Tony can bring it, reinforces the

fact that we were, in so many words, bought through Jesus' Blood and his act upon the Cross and are, therefore, not our own. And yet, we refuse to hand over to him the title to our life. Try emailing a request to: info@tonyevans.org or by calling (800) 800-3222.

Heaven's New Community, *a sermon message by Tony Evans from his radio broadcast, The Alternative*
Again, try to get this message by emailing or calling Tony Evans' organization. This is a wonderful exposition on our common need for renewal and newness from our life of sin into citizenship in heaven. It breaks down the differences of the human race and pegs us as ones renewed only through the power of God's grace. This is a resource which contains valuable context for our identity in Christ as we endeavor to give ourselves wholly into God's plan.

www.ingramcontent.com/pod-product-compliance
Lightning Source LLC
Chambersburg PA
CBHW072134090426
42739CB00013B/3191